EEC and the Third World: A Survey 3

The Atlantic Rift

edited by Christopher Stevens

HODDER AND STOUGHTON
LONDON SYDNEY AUCKLAND TORONTO

in association with the Overseas Development Institute
and the Institute of Development Studies

ISBN 0 340 32646 8

First published 1983

Represented in Nigeria and Cameroon by Nigeria Publishers Services Ltd,
P.O. Box 62, Ibadan, Nigeria

Represented in East Africa by K. W. Martin, P.O. Box 30583,
Nairobi, Kenya

Photoset by Rowland Phototypesetting Ltd,
Bury St Edmunds, Suffolk
Printed in Great Britain for Hodder and Stoughton Educational,
a division of Hodder and Stoughton Ltd, Mill Road,
Dunton Green, Sevenoaks, Kent,
by Richard Clay (The Chaucer Press) Ltd, Bungay, Suffolk.

Contents

Editorial Board

About the Contributors

Betsy Baker is a freelance writer on international trade policies, based in London.

Yves Berthelot is Director of the Centre d'Etudes Prospectives et d'Informations Internationales, Paris.

Lucy Blackburn is an economist with Lloyds Bank Group Economics Department, London.

Willy Brandt is Chairman of the Independent Commission on International Development Issues and formerly Chancellor of the Federal Republic of Germany.

Jim Fitzpatrick is a consultant with Davies, Dunne and Partners, Dublin.

Carol Geldart is a Research Assistant at the Institute of Commonwealth Studies, London.

Reginald Herbold Green is a Professorial Fellow at the Institute of Development Studies, Sussex.

Lee H. Hamilton is a member of the USA House of Representatives and Chairman of the Sub-committee on Europe and the Middle East.

Stephane Hessel is currently Interministerial Delegate for Co-operation and Development in the Prime Minister's Office, Paris; his previous posts include Assistant Administrator of UNDR and Ambassador to the UN in Geneva.

Adrian Hewitt is a Research Officer with the Overseas Development Institute, London.

Dr Michael Hofmann is a Fellow at the German Development Institute, West Berlin.

Fiona Merry is an economist with Lloyds Bank Group Economics Department, London.

Dr Joanna Moss is a Fellow at San Francisco State University.

Stefan Musto is a Fellow at the German Development Institute, West Berlin.

Roderick Ogley is Reader in International Relations at the University of Sussex.

Joan Pearce is Head of Policy Studies at the Royal Institute of International Affairs, London.

Dr B. Persaud is Director of the Economic Affairs Division of the Commonwealth Secretariat, London.

Dr John Ravenhill is a Fellow in the Department of Government and Public Administration at the University of Sydney.

Jan P. Pronk is Deputy Secretary-General of UNCTAD and was formerly Minister of Development Co-operation in the Netherlands.

Annette Robert is a consultant in international relations and development based in the Hague.

S. S. Saxena is Director (Foreign Trade) at the Ministry of Commerce, Delhi.

Thorvald Stoltenberg is a member of the Secretariat for International Relations at the Norwegian Trades Union Office.

Knud Erik Svendsen is Director of the Centre for Development Research, Copenhagen.

Karel E. Vosskühler is an official with the Netherlands Ministry of Foreign Affairs.

Jürgen Wiemann is a Fellow at the German Development Institute, West Berlin.

Addresses:

Institute of Development Studies
University of Sussex
Falmer
Brighton, BN1 9RE

Overseas Development Institute
10–11 Percy Street
London, W1P 0JB

Editorial Policy

The Survey provides an annual record of and commentary on major developments in the European Community's economic relations with the Third World. Its audience includes policy makers, opinion formers and academics in the ten member countries and the Commission, and in North America and the Third World. Its underlying philosophy is that the EEC and the Third World have mutual interests. Neither harmony nor conflict of such interests is regarded as inevitable.

The Editorial Board is responsible for determining that this work should be presented to the public, but individual members of the Board are not responsible for statements of fact and expressions of opinion contained therein.

Foreword

The third in an annual series, this *Survey* marks a departure from its predecessors. All of the *Surveys* aim to cover issues of contemporary relevance to the Third World and the EEC and, though their analysis is rigorous and securely founded, they do not eschew controversy. But the overall themes of this *Survey* are particularly controversial in the sense of being open to dispute. We can, and do, take a position on the merits of the Law of the Sea convention, the implications for developing countries of changes in the realm of export credits, and the impact of the Lomé Convention trade preferences. But the relative importance of East–West and North–South conflicts, and the desirable future direction of EEC development policy are more disputatious fare. They do, however, provide the framework within which the more specific topics of the past year must be viewed and interpreted.

The contents of this *Survey* deal with both types of issues. The scene is set by a collection of short, pithy viewpoints contributed by men of affairs and letters. Then, the more concrete events of the year are analysed in the now traditional *Survey* manner by acknowledged experts in their fields. The aim is not to produce a voluminous yearbook of events, but to survey the state of EEC–Third World relations focussing on key trends and events, as identified by the Editorial Board, in order to produce a well-rounded commentary and record.

The theme that runs throughout this *Survey* is the split between the Atlantic Partners on North–South issues. Is it real and growing, or is it only skin deep? The EEC Commission has been blunt in arguing the case that the USA's attitudes towards the Third World are bad not only for developing countries but also for the industrialised world in general and Europe, as a major trading bloc, in particular. The government of President Mitterand has also been critical of US positions both in the international arena and in respect of particular regions such as Central America. President Reagan has found himself isolated, in opposition to all the EEC member states, on some issues at a range of fora from Cancun to Versailles. Yet the three questions that spring to mind are:

how united are the EEC member states in their opposition to US policies; where differences between the Atlantic Partners exist, do these involve fundamental issues or are they, as Vosskühler argues, 'mostly symbolic and of limited consequence'; and are the tensions likely to increase or diminish? The chapters of this *Survey* provide answers to all of these questions.

The *Survey* begins with a forum in which three eminent political figures give their views on global strategy, the role of North–South relations, and the most appropriate stance for Europe and the USA. Part I then addresses conflicts and mutual interests at the global level. To set the scene, Vosskühler examines the politico-economic approaches of the USA and the EEC to world problems, and asks how substantial are the differences. Berthelot assesses the approach of the new government in France which has been, and will continue to be, both the chief architect of EEC policy on North–South issues and the most vociferous critic of US policies. The following three chapters address important events of the past year: the Law of the Sea convention, the new arrangement on export credits, Cancun and the other UN conferences on North–South issues, and the new multifibre arrangement. Part 2 transfers attention from the global arena to regional problems: Southern Africa, the Caribbean and the Middle East. The same tensions and interests are visible but are interwoven with local factors. All of these international and regional chapters ask not just whether conflicts exist but whether they will continue. The answer to this second question depends in part on the road taken by the EEC in its own development policy. This is the subject of Part 3. In September 1982 the Commission adopted a new and extensive statement of strategy towards the Third World, and in September 1983 this new strategy will be tested in practice as negotiations open between the EEC and the ACP on a successor to the Lomé Convention. When Lomé II was negotiated, the parties had little hard evidence of the impact of its trade and aid provisions to guide them. This is changing. Moss and Ravenhill provide a very thorough analysis of trade flows under Lomé I which makes uncomfortable reading not only for the EEC but also for the USA which has modelled its own Caribbean Basin Initiative on Lomé. Adrian Hewitt provides a similarly disturbing analysis of the performance of Stabex, jewel of the Lomé Convention. The negotiations for Lomé III will take place against this background, but they will also be heavily influenced by the perceptions of the negotiators about development strategy. Chapters 12 and 13 look into the future and show the (very wide) range of strategies currently being advanced.

Each *Survey* is based on extensive research and editorial work. We are very grateful to the Noel Buxton Trust, which has supported the *Survey* financially from its inception and continues to do so. The timely appearance of the *Survey* also continues to be due in large part to the efforts of Christine Palmer, ODI's publications officer, and Catharine Perry who compiled the Bibliography in addition to her stakhanovite efforts at the typewriter.

London
October 1982

List of Abbreviations

ACP	African, Caribbean and Pacific (signatories to the Lomé Conventions)
CACM	Central American Common Market
CADC	Central American Democratic Community
CAP	Common Agricultural Policy (of the EEC)
Caricom	Caribbean Community
CBI	Caribbean Basin Initiative
CET	Common External Tariff (of the EEC)
DAC	Development Assistance Committee (of the OECD)
ECA	Economic Community of Africa
ECOWAS	Economic Community of West African States
EDF	European Development Fund
EFTA	European Free Trade Area
EIB	European Investment Bank
G77	Group of 77 developing countries (now in fact 124 countries)
GATT	General Agreement on Tariffs and Trade
GSP	Generalised System of Preferences
ICA	International Commodity Agreement
IDA	International Development Association (a World Bank affiliate)
ldcs	developing countries
lldcs	least developed countries
MFA	Multifibre Arrangement
MSAs	Most seriously affected countries (UN classification)
NICs	Newly industrialising countries
OAS	Organisation of American States
OCT	Overseas Countries and Territories (of the EEC)
oda	official development assistance
OECD	Organisation for Economic Co-operation and Development
OPEC	Oil producing and exporting countries
SADCC	Southern African Development Co-ordination Conference
TNC	Transnational corporation
UNCTAD	United Nations Conference on Trade and Development
UNDP	United Nations Development Programme
WFP	World Food Programme (joint UN/FAO body)

1

Forum of Global Strategy: East–West and North–South

A Challenge for Europe

Willy Brandt

The world economic crisis is deepening and by the end of 1982 no major internationally co-ordinated effort was visible which might alleviate the problems besetting all countries. Recent suggestions for change and even promises contained in the communiqués of summit meetings at Versailles and Cancun have not led to any concrete steps. National governments seem to become more and more concerned with internal difficulties and look for domestic solutions to their problems, particularly that of unemployment. They are not yet ready to accept the thesis that internationally co-ordinated action and greater support for the developing countries might provide the real way out of the crisis.

Europe's role

In the prevailing situation the Commission of the European Community is trying to formulate a new strategy for its policy of co-operation with developing countries (see Part 3). The proposal prepared by the Commission calls for a certain reorientation and a concentration of effort on increasing food production in developing countries. At the same time European development efforts are to be based on a contractual system making assistance flows more predictable over a longer term. The essential philosophy is to be one of co-operation rather than aid, and overall the share of Europe's assistance handled through the Community is to be increased. The renewal of the Lomé II agreement will provide the opportunity to put the new policy to a test when negotiations start in September 1983. This new initiative represents a sign of hope.

Worldwide we face a general feeling of scepticism and a clear lack of leadership. International organisations in the development field encounter increasing criticism and try to live within narrowing (in real terms) budget limits – if they are not actually confronted with budgetary cuts. They have shelved recent plans for expansion of their activity in real terms. The major powers and main contributors are the most reluctant members, and their failure to live up to earlier promises cannot easily be offset by higher contributions from the smaller countries. And even in traditionally open-minded countries, some of which reached the 0.7 percent target years ago, there is now a growing pessimism and declining enthusiasm to support the demands of developing countries.

Under the prevailing circumstances Europe is seen by many as the only possible hope and the only political power potentially able to fill the leadership gap. In the past Europe has often been a follower rather than a leader and the hope for a change in its perception and role may not be bright. Nevertheless, in today's world nobody else seems capable or ready to take a fresh look and take the first step. It has often been said that Europe is more dependent on the Third World than either the USA or the USSR. It would be in its own interest therefore, not to neglect the developing countries as they could contribute to Europe's economic recovery if their own economies were given enough support to grow faster.[1] Among all industrialised countries Europe probably has the greatest immediate economic interest in reducing the constraints caused by scarcities and unstable modes of behaviour, to paraphrase a recent statement by the Commission. In my view, Europe clearly has the biggest political interest in co-operation with the Third World, and this becomes even greater the deeper the superpowers get entangled in the renewed East–West conflict. The field of North–South relations could provide another testing ground for European independence from the superpowers, if only in the sense that this time Europe would not follow the American lead nor use Eastern passivity as an excuse for abstaining from action. Rather, Europe should take the lead and, if necessary, start to act on its own thus perhaps recalling the Americans to their own tradition of compassion, generosity and internationalism.

A plan of action

Time is short, and every day counts. All the technical arguments have been made many times over. Rational solutions are within reach and we have it in our power to tackle the problems and disasters for which the world seems to be heading simply because they are either being ignored or treated with weak palliatives. A fraction of the annual expenditure on arms would relieve world hunger and enable the developing countries, in the near future, to meet the basic needs of their people. I believe it is now a matter of political will and leadership which must look ahead over decades and not just years. And I am confident that there is a chance for mankind to survive. But decisions must be taken soon and they will have to be bold. In its own interest and for the sake of the world Europe should respond to the current challenge.

What needs to be done? In my view three things are of particular importance: first is the education and mobilisation of public opinion. The present crisis is still widely seen as the result of misguided government policies alone – as if better national policies could easily do away with unemployment, inflation and stagnation. People must be made aware that we are going through a worldwide crisis of adjustment in which the pursuit of national adjustment policies can easily lead to a downward spiral of contraction for the whole world economy. There-fore, the world needs a joint effort of all countries to deal with the worldwide crisis. Only such internationally co-ordinated effort can lead to success. European nations and the EEC could set an example in this respect. I share the feeling of those who suggest that voters would reward leaders who move in needed directions, and I think that the chances in this respect are better in Europe than elsewhere.

Second, the remedies are neither hard to define nor impossible to execute; they are both familiar and unpopular. They include the avoidance of persistent large budget deficits, the granting of large resources to international financial institutions, and the opening of markets in the industrialised countries for the exports of the Third World. Perhaps one should add that international institutions, govern-ments and private banks will have to respect the conditions – appro-priately revised to take broader development objectives into account – imposed on recipients of IMF assistance.

Third, the world must wake up to the fact that we risk our future if we continue to waste our resources in unproductive arms expenditures while neglecting the urgent need for investment in such areas as energy, soil conservation, food production, and in population stabi-lisation. The only way to secure the necessary capital lies in a shift of budgetary funds – and a vast amount of talent – from the military sector. And I believe that governments all over the world, whatever their ideology, are now reaching the point where they are forced to decide between reducing military expenditures or lowering the living standard of their people.

Our values and priorities will have to change, including our tradi-tional understanding of 'national security'. Europe is in a unique situation in many respects and would appear to have the best oppor-tunity to lead the way in the process of change. Through timely adjustment it could avoid severe social and economic stresses. It would reap great benefits the longer others continue with, or fall back into, outdated policies. But the forces of traditionalism and the fears of the unknown are still strong. We can only hope that they will not force us to learn the hard way.

There will be change, there is no doubt. Perhaps it will be forced upon us as the result of a deepening crisis of a magnitude and intensity not seen since the 1930s. Alternatively, we could take the initiative and act to turn the tide; the global stimulation of the world economy and an end to the arms race are in the best immediate economic interests of all. And Europe should take the lead.

Note

1   Of course, Japan in many ways depends as much on the Third World as Europe does. But most observers just now would not expect new political initiatives to come from Japan.

An American Perspective

Representative Lee H. Hamilton MC

I write as Chairman of the United States House of Representatives Sub-committee on Europe and the Middle East and as a Member of Congress concerned with the problems and promise of international economic developments. From this perspective, there are a number of disturbing trends in the policy of the USA, and there is a growing divergence between the policies pursued by the USA and by a number of European states. Despite the criticisms levelled at European policy by other authors in this *Survey*, European approaches to the Third World display a greater awareness of contemporary realities. While there is clearly scope for improvement on both sides of the Atlantic, I argue that the divergence must be reversed and that the USA and EEC should increase the co-ordination of their international economic development programmes.

Recent trends in United States aid policy

To begin, US policy on international economic development is heavily influenced by our assessment of East–West rivalry. We have made the strategic and political relationship with the Soviet Union the principal reference point of foreign policy. Washington tends to interpret regional issues in terms of the Soviet factor; much less weight is given to indigenous factors, whatever they may be. Indeed, some have observed that the major purpose of our aid today is the suppression or elimination of conditions which invite exploitation by the Soviet Union or other communist states. It is becoming axiomatic that if a developing country is unable to present its needs in terms of East–West rivalry, its chances of receiving American aid are diminished.

A second trend is that the United States is setting aside proportionately less for assistance than are most other industrialised nations. In fact, among the seventeen nations of the OECD Development Assistance Committee (DAC) the United States was thirteenth in 1980 when ranked by percentage of gross national product. This state of affairs has come about slowly, but come about it has. UNCTAD recommends that the industrialised countries set aside 0.7 per cent of their gross national product for official development assistance. Although the United States does not accept the figure as an obligatory goal, our aid was above the average for members of the DAC until 1967. Since then, it has decreased to 0.25 per cent of GNP. The perception exists in the USA that American economic aid has burgeoned in recent years, but nothing could be further from the truth. Since 1960, it has declined some 42 per cent in real terms. General economic problems, widespread disillusion with the results of assistance, mistaken beliefs about the purpose of assistance, and a strong congressional desire to restrain spending are the primary reasons for the decline.

A third trend is that our aid is becoming more tightly tied to the advancement of narrowly defined security interests. With its net of security relationships, Washington seeks to repulse the threat of Soviet expansion and promote stability in regions possessing important resources for the West. It fails to recognise that security can be preserved and improved in many different, less tangible ways. Consequently, the amount of money available for military assistance has grown much faster than that available for economic assistance. Between 1970 and 1981, for example, financing for foreign military sales increased nine-fold to $3.1 billion while short-term economic aid to strategically important countries increased only five-fold to $2.1 billion. The narrow emphasis on security distorts our assistance and departs from our aims as we defined them in the 1940s and 1950s – aims which were much closer to those of our allies. Although security has always been a key consideration, promoters of assistance in those days tended to regard it as a humanitarian measure intended to lift living standards, increase material well-being, and encourage political stability. However, when one considers that in 1980 only 15 per cent of our aid went to the poorest countries, it is obvious that the humanitarian motive has become less important.

A fourth trend is toward geographical imbalance in our assistance. If Congress approves the legislation for 1983, three-quarters of the foreign military sales programme and three-fifths of the economic support fund programme will go to Egypt and Israel alone. These two nations have received one-third of all our foreign assistance since 1978. If the United States continues to channel so much of its military and economic aid into a handful of countries, the harm to our interests could be significant. The geographical imbalance is well-known, and among poor countries it has contributed to an understandable cynicism concerning our intentions. Some governments emphasise an identification with our security interests in order to get aid, but the fate of the Shah of Iran is a graphic reminder of how defenceless such governments can be in the face of internal opposition. It is true that our commitment to the Middle East is easily appreciated in light of the region's location and resources, but even in respect to resources it must be acknowledged that our assistance is badly distributed. After all, the Third World outside the Middle East supplies much oil to the USA and serves as a source of bauxite, manganese, cobalt, and other necessary minerals.

A fifth trend is the decrease in support of multilateral lending agencies. Americans are divided on the future of programmes of multilateral assistance administered by the World Bank, the International Monetary Fund, and other such agencies. The United States was instrumental in the genesis of these programmes and has played a central role in their evolution, but the Reagan Administration has sought to reduce our involvement in them. Early in 1982, the President revealed a plan to cut American support for the multilateral agencies by as much as 45 per cent. The reasons given include those pertaining to supply-side economics, a fear that multilateral aid gives too much power to the recipient, and a desire to promote private-sector initiatives in the Third World; yet an American retreat from support of these agencies means that only the most desperately poor nations will be able to get subsidised loans. From the perspective of the Third World, America's diminished role in the multilateral agencies reflects a wish to keep hold of the reins of economic power, a wish to prevent independent economic development. Critics in the Third World are bitter that the United States stands at the forefront of opposition to greater participation by the developed countries in the multilateral agencies.

A sixth trend is an increased preoccupation with the private sector as a vehicle for assistance. The promotion of private endeavours has always been an important aspect of US aid, and American companies and investors have made significant contributions to the Third World.

However, the heavy reliance on the private sector – a reliance which seems to be one of the cornerstones of the policy of the Reagan Administration – raises questions. It is doubtful whether companies will direct their resources into long-term development; many Third World hosts will view the influx of foreign business with suspicion and hostility. The legacy of the American private sector in many parts of the Third World is controversial and raises doubts about American sincerity.

The narrow emphasis on security, the attention to a few countries, the diminished support for multilateral agencies, and the heavy reliance on the private sector are characteristics of a policy which seeks the short-term fix more than the long-term accomplishment. A good illustration of the shortcomings of the American approach is Egypt, a nation which in recent years has assumed a vital place in our scheme for a durable peace in the Middle East. Besides the sizeable amount of money available to meet its military needs, Egypt receives significant assistance related to foodstuffs, raw materials, electric power, telecommunications, industrial development, private-sector growth, health, population control, and education. No one belittles the objectives of these programmes, but critics inside and outside of Congress question their effectiveness in addressing the fundamental problems of Egypt's economy and society. Basic economic troubles in Egypt are not being faced, and generous aid today may lessen the prospect that they ever will be. Government subsidies and structural deficiencies continue to retard overall improvement; progress in agricultural development is too slow; public deficits are growing; inflation is on the rise. Unless there is planning for the long term, we may actually accomplish very little of lasting value in Egypt.

Divergences between the USA and Europe

As one compares the policies of international economic development in place on both sides of the Atlantic, one sees that the United States and Europe are diverging. Much of this divergence originates in Europe's distinctive views of *détente*. It seems to me that while the Europeans fully understand the differences between East and West, they argue that the North–South dialogue between the developed and the developing nations is increasingly important in the modern world. An excessive focus on the Soviet Union distorts foreign policy and makes it more difficult to end regional crises and form closer ties with the Third World.

Europe also differs from America in its willingness to pay. Most European nations surpass the USA in the proportion of GNP they commit to official development assistance (oda). The Netherlands,

Sweden, Denmark, and Norway have contributed more than 0.7 per cent of GNP for purposes of development in recent years. France and West Germany are now actively seeking to increase their contributions. Only Great Britain has joined the United States in an intentional cutback of assistance to developing countries. The EEC has become in fact the world's most generous donor.

European attitudes toward security interests, geographical concentration of aid, multilateral agencies, and private-sector involvement in development are not running parallel to those of the USA. I perceive that the Europeans regard our assistance as aimed too much at the enhancement of American power. They question our obsession with the Middle East to the exclusion of so many other needy regions, including those on our own doorstep in Latin America. They disagree with American coolness toward multilateral assistance, arguing that multilateral agencies may be the most effective devices to provide economic aid to the developing countries. They are confused by the American preference for an extensive private-sector role in development, which they find to be anachronistic and insensitive. European critics have suggested that America's difference with Europe results in part from a deeply entrenched American uneasiness with state support of human welfare. Such support, these critics respond, whether it be domestic or foreign, is a moral responsibility, and the polls reveal that large numbers of Europeans feel a strong moral obligation to help the Third World. It is hardly surprising that European programmes tend to be more humanitarian and more orientated towards the long term.

None of this is to say that the Europeans share no shortcomings with the USA. They have their problems, too. Much of France's assistance, for example, is aimed at former colonies, so it serves very definite political interests as well as humanitarian ones. What is worse, Europe must accept part of the responsibility for the rising tide of protectionism which is closing the markets of the West to manufactured exports from the Third World. When the issue is economic development among the poor nations, there is enough blame for inaction to go around.

Recommended changes in US policy

To correct the problems of its programmes of international economic development, the United States should implement a policy that is at once generous in its scope and hard-nosed in its conditions. In applying conditions to aid, the United States would be following a course already charted by the multilateral agencies. We would certainly be justified in expecting foreign governments to introduce the measures needed to promote long-term economic growth even when those measures are painful, as they often are. Such conditions, of course, should not be so rigid that they demand the creation of 'little Americas' throughout the world. Unrealistically high expectations – expectations formed in ignorance of cultural and historical traits as well as of contemporary needs – could do much damage to our image.

Other changes are in order. American assistance should be given out less for its effect in the East–West context and more for its potential to achieve the goals of development. Too little of our money is going to the neediest countries; too much is going to countries merely to meet narrowly defined security interests. However, in channelling additional funds into developmental assistance the United States should not repeat the error of neglecting long-term economic growth and political stability. As it strengthens its economic assistance, the United States should try to distribute it more widely and ensure that it affects recipient countries more deeply, helping to cure the fundamental ills which lie at the heart of much economic stagnation and political turmoil.

It follows from these observations that the huge share of American assistance committed to transfers of weapons should be trimmed. Foreign military sales are a necessary component of our aid, but they are seriously counterproductive when they fuel regional hostilities or prompt repressive regimes to intimidate their populations. The United States will sell approximately $25 billion in weapons in 1983. That we will be such an aggressive salesman of arms is discouraging news to most Americans.

America should not retreat from its support of multilateral agencies, nor should it fail to understand the crucial link between the condition of public infrastructure and the success of the private sector. Historically, the multilateral agencies have been important sources of aid to the poorest countries, and their resources have been committed to valuable, long-term objectives. They fulfill a need which cannot be readily fulfilled by the private sector. If the United States moves further away from multilateral assistance, it will compromise its international reputation and weaken the chances for significant, long-term development in the Third World. The chances for such development must be strengthened, not weakened. To funnel money into short-term economic projects and 'quick-fix' military endeavours is only to delay for a brief time events that will endanger world peace. A return to long-term objectives would be an important concession to the ideals which moved the United States to extend its magnanimous hand to the war-ravaged nations in the aftermath of World War II, and it would greatly improve the standing of the United States among rich and poor nations alike. It is a fundamental premise of this point of view that for the remainder of the century at least, the security interests of most nations will be defined less strictly in military terms and more amply in terms of economic development.

As the United States and Europe consider their growing dependence on the Third World as well as on one another, they should see that their programmes of international economic development must be more, not less, co-ordinated. A common approach to development would benefit both the donor and the recipient. Continuation of current trends in our programmes of aid, however, will lead to unsettling tensions in the Atlantic Alliance and to further impoverishment, suffering, and destabilisation in the developing nations.

The Perspective from Outside the EEC

Thorvald Stoltenberg

The need for a European strategy

The United States is the only country which has the political, economic and military capacity to pursue a global strategy in practice. The Soviet Union is building up sufficient military power to be present in all the world's waters, but its economy does not allow it to pursue a truly global strategy. Naturally Europe would be even less able to indulge in one even assuming that such a strategy could be agreed upon by all parties. So far Europe has not been able even to formulate and maintain a reasonably homogeneous policy to any degree; rather the tendency has been to deplore or criticise the policies of the USSR and the USA without presenting constructive alternatives.

In the long term we would like to see a European policy which includes the real Europe – both East and West, but this is a long way down the road. In the immediate future, however, there is a great need for at least a consistent European policy to which all the countries of Western Europe can feel committed. In practice this means, first and foremost, an agreed EEC strategy in the formulation of which we who are not members of the EEC will participate only through those channels and possibilities open to outsiders. This raises problems. While such channels do exist in some numbers, anyone who has participated in the forming of policies internationally knows that, when all is said and done, there is no substitute for actually sitting at the negotiating table until the final full stop in the joint agreement has been written. Hence political co-operation within the EEC is becoming an increasing challenge to those European countries which are outside the Community, particularly since such co-operation increasingly includes aspects of military security. If the United States and the EEC were ever to combine under the auspices of NATO with clear and definite positions on defence strategy, the non-EEC countries' influence in such vital areas would be very limited.

Despite such problems, the countries of Western Europe, EEC and non-EEC alike, feel a growing need to co-ordinate their foreign policies so as to strengthen their influence on world development. The time is ripe, therefore, for the EEC to respond to this pressure for better co-ordination of its foreign policy. Despite their strength, the superpowers' influence is declining, not least because of the increasing self-assertiveness of the periphery and its growing ambitions to participate in the international decision-making process. There are, of course, still exceptions. The Falklands and Lebanon conflicts would appear to be sad illustrations of the limits to the influence that the periphery can wield, because words remained words and were not translated into actions. Support for Argentina from Castro's Cuba and Pinochet's Chile alike never went further than speeches: the Argentinians received very little in the form of positive action from their Latin American friends. Similarly, the Palestinians feel the gap between words and actions from the Arab world. Nevertheless, these two conflicts may turn out to be important steps in the development of a political solidarity in the periphery which has international implications.

The importance of the Third World

Europe has a wealth of experience to draw upon when shaping future policies. Historically, it has been in the front line for the policies of the superpowers, which have sometimes resulted in disagreements and war, and sometimes in agreements and new alliances. Yet our attention has been concentrated on relations between countries with influence in international decision-making, which means the industrial world. The rest of the world, that is the majority of the world's population, have either been colonies or, as lately, receivers of smaller or larger alms. In neither case has it been taken seriously, in the sense of being considered important for our own economy, employment and security. Until it is recognised both in the East and the West that Third World development is important for us as well as for them, we will continue to focus on traditional East–West conflicts and will neglect the greater danger inherent in such an ostrich-like policy *vis-à-vis* the developing countries of the South.

Two examples will indicate what I mean. The first is the meagre results from the endless negotiations on mutually beneficial economic co-operation. One of the few positive results was the establishment of the Common Fund, with the declared aim of securing stable prices for producers, and stable supplies for consumers. These negotiations were helped by the fact that the division between consumer/producer is not the same as the division between industrialised/developing countries. This mixed interest grouping provided a positive base for success and there was in fact a formal result – the establishment of the Common Fund. Yet this formal measure has not been followed through in practice. The existing structure of the international raw material markets appears to be so strong, and the actors in it to have such distrust of the Fund, that it does not seem to be able to make the step from being a document to an activity. This causes political and economic frustration in both industrial and developing countries. Indeed, in the extreme, it can be interpreted as a threat to security since such a situation strengthens the position of those who do not believe in negotiations and political solutions, but who believe that the use of force and weapons is the only possible way to lift the majority of the world's population out of poverty and misery. There are a variety of motives behind calls for change. Not everyone who claims to represent the poverty-stricken can be said to do so, when one analyses the policies they follow. One thing is certain, however. It is that there is a powerful desire in the periphery to participate more fully in the international decision-making process.

The problem, therefore, is not only a social one – that the majority of the population in a rich world should not live in poverty. It is also a political one – that only a few countries are involved in taking decisions that are of paramount importance to many countries. There is little doubt that this situation will change, given time. But the important question is how it will happen: by means of negotiation and co-operation, or by a shift towards more chaos, force and militarism.

Peace, arms control and nuclear weapons have taken a central position in the political debate of Europe and the United States. This is natural, and it is important that we reduce our dependence on nuclear weapons in order to reduce the threat of war and the danger that they may be used. Results may be reached by getting the nuclear powers, first and foremost the USSR and the USA, to agree to disarmament rather than continue with the vicious circle of the arms race. The results of the negotiations in Geneva and Vienna will have a major impact on Europe's position to the end of the century.

It is, however, unfortunate that by focusing on disarmament and on a reduction of the tension between East and West, we ignore other dangers that may result in armed violence in the coming years. A confrontation between the superpowers will hardly be a result of rational evaluation in Washington or Moscow. Both sides have everything to lose from such a confrontation. Both Mr Reagan and Mr Andropov have more to gain by utilising their countries' resources to solve domestic problems – in co-operation with other countries of the world. The danger of a confrontation, as has been pointed out time and time again, lies in errors which end in misunderstandings. Naturally, everything must be done to prevent this from happening, but it is not necessary to elaborate in this essay on what is required. The other danger, which is ignored both in the East and the West, is that continued frustration among the majority of the world's population may result in a growing belief that armed violence is the only possible way to force through the changes needed for a better existence for themselves and their fellows. This frustration will come from the fact that they can see no improvement in their situation, that a decade's negotiations have not produced the hoped-for results, and that the industrialised countries in the East and the West appear to have lost interest in their problems. We know that this frustration is increasing, as is the danger of nuclear weapons proliferation. Who can produce nuclear weapons? Which countries have such weapons today that we are not aware of?

This combination of rational thinking on the part of the developing countries, leading to the conclusion that force is an appropriate response, together with the possibility of the use of nuclear weapons opens up frightening perspectives. I am not thinking about a collective rising by the Third World against the Second or First World. That is unrealistic, both politically and militarily. I am thinking instead of terror situations, of which we already see the outlines and which by the end of this century may be our greatest security risk. We fear violence and war primarily because of the insane waste of human life involved. Yet, in many developing countries, many people are already today suffering from such a 'state of war', not because they are being killed by bombs and shells, but because of a shortage of food and medicines. In a situation where a high proportion of the babies in a village die before they are one year old, perhaps war is not as frightening a prospect as it is for us with a life expectancy of 70–80 years.

With this in mind, Europe must expand its conception of security beyond considerations of satisfactory defence, *détente* and disarmament, to include the solution of national and international socio-political problems. Unless we give great weight to these concerns, we will not increase our security; we will reduce it. From this perspective one could argue that the Afghanistan conflict is more dangerous to world peace than is Poland. The situation in Poland is, of course, extremely serious, for the Poles, for the stability of Europe, and for a return to European *détente*. But it is not accidental that post-war Europe has been the most peaceful area in the world; it is by design. European security has been cold-bloodedly orchestrated, with *realpolitik* the dominant theme. This certainly has some unsatisfactory corollaries, but it does mean that both East and West know that they risk catastrophe if they tamper with the borders of the two blocs. That is why they have not done so. Afghanistan's position is not so clear. It is true that it had a regime friendly to the USSR but it could not be described as belonging to the Soviet Union's sphere of interest. Therefore the USSR took a serious risk by entering Afghanistan. One of the costs it has had to bear as a result has been the critical international response. In a rare example of unity, the Third World reacted more or less unanimously in the UN to condemn the Soviet intervention. It was a strong reaction, and, for the USSR, an unexpected one. However, we in the West in fact helped Moscow off the hook of this East–South conflict by bringing it into the traditional sphere of East–West conflicts. In Western Europe there was some opposition to such short-sighted reactions, but experience and knowledge lost out against the strength of immediate feelings. In this case a stronger, better and more well-established Western European system of co-ordination might have given Europe's views a better chance of being heard in Washington.

Relations between Eastern and Western Europe

What should our Eastern Europe strategy be? Policies of sanctions rarely give the desired results. Sanctions against Poland break down the co-operation Poland has had with the West and make Poland more dependent on the Soviet Union. Is this what we really want? Moreover, the policy of sanctions has resulted in disagreements between the Western allies. Thus, we get yet another West–West conflict. If we accept that the conflict between the USA and the USSR is not an ideological conflict between communism and capitalism, but a conflict of interest between two superpowers, we have a reasonably sober basis for devising an appropriate position. Let us not forget that economic problems do not affect only the West; they also haunt the Soviet Union and Eastern Europe. Because of this, and of a growing popular demand for change, a number of Eastern bloc countries are altering their economic course dramatically towards increased decentralisation and more private sector activity. Industry and the banks are being made to work in line with profitability norms as we know them in the West. In the long term this should permit a more balanced economic co-operation between Eastern and Western Europe. All the post-war experience of a divided Europe suggests that *détente* and co-operation have not only served the cause of peace, but have also aided the development of human rights in Eastern Europe.

It is readily apparent that the open democracies in the West have no reason to fear open co-operation with Eastern Europe. Therefore policies aimed at closing and isolating authoritarian states in the East are contrary to our own interests and principles. This does not mean that there will not be situations where our emotional reactions are so strong that we indulge in sanctions, even though these may not be politically rational. Examples such as Hungary in 1956 and Czechoslovakia in 1968 show this. But our main line of policy must be to promote open co-operation between Eastern and Western Europe. There appears for the most part to be agreement on this in Western Europe.

Does this mean that we should simply accept today's divided Europe, with the demands this makes on millions of people? The answer is a definite no – because such a policy is neither desirable nor possible. An unchanging policy in a rapidly changing environment will not serve its purpose. Equally clear, however, is the fact that the people of Western and Eastern Europe have little to gain from brinkmanship. If we accept that the conflict is not ideological, but one of interest, and if we further accept that the USSR has genuine security interests, the basis should be formed for a realistic policy. The new generations growing up in Eastern Europe do not appear to be any more willing to accept their situation than were the earlier generations behind the uprisings in East Germany in 1954, Hungary in 1956 and Czechoslovakia in 1968. The opposite is true, and Poland today is a good example. Youth does not turn to the Communist Party, but to Solidarity and to the church. The security that Eastern Europe provides for the Soviet Union is extremely fragile. If it were put to the test, it is doubtful that Moscow would derive much support from its allies. Indeed, Eastern Europe is developing into an economic, political and security strain on the Kremlin. It is possible, therefore, that the Kremlin is now evaluating other forms of co-operation which will provide the Soviet Union with more tranquillity and stability in its immediate surroundings. If they look around they will see that their democratic and independent neighbour, Finland, has given them far fewer worries than the Moscow-dominated Eastern European countries. A so-called 'Finlandisation' of Eastern Europe, whilst maintaining the Warsaw Pact, may be a development that is in the Soviet Union's interest. This would then open new perspectives for European co-operation across East–West borders. Western European strategy must avoid policies that counteract such a development in Europe.

Part 1

EEC and USA – the International Arena

2

The EEC and the USA – Differing Politico-Economic Approaches

Karel E. Vosskühler

Since the 1973 oil crisis there has been a vivid awareness amongst Western nations that developments in the Third World could pose a threat to global security as well as to various Western interests. Perceptions of the nature of 'the threat from the Third World' have evolved over the years, partly in response to actual events and partly as a result of changes in philosophical outlook. Significant differences *appear* to have emerged between the perceptions of the Atlantic partners and the policies that they derive from these perceptions. How far are such appearances borne out in reality? This chapter examines the underlying politico-economic philosophies of the USA and the EEC to assess how deep-seated are the differences and whether they are likely to grow.

North–South and East–West

Many observers of the North–South confrontation that accompanied the oil crisis – culminating in the debate about the New International Economic Order (NIEO) – foresaw an extended period of radical posturing by a Southern bloc, a trade union of poor countries attempting to emulate the successful OPEC example.[1] As the North–South dialogue developed, however, it became clear that Third World unity was primarily rhetorical and that confrontation had only limited success given the international balance of power and the weakness of the decision-making machinery of the United Nations system. The focus shifted from broad concepts of a world-order nature (as exemplified by the RIO project[2]) to more pragmatic notions of interdependence between North and South and to a more incrementalist approach to international reform (as advocated in the Brandt report[3]).

As the 1970s progressed, Western perceptions of possible threats from the Third World also changed. There was a growing awareness that regional instability in the Third World might pose a graver threat to world peace and to vital Western interests than confrontation between the North and the South as such. Growing economic interdependence has made the advanced Western countries extremely vulnerable to the disruption of international flows of energy, raw materials and manufactured goods, not to mention financial flows. Given the stake that many developing countries (or their ruling élites) now have in the continuation of such flows, wilful interruption on their part has become less likely than interruption due to interstate conflict or domestic turmoil.

Regional instability *per se* can cause considerable damage to Western interests. Whenever events in the South have appeared to touch upon East–West relations, Western governments, not just the US Administrations, have taken a particular interest. The ability of the Soviet Union to intervene outside its borders has increased markedly during recent years, particularly in terms of its naval and air capability. The recent pattern of Soviet behaviour *vis à vis* the Third World suggests two distinct dynamics: the traditional interest in expanding Russian influence in its southern periphery, and a degree of opportunism in exploiting situations of crisis and instability anywhere in the Third World (if necessary through proxies such as Cuba).

During the 1970s there were several instances of Soviet bloc intervention in the Third World, often at the invitation of the ruling government and with the consent of most regional actors (for example Ethiopia, Angola). For primarily domestic reasons US governments in the 1970s chose more or less to ignore these developments. It took two major events in South–West Asia to change the American attitude. The Soviet invasion of Afghanistan and the ousting of the Shah from Iran have shattered the two main premises of American security policy in the area around the Persian Gulf: that the Soviet Union would not intervene militarily on a massive scale in that area and that 'local policemen' could be relied upon for maintaining regional stability. The return to a more assertive US stance opposing Soviet expansionism in the Third World clearly pre-dated the Reagan Administration. On 23 January 1980, President Carter declared that 'an attempt by any outside force to gain control of the Persian Gulf region will be regarded as an assault on the vital interests of the United States of America and such an assault will be repelled by any means necessary, including military force'. It was under the Carter Administration that the build-up of the Rapid Deployment Force was started.

The globalist and regionalist approaches

It was with rather great hesitancy that the Carter Administration acknowledged the East–West dimension of regional conflicts in the Third World. Initially even Zbigniew Brzezinski was more inclined to embrace what may be called the regionalist approach.[4] The regionalist approach to Third World conflict accepts and values the continuing diffusion of power, appreciates the unique nature of the various regional alignments, assumes rather limited objectives behind Soviet policies in most Third World areas, relies heavily upon diplomatic and economic initiatives, favours maximum dissociation from regional conflicts and relies rather more on multilateral diplomacy, particularly within the framework of the United Nations. The regional approach can be contrasted with the globalist approach which tends to situate Third World conflict in an East–West context, assumes global aspirations on the part of the Soviet leadership, relies heavily on military force, attaches great value to formal alliances and, at the same time, shows a preference for bilateral diplomacy. Clearly, the events in South-West Asia of 1979 caused a shift in US foreign policy from a regionalist to a globalist stance.

Under the Carter Administration, this shift was pragmatic and, wherever possible, the regionalist approach was allowed to prevail (as in Southern Africa and Central America). The accession of the Reagan Administration strongly reinforced the globalist tendencies in the US approach. A wide variety of factors account for that change. First, a confrontational attitude *vis à vis* the Soviet Union can count on wide popular support in present-day America. There is a general disenchantment with *détente*, which has not led to greater Soviet moderation in its external policies and, it is believed, has resulted in an unfavourable shift in the arms' balance. Moreover, the proclaimed goal of the Reagan Administration to restore US military strength offers an ideal focal point for the restoration of American self-confidence, so badly shattered after Vietnam, Watergate and the hostage-taking in Tehran. A good part of the new American assertiveness seems to be negatively motivated and to derive from frustration with a loss of direction within American society, a lack of new challenges and frontiers, and declining economic productivity. Traditionally, American disenchantment with the outside world has fostered isolationist tendencies in its foreign policy orientation. For the moment, however, American frustrations are translating themselves into a more expansionist posture. In the economic sphere, the first two years of the Reagan Administration revealed both a certain ideological messianism with a populist undertone, espousing the advantages of free enterprise and the free market, and also unilateralist tendencies that seemed to be inspired by an 'America first' mentality. In the various multilateral fora for North–South negotiations, this mixture of ideological messianism and unilateralism was clearly manifested, for example, at the Law of the Sea Conference, the LLDC Conference in Paris, the Energy Conference in Nairobi, and at the World Bank/IMF (see Chapters 4 and 6).

Second, the US position is, of course, heavily influenced by structural factors. The status of superpower carries a number of obligations that cannot be ignored with impunity. Even though the age of the Pax Americana may have ended, the USA remains a crucial actor in a number of regional theatres. In South-West Asia, for example, much more is at stake than direct American interests, which are not particularly great – as much as 89% of US energy consumption is met from domestic sources, and for the remainder only 15% of energy imports come from the Middle East. The prime consideration for US policy in South-West Asia is not the safeguarding of US oil imports, but the wish to deny the Soviet Union an expansion of influence in the area and to prevent it from gaining leverage over Western Europe and Japan in that way. US foreign policy objectives in South-West Asia, therefore, almost necessarily contain a strong globalist element.

Third, there are certain systemic factors in the policy-making process in Washington that are biased against the regionalist approach. These include the concentration of decision-making with a small group of advisers in the White House, most of whom lack diplomatic training and detailed regional expertise. Yet the importance of such systemic factors in relation to structural ones should not be exaggerated. Perceptions and policies *vis à vis* Central America during the first years of the Reagan Administration were only partly influenced by a lack of adequate information. The adoption of the globalist approach to El Salvador and Guatemala was inspired primarily by doctrinaire strategic considerations, notably the wish to halt 'Soviet expansionism' by putting pressure on local agents and proxies at a minimum cost and with a maximum effect on public opinion in the USA and the world at large. To that end, the nuances of the internal balance of forces in these countries were deliberately ignored.

Differences between the USA and Europe

Because of the continuing importance of structural factors, it is important not to exaggerate the extent of the changes in US Third World policy since the accession of the Reagan Administration. Nevertheless, under the Reagan Administration irritation and friction between the United States and Western Europe has increased, not least as a result of differences over the handling of Third World conflicts, notably in Central America and South-West Asia, and over aspects of the North–South dialogue. There is, of course, a link between perceptions of the nature of Third World instability and questions of burden-sharing in addressing it. Many years ago, Henry Kissinger wrote: 'Countries do not assume burdens because it is fair, only because it is necessary . . . Even with the best will, the present structure favours American unilateralism and European irresponsibility'.[5] The first two years of Reagan's foreign policy were marked by strong globalist and unilateralist tendencies: its central concern was to confront Soviet expansionist tendencies wherever they seemed to occur by strong American initiatives and to press the Western allies to follow suit.[6] This uncompromising American stand caused concern both amongst regional actors in the Third World and among the Western partners. The moderate nations in the Middle East showed concern about the American subordination of the Palestinian problem to its geopolitical ambition of forging a 'strategic consensus' against Soviet expansionism in the area. Some states (Egypt, Oman) provided the USA with limited facilities for the expanded Rapid Deployment Force, but the attitude of most pro-Western local governments was very ambiguous ('Go away a little closer'). In South-East Asia the ASEAN countries were concerned to minimise superpower rivalry in the region by moderating the Indo-China conflict and by attempting to maintain a certain power balance between the Soviet Union, China and the United States. In Central America, Mexico continued to play an independent role by showing considerably more flexibility in the face of leftish insurgency than the Americans would have liked to see.

The position of the Western European nations in addressing situations of regional instability in the Third World is highly complex. First of all, they are far more vulnerable to the effects of regional turmoil than is the USA with its more autarchic economy. Whereas the USA's import dependence on strategic raw materials (other than oil) is about 15%, for Western Europe the figure is 80%, and for Japan it is 95%. Dependence on foreign suppliers has been a long-standing tradition for Western Europe, while for most Americans it represents a rather unsettling new reality. Apart from France and the UK, European states have an extremely limited capability for manifesting themselves in distant parts of the world, and the inclination to assume military burdens abroad is in most countries very limited. (West Germany is constrained by its constitution from undertaking such burdens.)

After the oil crisis of 1973 most West European countries showed an increased awareness of their vulnerability to pressures from the Third World. They reacted in a variety of ways. First, they accorded increased priority to the North–South dialogue in order to dispel Third World confrontation. Second, they took measures to reduce their dependence on OPEC oil (conservation, diversification), or their vulnerability in the case of sudden supply interruptions (stockpiling, emergency distribution schemes, etc.). Thirdly they sought preferential arrangements on a bilateral basis with certain oil-producing countries (a line of approach that was followed particularly vigorously by the French and the Italians). Fourth, they befriended the Arab states at the expense of ties with Israel. All of these steps exhibited, and reinforced, a regionalist approach to the Third World. When the Soviet Union invaded Afghanistan there was limited enthusiasm amongst West European nations to turn it into an outright East–West confrontation. So far, Western Europe has only taken note of the American build-up of the Rapid Deployment Force without fully endorsing it, let alone joining it. It can be safely assumed that some contingency planning has been going on between the Americans, the French and the British naval forces in the Gulf area, but there seems to be no unified support in Western Europe for joint US–European endeavours for safeguarding common interests outside the area covered by NATO. Arguments for such co-operation have been put forward from various sides in the recent past, most notably by a quartet of foreign policy intellectuals from the USA, the UK, France and West Germany:

> The days of the old Atlantic system, based on US predominance and, its corollary, European reluctance to take wider responsibilities, are over. Given today's international realities, neither the US nor Europe can be expected to face the challenges of the 1980s on its own. A new transatlantic political and military bargain is required to close this gap. The US should be more sensitive to European interests and accept a greater European share in alliance decision-making . . . In exchange Europe should accept more responsibility in dealing with the Soviet threat and with the Third World.[7]

Although the suggestions for contingency planning for Third World theatres by 'core groups' of Western nations have not met with much of a response, one observes an awareness in Western circles that some policy co-ordination amongst the partners will be necessary to deal with situations that pose a threat to common interests and to ensure that disunity does not undermine the Alliance's cohesion and weaken its posture against the Eastern Bloc. In some areas, where vital Western interests are at stake, tolerance towards diverging perceptions and initiatives seems to be very limited. Although critical of the Camp David formula, Western Europe has generally avoided conflict with the Americans in the Middle East. In Central America, however, there appears to be considerable room for differences in analysis and behaviour (as exemplified by the French arms shipments to Nicaragua). What seems to be blatantly unacceptable to the Americans is Europeans trying to gain unilateral advantages in Third World areas where the United States sees itself forced to play an unpopular role, as was the case when the French sought preferential treatment from Arab oil suppliers after 1973. Since the arrival of the Reagan Administration there is also less tolerance for European 'window-dressing' in international fora: taking popular positions on North–South issues without any real intention of acting accordingly, in the knowledge that American vetoes will prevent implementation of the Third World proposals.

The formula that is emerging for accommodating divergences between the United States and Western Europe over the Third World can be summed up as regional specialisation and complementary action. During the 1979 summit conference *à quatre* in Guadeloupe, Chancellor Schmidt assumed responsibility for contributing to stability in Turkey and Pakistan through the German aid programme. France remains committed to Africa ever since the accession of the Mitterand government which has not yet led to any substantial change in the French African policy, although one might expect that the inclination to intervene militarily will have diminished.

Prospects for Atlantic harmony or conflict over the Third World

To what extent are American and European interests in the Third World compatible? Undoubtedly, there are significant differences between them in terms of dependence and vulnerability, global capabilities and ambitions, foreign policy traditions and political temperaments and intuitions. The United States is an eager superpower that is losing control, not so much due to the ascendancy of Soviet power or the unwillingness of its European partners to follow its lead, but mainly due to the diffusion of power to other parts of the world. This is a logical consequence of the slow but certain political and economic emancipation of the Third World. In some areas, most notably in South-West Asia, the Soviet challenge could be real and poses a dilemma: can it be met by fostering regional stability through political and economic means, or are elements of military deterrence indispensable? Here, it seems likely that Western Europe will follow the American lead, albeit hesitantly and at a distance, mostly because it cannot safeguard its interests in any other manner. In most other Third World areas Europe is less acutely vulnerable and alternative options for dealing with threats are available. In Africa and Latin America there are reasonable prospects for regional security systems to emerge, while in South-East Asia the maintenance of a reasonably stable power balance between the major powers would seem to be the best bet for minimising the effects of regional instability. Although energy and raw materials supplies could be jeopardised in the short run, the greatest threat to trade in manufactured goods, investment and financial interests is likely to derive from economic and political disruption over an extended period of time.

The post-war liberal trading system is under heavy siege, and on both the economic and political fronts the United Nations system has failed to contribute significantly to international order. It is hard to avoid the impression that the differences between the American and European stands in the UN economic fora are mostly symbolic and of limited consequence, even where they seem to reflect major ideological and political disagreements. Mostly, they concern items of institutional gadgetry that apply to minor segments of the world economy (funding mechanisms, management formulae, decision-making procedures) which, although indicative of a philosophical attitude, remain marginal to the mainstream of North–South relations. When it comes to concrete situations and difficult trade-offs must be faced, there is no guarantee that the Europeans will be more forthcoming towards Third World demands than the Americans.

And yet there remains the possibility that tensions between the USA and Europe over Third World issues will increase in the near future, not as a result of basic differences over long-term goals and philosophies, but due to frictions that might develop as part of the crisis in the liberal trading system or in the process of conflict management in the Third World. Such frictions could inflate existing differences and, inadvertently, cause partners to set off on diverging paths. If this were to happen, there is no reason to assume that EEC member states would stick together. Their interests and inclinations are, in principle, as diverse as those of the USA on the one hand and Europe on the other. In the economic sphere the Germans, British (under Conservative rule) and the Dutch will continue to favour free trade, while the French and most other Latin nations, with their interventionist tradition, will be more inclined to 'organised free trade'. On concepts of world order and international interventionism, the Dutch and the Scandinavians will generally join the French camp, as for example on the law of the sea, international finance, etc. The Northern European bloc of free-traders will be less favourably inclined than the Southern Europeans towards regional compacts with segments of the Third World, as exemplified by the Lomé Convention and Giscard d'Estaing's proposals for a Trilogue with Africa and the Arab nations. In the political sphere other sub-divisions within the EEC are likely to occur. In the face of Third World conflict, the UK is the most likely to pursue its security interests by grabbing at America's coat tails. Neither the British nor the French would ultimately shun military intervention, but the French would be much less inclined to subordinate their policies to American views and behaviour. The Germans and most smaller European nations would prefer to stay out of Third World conflicts and would stress the need for international solutions in the framework of the United Nations or the Non-Aligned Movement.

Thus, the USA and Europe share an interest in maintaining an open world economy and global stability. If free trade collapses and Third World conflict increases this could cause rifts in the Atlantic partnership. However, it would seem most unlikely that this would result in the emergence of an independent and coherent European response to the Third World, be it on the global or the regional level. European security interests in the Third World are tied up in an intricate web of dependencies globally, regionally, and in the context of its Atlantic relations.

Notes

1   Along these lines see for example Fred Bergsten, 'The Threat from the Third World', *Foreign Policy,* Summer 1973.
2   J. Tinbergen *et al, Reshaping the International Order*, New York, 1976.
3   Willy Brandt *et al, North–South: a Programme for Survival,* London, 1980.
4   Zbigniew Brzezinski, 'America in a hostile world', *Foreign Policy,* Summer 1976.
5   Henry Kissinger, 'Central issues of American foreign policy' in Kermit Gordon, *Agenda for the Nation,* Washington DC, Brookings Institution, 1968.
6   Stanley Hoffman, 'Reagan abroad', *New York Review of Books*, 4 February 1982.
7   Karl Kaiser, Winston Lord, Thierry de Montbrial, David Watt, *Western Security: What has changed? What can be done?,* London, 1981.

3

France's New Third World Policy: Problems of Change

Yves Berthelot with D. Besnaiou

Three gestures by the new French government illustrate the changes they aim to introduce into France's relations with the Third World. The first, a political gesture, came from the joint declaration by President François Mitterand and President Lopez Portillo, made during the former's official visit to Mexico. In emphasising the need for greater justice in Central America and the Caribbean and condemning the situation in El Salvador, the French President wished to demonstrate that he considers the principle of justice more important than a cautious non-interference in the internal affairs of other countries. By distancing himself from the US approach, however, he also indicated that, if necessary, he was prepared to break ranks with the Western powers and align himself with the Third World.

The second gesture was an economic one: France agreed to pay a price for Algerian gas that was higher than the current market rate. By this action the French government hoped to show that, over and above the direct interests of France and Algeria in these negotiations, it recognised the importance of Third World countries being able to finance their own development by the export of raw materials, and that, even where there are no international agreements, they are prepared to make bilateral agreements to pay more than the market price.

The third gesture, a less public one since it will only be noted by experts, was the omission from the French report to the Development Assistance Committee of the OECD of transfers made to the Dom-Tom (France's overseas possessions); thus French aid to the Third World as a percentage of GNP is shown to be only slightly above the average for all DAC countries. This new method of calculating the aid figures, coming as it does after the commitment to reach 0.7% of GNP by 1988, demonstrates that the government is not taking the easy option, but is determined to make a very significant drive to increase aid. These indications of change are, however, offset by the continued application of measures designed to restrict imports of 'sensitive' products originating in Third World countries. The measures, aimed at preventing factory closures and increased unemployment in France, contradict the government's declared view that Third World countries need to export.

These examples illustrate both the government's will to change, and the need to harmonise France's relations with the Third World into one coherent policy although, as the last example shows, this will be difficult to achieve. The interaction of sometimes contradictory interests, objectives and principles demonstrates that creating a new policy can be neither rapid nor spectacular.

France's economic interests in its relations with the Third World

Towards a new balance in trade

Despite its long tradition of trade and development co-operation, France is not renowned as an open market for products from ldcs. The share of Third World countries in French imports was only some 14% in 1980 (8% if only manufactures are considered). The proportion is much greater for the USA, Japan, West Germany and the UK. However, it is worth noting that the proportion of imports is not a good indicator of a country's openness to the Third World since they may only represent a small part of national income, as is the case with Japan and the USA. In fact during the 1970s, France opened up considerably to Third World products and has thus lessened the gap between it and other trading partners (see Table 3.1).

Nonetheless, France is still not a primary market for developing countries apart from those in Francophone Africa. On the other hand, the Third World is a vital market for France. Indeed, it is only with the Third World that France runs a surplus in its trade of manufactured goods; it is in deficit with all the other major areas – the EEC, the USA, Japan and the Eastern bloc countries. This surplus is vulnerable because of the geographical orientation of trade within the Third World; exports mainly go to Africa and the Middle East, but Africa's absorptive capacity is weak and all the international organisations agree that it is likely to remain so. The OPEC countries are now experiencing financial difficulties and a degree of saturation which is slowing down their rate of import penetration. On the other hand, France has been unable to gain a sufficient foothold in the more promising markets of Asia and Latin America.

Table 3.1   *Growth in imports from the Third World of various OECD countries*

| | Share of Third World in manufactured imports (%) | | Imports from Third World, per capita (1975 $ prices) | | | |
| | | | manufactures | | textiles | |
	1973	1980	1973	1980	1973	1980
France	5.4	8.2	21	90	0.9	11.0
West Germany	7.3	9.5	28	115	4.9	33.6
UK	10.4	9.7	53	90	7.2	17.6
Japan	29.7	30.5	22	88	1.0	7.6
USA	19.3	27.3	45	131	5.8	17.6

Source: CEPII – CHELEM.

Note: These figures mainly comprise annual exchange flows gathered since 1967 in matrices of 32×32 countries or groups of countries and 71 categories of products. This data base is put together by CEPII (Centre d'Etudes Prospectives et d'Informations Internationales) using another data base CHELEM (Comptes Harmonises sur les Echanges et l'Economie Mondiales).

A second reason for the vulnerability of France's exports is the method of financing. Exports to the Third World rely on commercial credits and various guarantees for the exporting companies established under the 'grands contrats' policy (see Chapter 5); from 1975 to 1980 these covered more than half of capital equipment exports to the Third World. Criticisms have been made, however, of facilities which are designed solely to increase France's level of exports with no consideration of either their appropriateness for the development of the importing country or for the risks inherent in increasing ldc indebtedness. During 1981–82 the rate of approval of such 'grands contrats' slowed down, not because of any examination of the developmental effects of projects financed in this way, but because ldcs, which are the countries most affected by the world economic crisis, have had to avoid taking on further debts. Furthermore, direct investment overseas, which is supposed to promote export growth and avoid major fluctuations, remains relatively limited; in the world league table France is only seventh in overseas investment, and industrial investment in the Third World only accounts for 1% of industrial gross fixed capital formation. In Mexico, for example, a large country which France hopes to gain as one of its major partners, French investments represented only 1% of total foreign investments in 1981. This weak French presence cannot be rectified by aid.

The object of aid and development co-operation is to contribute to development, and this is the chief reason for the government's current changes in attitude. Before considering it from this angle, however, it must be borne in mind that the impact of aid on trade is not negligible,

Table 3.2 *Breakdown of trade* (in 000 mn FF, 1973 prices)

	Africa south of the Sahara		North Africa		Middle East		Far East		Latin America/ Caribbean		Total All areas	
	1973	1980	1973	1980	1973	1980	1973	1980	1973	1980	1973	1980
Semi-finished products	0.1	0.6	1.1	1.8	0.7	2.4	0.1	—	0.3	0.4	2.2	4.9
Technical equipment[a]	1.6	4.0	1.8	4.6	1.2	4.4	0.1	-0.6	1.5	2.4	9.6	22.2
Household equipment	0.1	0.1	0.1	0.1	—	0.2	-0.1	-0.5			0.2	—
Vehicles	1.0	2.1	0.7	1.5	0.4	1.0	0.1	—	0.3	0.7	2.6	5.5
Current consumption	0.8	1.0	0.7	0.8	0.4	1.2	-0.3	-1.6			1.0	0.3
Total industrial sectors	3.6	7.8	4.4	8.8	2.7	9.2	-0.1	-2.7	1.7	3.4	15.6	32.9

[a] Armaments included in the total only

Source: Ministry of the Economy – Forecasting Department

although it may be difficult to measure. Aid is financed from various budgets: cultural and technical assistance, the aid and co-operation fund (FAC), the Caisse Centrale de Co-operation Economique (CCCE) and Treasury loans. These different instruments have resulted in exports in different proportions: approximately 70% for the FAC, 70–80% for the CCCE and 100% for Treasury loans. Similar calculations of the rates of return obtained from projects financed by multilateral aid show that this varies between 80–85%.

Competition and jobs

In a period of rapidly rising unemployment, the government is very aware of the effect on employment of trade with the Third World. A study commissioned by the Ministry of Planning and the Ministry of Development and Co-operation has just been completed on this subject and its findings will be taken into account in the evaluation, involving all the relevant ministries, of France's overall relations with the Third World, which is due to take place before the end of 1982. This study shows that the job-creating potential of Franco–Third World relations is in decline.[1] From 1973 to 1980 the number of jobs created by the rise in exports to the Third World was between 220,000 and 360,000. The link between jobs and exports is clear; less obvious, however, despite general opinion to the contrary, is the link between job losses and a rise in imports, since one has to distinguish between complementary and competing imports. The former are necessary to production and hence to jobs; the latter, on the contrary, bring about a reduction in jobs. By using various methods of evaluation, job losses associated with a growth in imports from the Third World between 1973 and 1980 have been put at about 70–100,000. Thus over the whole period the balance between jobs created and lost is positive and according to the estimates used, is between 150,000 and 250,000.

This positive balance is under threat. The export growth rate to the Third World actually flagged after 1978, whereas import growth continued to increase. The very positive balance of 1973–75 had become slightly negative by 1979–80. The root cause of this deterioration is (and will continue to be) the fall in exports to the Third World rather than the rise of imports. Forecasts made indicate that in 1987, a reduction of 20% in imports from the Third World could lead to 24,000 jobs being created, whereas a drop of 20% in exports would cause 107,000 job losses.

Of even more concern than the import penetration of the French market is the competition that French exports face in third markets, particularly in West Germany. Competition has been most severe in the textile industries, wood and paper industries, and also engineering, electrical goods, electronic components and electronic consumer hard-

Table 3.3 *Level of jobs in trade in industrial goods between France and developing
countries.*

	1973–75	1975–78	1978–80	1973–80	France–World 1973–80
Gains linked to exports	179.1	49.3	35.2	263.6	591.0
Losses linked to imports	18.1	33.4	52.9	104.4	271.7
Balance	161.0	15.9	−17.7	159.2	−180.7

Source: Y. Berthelot and J. De Bandt 'L'impact des relations France-Tiers-Monde
sur l'économie française' to be published by the Documentation Française.

ware. It is estimated that 30% of market losses suffered by French
companies can be attributed to Third World exports.

This phenomenon, the extent of which has not hitherto been measured, has one major consequence. If French production is, in the final
analysis, threatened by competition from the Third World more in
foreign than in domestic markets, then maintaining employment in
France requires a policy for industry rather than a policy of protection.
At best the latter could only protect jobs linked to competing imports;
it would be ineffective in regaining foreign markets.

In conclusion, changes in jobs due to trade with the Third World are
small by comparison with changes due to trade with other countries, to
productivity-induced restructuring, and to lack of demand. French
exports to the Third World are partly concentrated on countries where
aid is important, but this link is a source of concern since the African
and the Middle Eastern markets have poorer prospects than do those
of Asia and Latin America.

New directions in development co-operation policy

Relations between France and the Third World are a priority which the
French President affirmed from the first day of his seven-year term in
office and which he confirmed at the conference of lldcs at Paris in
September 1981, at Cancun and at the Versailles summit (see Chapter
6i). The importance attached to North–South relations by the Socialist
Party is long-standing, partly because, unlike other parties, its beliefs
are based on an explicit doctrine, set out in a book (*Les Socialistes et le
Tiers-Monde*) by Lionel Jospin, who is today First Secretary of the
Party. In addition the Socialist Party has occasionally adopted aid to
the Third World as a campaign theme when many considered it
scarcely an electoral issue.

Criticism of the past

Once in office, the new government decided to make an evaluation of past action, and therefore turned its attention to the development policy of its predecessors. The reforms that the government will attempt to carry out are consequent upon the criticisms made in this evaluation. The deputy responsible for the co-operation and development budget, Alain Vivien, has spoken of a difficult policy inheritance in which 'generous talk' is 'contradicted by a more sombre reality'.[3] According to Alain Vivien, talk continues, but it has not progressed: France has talked for a long time about inequalities between nations, the lot of the poorest countries, the current price of raw materials, balanced development, the reform of the international monetary system and the need for a growth in aid. But progress is slow and France's influence is limited by its lack of a coherent policy. Decision-making is divided between numerous ministries and organisations, and French aid is small if the Dom-Tom are excluded. Furthermore, the evaluation report considers that the burden of Treasury loans is excessive, as they have 'financed a frenzied policy of exports rather than a policy of internal development in the recipient states'. As A. Bellon, speaking on behalf of the Foreign Affairs Commission of the National Assembly, has said, 'the absence of long-term perspectives has brought about the abuse of one-off interventions which correspond more to crisis support than to creating a healthy economic base'.

Solidarity and French interests

The new development policy will aim to be coherent, not only by integrating its different components, but also by co-ordinating development policy with other national policies. Jean Pierre Cot, the minister in charge of development co-operation, has demonstrated this concern at numerous conferences: 'The imperative of solidarity, which determines the whole of the government's policy, cannot end at our country's borders. Why should our support of the most disadvantaged end at the limits of our national territory?'

'In addition economic relations with ldcs are particularly vital for our country. France is one of the chief creditors of the Third World, one quarter of its foreign trade is conducted with it, and ldcs absorb over 50% of our production of some types of capital equipment. Of special importance is the contribution of these economic relations to employment. In the future the economies of these countries should grow faster than those of the industrialised countries; their expanding import needs will offer important possibilities for the development of our exports and hence for the promotion of employment in our country.'

By this account the minister has shown himself clearly to be in favour of liberal treatment for imports and has called for the restructuring of

French industry. On this question, however, debate is continuing between members of the government.

Nevertheless, the aid objective of 0.7% of GNP has been affirmed on numerous occasions by the President and 1988 is the date set for its achievement. A secondary objective of 0.15% of GNP as aid to the lldcs is to be reached by 1985. These ambitious objectives will not easily be achieved as is clear from an examination of the 1982 and 1983 budgets (see below).

Priorities and geographical choices

France has always wanted to play a global role, and the first declarations made during the President's visit to Mexico might have led one to believe that a global redistribution of development co-operation was envisaged. In fact these ambitions have come up against the same limitation encountered by General de Gaulle when he wanted to follow up his tour of Latin America with concrete actions – lack of resources. The new government is therefore more cautious and seeks a modulated response. Jean Pierre Cot expressed this prudence when he said 'we have to admit that France is a country of modest size, with modest resources'. Thus it is necessary to choose privileged partners.

Priority action in favour of Africa is being maintained; but this will no longer be limited to French- or Portuguese-speaking Africa, and will be extended to English-speaking Africa. The second priority is the poorest countries which should benefit from the growth in aid to the lldcs, and the third priority is multilateral aid, as this can contribute to a country's development where France's bilateral action alone would be insignificant. Similar considerations apply beyond the sphere of aid narrowly defined; it is only on a multilateral basis that commodity agreements can be made and world financial and monetary problems tackled. It is progress in these areas, more than aid, that promotes development. Thus the government hopes to be more active in its proposals within international organisations and, to this end, has decided to increase French contributions and to encourage other countries to continue supporting these organisations.

Finally, as a new venture, certain countries will be chosen for experimental forms of development co-operation which hopefully will serve as examples for the rest of the world. The terms employed – 'plan agreements' and 'co-development' – show a concern to establish planned relations and to put back a little of the original meaning in the word 'co-operation'.

Development strategies and responsibilities

It is the view of those now in charge of development co-operation that the failures in development strategies over the last two decades or more have their origins in the excessive dependence of the Third World on prices and international markets. They therefore advocate 'forms of development less dependent on the fortunes of the external world, based on giving priority to expanding domestic markets, to creating structures of production adapted to those markets, and utilising appropriate technologies'.

The policy of development co-operation which aims to promote this 'self-centred development' is based on four priorities: self-sufficiency in food, fulfilment of basic needs, energy and appropriate indus-trialisation. The first priority, self-sufficiency in food, is justifiable because, with a few rare exceptions, no country has achieved lasting development without first creating a sound agricultural base. French aid will be concerned with defining integrated national and regional programmes involving land reform, policies of price incentives for producers, research, extension services, storage, irrigation and train-ing. The government, however, does not envisage ending food aid where this is necessary, but aims to find a way of avoiding disincentive effects on local production.

In the same way, a basic needs strategy should be aimed at the poorest strata of the population. As regards health, priority should be given to primary health care, and France will support any project encouraging birth control. Projects for the supply of drinking water, improving rural housing and for secondary road-building will be given preference over more spectacular infrastructure projects. Finally, education programmes will concentrate on primary and vocational education. In the energy field, development co-operation will aim to reduce the cost of imported energy by focusing on compiling inventor-ies of resources, assisting tariff setting, helping to increase supply of traditional energy to meet demand by developing new energy sources, and increasing the thermal output of cooking equipment.

Industrial development will differ from one country to another, depending on the degree of industrialisation and the level of training of the workforce and staff. Recipients will include nationalised com-panies, private firms and civil engineering bureaux. The government hopes to encourage Third World enterprises to join together to give priority to those industrial projects which aim to satisfy domestic needs.

When French development co-operation was examined in February 1982 at the OECD, the presentation of this policy led to numerous questions. What is the difference between 'self-centred' development and basic needs? Is 'self-centred' development synonymous with self-sufficiency? Is this concept not opposed to the ideas of some development experts? Even if it is more a question of import substitu-tion than true autarky, is not any tendency towards protectionism irrational and in any case harmful to the interests of all exporting countries, especially if France extends the concept to middle-income developing countries? Along the same lines, will not the French policy of 'winning back the domestic market' have the effect of reducing imports from ldcs? How do you reconcile the idea of self-centred development and expansion or, more concretely with *crédits mixtes* (see Chapter 5), which are directly aimed at stimulating exports? More generally, how can the French hope to avoid the charge of paternalism, when the government talks more about development strategy than the strategies of Third World countries?

Only experience will provide answers to the first set of questions. How the stated principles will be applied will emerge only from a case-by-case analysis of each aid request or each credit file. It is hard to prejudge the issue. But what can be said is that having these guidelines will enable more coherent decisions to be taken. In any case, 'self-centred' does not mean autarky. On the contrary, it is arguable that a more 'self-centred' development will promote growth and thereby increase the demand for capital equipment and consumption goods, necessary to sustain growth in the long run.

On the question of paternalism, Jean Pierre Cot has replied elsewhere to representatives of Francophone African countries: 'we claim the right, and indeed we affirm it to be our duty, to have a concept of development; would it be better to act in an unconsidered way, would it be better to be silent accomplices, ashamed and a little scornful of projects we regard as ill-starred, would it be better to rely on the logic of the market which in any case corresponds to a concept of development no less real for being unexpressed? No, we do not plead guilty to the charge of "interference".'

Provisional evaluation

The first year of the new government, as far as relations with ldcs are concerned, has been characterised by a number of gestures and reflections. The more significant gestures were described at the beginning of this chapter; the reflections resulted in a realisation of the diversity and scope of Franco–Third World relations and in the definition of guidelines. The achievements so far can only be modest, and as has been emphasised, only experience will permit a judgement on the application of the principles. A provisional judgement can however be made on the basis of the 1982 and 1983 (projected) budgets, the re-organisation of the machinery for development co-operation, arms sales and decisions taken on trade.

Development co-operation budget

The aim of improving relations with ldcs, which was incorporated in the 1981 budget by the previous government, was put into practice through an appreciable rise in the resources available to development co-operation agencies. The total resources assigned to official development assistance (oda) increased by 34% between 1981 and 1982. All the institutions concerned with aid (see Table 3.4) witnessed an increase in their budget grants. However, the budget of the Ministry of Co-operation, which administers one-third of oda[3] increased by less than the rise in the overall budget in 1982: 19.2% as against 23%.

Table 3.4 *Official development assistance (oda): contributions from French institutions*[a] *(million FF)*

	1981	1982	1983
Oda financed from budgetary resources:	8896	14576	14024
– Ministry of External Relations	1861	5274	4160[b]
– Ministry of the Economy: France's contributions to multilateral financial organisations	2926	3685	3743
– Ministry of Research and Industry: overseas scientific research (in Dom-Toms)	552[c]	715	877
– Ministry of Development and Co-operation	4109	4897	5244
Oda financed by the Treasury of which			
– Treasury loans	2685	3000*	3200*
– CCCE	1280	2000*	2800*

[a] The figures for 1981 and 1982 correspond to credits voted. Figures for 1983 will be submitted for examination to Parliament. Their breakdown is approximate due to internal modifications in the areas of competence of the different institutions.
[b] Including the payment for Algerian gas (FF1.4bn in 1983 and FF2.8bn in 1982).
[c] In 1981 credits for overseas research were part of the Ministry of Development and Co-operation budget.

* Estimates

The guidelines laid down for development aid have resulted in the following initial applications.

(a) Priority for Africa, and specifically the least developed countries, has been effected, by a growth in the grants made by the Ministry of Co-operation and in loans by the CCCE. The share of countries with a per capita GNP of less than $250 was 25.3% of CCCE loans in 1981 compared with 16.5% in 1979, with relatively low interest rates. Other countries with a higher per capita income, but whose economic situation is causing concern, have also benefited from exceptional transfers. These serve to ensure the functioning of state machinery and have increased greatly in sub-Saharan Africa where the situation is particularly critical.

(b) The emphasis placed on self-centred development has been demonstrated by increased aid to agriculture, rural development and the promotion of local energy sources. Thus in 1981 42% of assistance was allocated to rural sectors compared with 33% in the preceding years. This has taken the form of finance for agro-industrial projects like the Diama dam on the Senegal or the integrated development project, based on cotton, in the Zambezi, Mozambique.

(c) Efforts to join with foreign partners, notably the Arab Funds, in bilateral projects have not seen any real change, despite the emphasis put on them. The growth in French contributions to multilateral and financial organisations is of greater significance. The parameters for these contributions are now budgetary rather than political, but one cannot expect a rapid transformation in the distribution of aid between bilateral and multilateral agencies, nor that, even in the long run, the share of the multilateral agencies will be significantly greater than it was in 1982 (26%).

The figures for 1981 are relatively satisfactory, thanks to the package voted in the summer of that year, as are those for 1982. For 1983, the budgetary forecasts are not favourable and the objective of increasing aid may not be adhered to. The draft budget only envisages a 7% growth in current prices compared with 19% for 1982. This development would mark a great reduction in aid unless the loans from the CCCE and the Treasury were increased significantly.

Table 3.5 *Ministry of Co-operation: budgetary credits* (million FF)

	1981	1982	1983
Category III			
Resources of central administration and external services	245 888	295 889	343 440
Category V			
Investment on behalf of services	11 000	12 900	11 600
Total allocated to services	256 888	308 789	355 040
Category VI			
State assistance	2 890 590	3 493 843	8 791 700
of which:			
Aid in personnel	2 036 134	2 449 287	2 651 718
Military technology	274 195	304 195	317 520
Financial assistance	287 153	391 153	447 945
Civil co-operation	293 106	349 206	374 516
Category VI			
Investment subsidies	962 000	1 095 000	1 097 330
of which:			
FAC	825 967	914 250	769 530
Exceptional operations	96 033	140 750	300 000
military aid	40 000	40 000	27 800
Total resources allocated to aid	3 852 590	4 588 843	4 889 030
Total allocation to Ministry of Co-operation	4 109 480	4 897 632	5 244 431

Co-ordinating development co-operation policies

The government very quickly established an inter-ministerial delegation for development, under the authority of the Prime Minister.
Stephane Hessel, who, as ambassador to the UN at Geneva, had
played a large part in finalising talks on the Common Fund, was given
responsibility for attacking the formidable problem of inter-ministerial
co-ordination on development (he is a contributor to Chapter 12). He
has succeeded in ensuring that, on important issues, whether concerning principles, international conferences or projects, an agreed position should be reached by the ministries concerned and that a common
stance should be laid down and adhered to.[4]

One of the reforms to which the delegation will contribute concerns
the Ministry of Development and Co-operation. Traditionally the
ministry's competence was limited to sub-Saharan French- and Portuguese-speaking Africa. Now, under the authority of the Ministry of
Foreign Relations, it covers the whole range of development problems. This integration of development co-operation is necessary for
the formation of a global policy covering all the Third World. However, financial questions still remain with the Ministry of the Economy,
which has traditionally dealt with them, as do the famous Treasury
loans and *crédits mixtes*, contributions to international financial organisations, and questions concerning debt. Finally, a geographical dichotomy remains, since those countries which obtain Treasury loans are
not eligible for loans from the CCCE. It is clear that very politically
significant changes have been made, but inter-ministerial co-
ordination still has some way to go.

Trade and armaments

Despite some fears expressed by France's trading partners, the move
to regain the domestic market is more a sign of competitive drive than
an indication of protectionist wishes. In fact the government has not
increased the protectionist measures adopted by its predecessor – but
neither has it lifted them. The most critical aspect of the renegotiation
of the Multifibre Arrangement is not that France contributed to a
hardening of the terms, but that it did not seek to replace the
traditional system based on relations between unequal partners with a
contractual organisation of trade.

Some observers claim that the question of arms sales represents
another dichotomy between the intentions of the government and its
actual practice. Arms sales are, at the moment, an important component of French exports, representing 41% of the industry's turnover.
One gesture by the French President has given the impression that he is
opposed to such sales: when attending the aeronautical show at
Bourget he asked that offensive weapons should not be displayed. In

fact in an interview with the BBC, the President himself stated that the export of military equipment would only be prohibited to 'fascist or racist countries'. Arms sales may even allow France's partners 'to increase their margin of independence by not having to turn to one or other of the two superpowers with all the consequences such a liaison entails'.[5]

The arrival of a new party in power has led many ldcs to hope for a new style of relations, a deeper understanding of the fundamental problems of development, and action to advance North–South negotiations. Speeches, gestures and actions have corresponded with this expectation; the limits imposed on France by its size, its budgetary and financial constraints, the complexity of the records which the new government discovered, all explain the slowness, contradictions and back-tracking. But beyond the disappointments and the renunciations, the essential orientation remains, and only time will establish the changes. It is thus too early to draw up a balance-sheet.

Notes

1   *L'impact des relations France-Tiers-Monde sur l'economie Française*, Y. Berthelot and J. de Bandt, to be published by Documentation Française.
2   Assemblée Nationale, ordinary session 1981–82, report on the Finance Bill 1982.
3   Excluding aid to Dom-Tom.
4   M. Hessel was promoted to the Haute Autorité de l'Audio-visuel on 1 September 1982.
5   Lecture by the Prime Minister to the Institut des Hautes Études de la Defense Nationale in September 1981. Quoted in *The Policy of Defence in France and the New Government,* Yves Boyer, Institute of International Studies, Lausanne.

4

The EEC, USA and the Law of the Sea

Roderick Ogley

Some fifteen years of negotiation came to a climax in April 1982 when a new Law of the Sea Convention was adopted. This climax was, however, marred by sharp differences between the EEC and the USA, and among the EEC member states. Denmark (with the other Nordic countries), France, Greece and Ireland voted for the convention; Germany, the Benelux countries, Italy and UK abstained; and the USA voted against. Before it can come into force, the Convention must be signed and this is scheduled to take place in December 1982 in Jamaica. At the time of writing most EEC governments had not taken a final decision whether to sign. But the USA had indicated that it would not sign. The conflicts may, therefore, continue well after the Jamaica meeting and continue to create divisions within Europe and between Europe and the USA. Since the issues are highly complex and State positions are still fluid, this chapter provides the information and analysis needed to assess developments in 1983 and beyond. It explains the issues at stake, the positions taken by the main actors, and the consequences of the most likely outcomes.

Third World interests in UNCLOS

The law of the sea has been a prominent concern of the Third World since 1967, when the Maltese representative brought before the UN General Assembly a proposal for making that part of the sea-bed 'beyond the limits of present national jurisdiction' the 'common heritage of mankind'. This proposal led, via six years of Sea-bed Committee meetings, and then eleven sessions of the Third United Nations Conference on the Law of the Sea (UNCLOS III), to the adoption on 30 April 1982 of the Law of the Sea Convention, by 130 votes to 4 with 17 abstentions. This has not been, by any means, the sole theme of Third World interest at UNCLOS III. In 1970 the General Assembly, in endorsing the 'common heritage' principle[1] also decided that the Conference to implement it would be a comprehensive one, charged with a complete overhaul of the existing law of the sea, in the making of which most developing countries had played little if any part.

The chief fruits of all this endeavour were the legitimisation and acceleration of a trend towards wholesale extension of coastal state jurisdiction over the sea as well as the sea-bed, which was tempered in the Convention by a complicated and finely-balanced set of constraints and assurances. This helped many Third World states, among others, to set the terms on which foreigners might exploit the often rich resources off their coasts. It was, however, differences over the application of the 'common heritage' principle that were chiefly responsible for the Conference lasting so long and failing, in the end, to achieve consensus on a text.

This principle, and the International Sea-bed Authority that was to embody it, were important for North–South relations both economically and politically. Because of these rapidly expanding coastal state claims the area of the sea-bed beyond national jurisdiction – 'the Area' – is now much smaller than it was in 1967, or even 1970, but it still contains much mineral wealth: manganese nodules lining much of the ocean's floor, whose value lies more in their nickel, cobalt and copper content than in their manganese; and polymetallic sulphides, discovered only last year in the crests of some Pacific oceanic ridges, which are particularly rich in copper.[2]

The economic relevance of a Sea-bed Authority to North–South relations is threefold. First it could be expected to contribute, probably very modestly, to the global redistribution of wealth. The Area would be exploited through a 'parallel system'. Each private or state applicant for a site would have to offer the Authority a choice of two, and the Authority would be able to exploit its chosen site directly, through its operating arm, the 'Enterprise'.[3] The private and state miners would pay royalties or a share of their net revenues to the Authority and it is hoped that the Enterprise would make profits. In addition, although the Area is not expected to contain commercially attractive deposits of hydrocarbons the Authority might still benefit from their exploitation, since after a five year grace period it would receive a share of the value of any minerals produced by coastal states from parts of their shelves that lie outside the 200-mile zone. Such exploitation would probably be more costly and formidable than any so far undertaken, but it could not be ruled out as impossible.

Second, the Authority would be assured of the technology to exploit the sites it had banked, if necessary by 'compulsory purchase' from private and state contractors, on terms to be set by agreement, or failing that by arbitration. This is very important for those developing countries that hope to move into ocean mining, since the Authority could assign to one or more of them any site that it was not itself planning to mine, and with it the technology it had acquired.

Third, and perhaps even more importantly in the eyes of the Group of 77 (especially those members who are actual or potential producers of the minerals in question), the Convention imposes an interim limit on sea-bed production, to apply for twenty years after commercial production has begun, derived by a precise and elaborate formula from the growth segment of the nickel market (see box). It also authorises the Authority to conclude commodity agreements 'in respect of production in the Area', provided that 'all interested parties including both producers and consumers' participate in them. Thus the Sea-bed Authority could play its part in the negotiation of an Integrated Programme for Commodities.

Limits on sea-bed mineral production

The effect of the interim limit would give nickel producers the assurance that, in this initial period, the nodules mined would yield no more than 60–100% of the growth segment of the nickel market. In fact, sea-bed miners do not seem to expect that it would be profitable to exceed this limit anyway in these early years. Since the copper content of this quantity of nodules would form only a tiny share of the world market, copper exporters are also well protected, although since the limit applies only to nodule mining, any large-scale mining of sulphides with high copper content would be a different matter. The cobalt and manganese content of nodules, on the other hand, constitutes a much larger percentage of their respective world markets. If the production limit was reached, the price of cobalt could fall drastically, probably down to that of nickel. If that happened, the Authority would be empowered to institute compensation schemes, but, because the gap between cobalt and nickel prices has sharply widened in recent years, it could hardly afford to reimburse cobalt exporters fully. The effect of nodule mining on the manganese market is more obscure. Though nodules contain 25–30% manganese, land-based ores frequently contain more, and it may not prove profitable to extract the manganese. If it is, though, manganese exporters could suffer.

Politically, the Convention is important both for what it contains and for how it was produced. It was the product of *negotiations* and not, until the last vote in April 1982, of the outvoting of minorities by majorities. Moreover, it was based on a text which, in 1980 in an admittedly incomplete form, had given general, if not universal, satisfaction to the Group of 77, the socialist states, and the West. Though often described as an element in the New International Economic Order, it is not closely linked with the General Assembly's resolutions of 1974. Yet if it leads nowhere it will deal a heavy blow to the constructive rather than the confrontational approach to North–South issues. If it is accepted, it will give a boost to other attempts at North–South dialogue. Moreover, to give effect to the 'common heritage' principle, the Convention had to define 'mankind' institutionally. By 1980, it had somehow solved the seemingly insoluble riddle of how to reconcile the Group of 77's confirmed opposition to any form of weighted voting with the West's refusal to allow the Authority to be controlled by the Group of 77's ever-growing numerical strength. It did this by reserving the most crucial decisions to a Council, half of whose members represented 'interests', rather than to the Authority's membership at large, while at the same time giving every one of the Authority's thirty-six members a veto, thus making these decisions a matter of further negotiation. If an Authority of this kind were to be generally accepted, and to work with reasonable efficiency and profit, the functions it would perform in the management of the sea-bed could make it both a model for dealing with other common terrains (Antarctica, the Moon) and a not negligible force for global political integration in its own right. These functions would include the unequivocal grant of title to mine, regulation and inspection of operations, distribution of revenues, and in the case of the Enterprise, the role of a mining entrepreneur.

USA and EEC positions

Until 1981 it had usually been the United States, rather than the European mining states, which had taken the lead in attempting to reconcile the interests of ocean miners with the concept of the 'common heritage of mankind'. President Nixon's Draft Convention of 1970, for instance, included the most generous proposals, in terms of the revenues that would thereby accrue to an International Authority, ever made by a mining state.[4] At Caracas in 1974 American proposals for the system of exploitation were uncompromising in their adherence to the principle of 'open access' to the Area by miners; but those emanating from eight of the nine Community members (Ireland being the exception) were very similar to, and certainly no improvement on them. It was the leader of the US Law of the Sea Delegation, Leigh Ratiner, who with some decisive interventions from the then Secretary of State, Henry Kissinger, laid the foundations of the parallel system in 1975 and 1976. When, under Carter, Leigh Ratiner was replaced by Elliott Richardson, the latter's record almost entirely confirmed America's position as the most far-sighted of the major industrialised

Western countries. In 1978, a direct comparison could be made with the EEC since the Community made a joint proposal on the question of what payments private and state miners should make to the Authority. It was the most niggardly of the seven then made. The next lowest, by some distance, was Japan's; then, again by a considerable margin, that of the USA; then the USSR's; then two by Norway; and, highest of all, India's.[5]

There was only one episode during these years when the USA was in some danger of coming to a major confrontation with UNCLOS III. This was in 1977 when, following the publication of the original Informal Consolidated Negotiating Text (ICNT) after the end of the Sixth Session, Richardson instituted an inter-agency review of US law of the sea policy. He conceded in answer to a question at a press conference, that US withdrawal from the conference could be one of the conclusions drawn by the review.[6] Negotiations on sea-bed mining at the Sixth Session had effectively been in the hands of the Norwegian, Jens Evensen, who believed that he had managed to construct a text acceptable to both the developed and the developing states; at least as a basis for negotiations. But the official chairman of the committee concerned, Paul Engo of Cameroon, made a dozen or so significant changes when incorporating it into the ICNT, all of which leaned towards the Group of 77 position and were unacceptable to the West. The US view was that this made nonsense of the session's negotiations. This view was widely shared by the Europeans, but Britain, in particular, urged the more sober response of continuing the argument within the conference.

Although Richardson did, after much inter-sessional consultation, keep the USA within the conference, he did change his policy in one respect. Since 1971, there had been bills before Congress to authorise the US government to license mining in the Area. Their sponsors had claimed either that such mining was a 'freedom of the high seas' and therefore did not need to wait upon an international agreement of the type UNCLOS III was seeking or, less contentiously, that before a global agreement could come into force, interim legislation was necessary to give mining consortia the comfort of knowing that their investments in specific sites had the weight of the United States behind them. Either way, the passage of such legislation, and still more the actual issue of a licence for a specific site under it, would have tied the US Administration's hands at UNCLOS III. Moreover, it was seen by the Group of 77 as illegal. Until the Sixth Session, these bills had been opposed consistently by the Administration, not so much on principle as on the grounds that UNCLOS III ought to be given a chance to find an international solution. After the review, Richardson gave them his support, so long as the terms on which licences were to be granted were not too different from those which the convention looked likely to prescribe for mining contracts with the Authority. Even with Administration support, however, a bill was not enacted until 1980. Similar legislation followed in Germany immediately and in Britain and France in 1981. Thereafter, such states were bound to insist that the Law of the Sea Convention included, or had attached to it, some provision for recognising title to sites based on the legislation they had passed. This raised the question of 'Preliminary Investment Protection' (PIP), one of the few issues remaining to be settled after the euphoric Ninth Session of 1980 when the delegates reached a wide measure of agreement on a draft convention. Neither the PIP nor any of the other remaining problems was expected to cause great difficulty, and only one further session was scheduled to resolve them.

It thus came as a jarring shock, not just to the Group of 77 but to most of the developed world as well, when in March 1981, on the eve of the Tenth Session of UNCLOS III, the Reagan Administration abruptly sacked several members of the US Delegation who had worked under Richardson (who himself had resigned the previous November), reinstated Leigh Ratiner, and announced another and more fateful review of its position which, to make matters worse, would not be completed in time for the resumption of the session at Geneva in August.[7] The Group of 77 responded by refusing to discuss PIP until the US position was clear. At the resumed session of the Conference it was decided by consensus to 'formalise' the 1980 text in a slightly amended version, to reserve the first three weeks of the 1982 New York session for further negotiations, and to commit UNCLOS to the adoption of a convention by the end of that eight-week session.

Not until 29 January 1982 did President Reagan announce that the USA would return to the conference and, if it secured the changes it wanted, would recommend ratification of the convention to the Senate. In a paper of 24 February 1982 the US delegation listed some twenty problems it had with the 1981 text, and suggested a variety of ways in which each could be 'solved'. At the time of this seemingly constructive approach, the delegation had not yet received its instructions.[8] These, issued on 8 March apparently without further reference to Reagan himself, drastically reduced the delegation's freedom of action. The amendments sought by the USA included the entire elimination of the production limit which was, in Ratiner's words, a 'cosmetic provision' unlikely to impose any real restriction on the scale of ocean mining though the land-based producers attached great importance to it; and a provision that would give the seven largest contributors to the UN the ultimate power to adopt or amend, by simple majority, the Authority's 'rules, regulations and procedures'. Because of the seemingly wholesale character of the proposed demands, and the perceived inability of the US delegation to make compromises, the Group of 77 would not entertain these amendments, even though they were now supported by Belgium, France, Germany, Italy, Japan and the UK. The rest of the conference, as Ratiner was to put it, was persuaded that 'the US appetite was too great – no improvements were likely to satisfy us that could also be swallowed by the Third World'.

On 19 March, a number of lesser industrialised Western states (including three EEC members), calling themselves 'the Friends of the Conference', circulated a set of suggestions for bridging the gap between the seven and the Group of 77.[9] These would have allowed dissenting states to have opted out of amendments adopted at the Review Conference, even after they had come into force, without thereby denouncing the rest of the Convention; ensured that the developed Western members of the Council could, if united, have vetoed the Authority's budget; reduced the scope of the Council's Legal and Technical Commission for refusing to approve an operator's plan of work; and have limited the operator's obligation with respect to transfer of technology so that it covered only that technology which it had made available, or was willing to make available, to third parties.

These were substantial modifications to the 1980 text. There were indications that the Group of 77 might have negotiated on the basis of them if they had been regarded as sufficient to secure the USA's acceptance of Convention; but the USA emphasised their insufficiency so strongly that such negotiations were discouraged.[10] Later, when the US delegation had managed, with some difficulty, to get its instructions altered, there were intense negotiations which came close to success but in the end broke down on two vital issues. One was the contractor's obligation to sell technology, at independently assessed prices, to the Enterprise, until the latter was firmly in business. The USA simply wanted to replace this with an obligation on the part of *states* undertaking, or sponsoring, ocean mining, to assist and advise the Enterprise in the acquisition of technology. The other was a provision to allow the convention's sea-bed mining provisions, apart from certain fundamental features of the system, to be amended after a Review Conference. The Review Conference would be held fifteen years after commercial production began, and if it had not reached agreement after five years, could adopt amendments by a two-thirds majority which would then come into force, for all parties, when ratified by two-thirds of them. The USA objected to this and sought that they should come into force only after being ratified by all members of the 36-member Council of the Authority.

The Group of 77, having over the previous eight years negotiated the compromise that resulted in the text of 1980, was now called upon to undo that compromise and make a different and less favourable one at short notice. It was not surprising that it was not prepared to make enough concessions to do so. A swift, unilateral shift in its position would no doubt have weakened its credibility elsewhere, notably in UNCTAD. But with hindsight, although this reaction was understandable it may not have been the right one. Had it given way on these two points, the convention would still have contained much of the 1980 compromise, including the financial terms of contracts and the parallel system, and such a convention with US participation would have been better than the present one if it is not widely accepted by mining states.

In the event, *some* concessions were made. The amendment process was altered to require ratification by three-quarters, rather than two-thirds, of the parties; and the entitlement of the USA to a *de facto* permanent place on the Council, in the guise of 'the world's largest consumer' of sea-bed minerals, was made plain to the most hostile critic, though it had never been in any doubt among the negotiators. In addition the Group of 77 took an accommodating line on PIP which was being discussed for the first time so that positions were not complicated by previous compromises. The Group of 77 accepted a suggestion of the conference president which would recognise at least eight pioneers: four consortia, and state enterprises from France, India, Japan and the USSR, and would even permit a pioneer firm to change nationality, provided the state whose nationality it adopted had 'effective control' of it. These concessions did not go far enough for the USA or for four of their European allies (Belgium, Germany, Italy and the UK). These five wanted the resolution to permit the pioneers to begin commercial production by 1988 even if their sponsoring states had not all ratified the convention by then; the convention requires that ratification comes first. They also wanted to reduce the information that the applicant had to supply to the Authority before it made its choice from the two sites; and, more importantly, to transfer the obligation to assist the Enterprise in the exploration of its 'pioneer' sites from the pioneer investor to the sponsoring state. On all these points, however, France and Japan stayed aloof, and their difference of view here may account for their positive vote on adoption.

The PIP Resolution requires each of the pioneer investors (or, if consortia, their sponsoring states) to ensure that the area it claims does not overlap with that claimed by any of the others or, if it does, to resolve the potential conflict if necessary by referring it to arbitration in accordance with UNCITRAL arbitration rules no later than 1 March 1983. Thus, in Ratiner's words, the convention 'now authorises, even commands, a mini-treaty', but that must be among the states that sign it. The convention requires that any claim, acquisition or exercise of such rights outside of it shall not be recognised (Article 137); and, Ratiner says, 'the President of the Conference has vowed to challenge any alternative mini-treaty before the UN General Assembly and to seek an opinion of the International Court of Justice'. It would seem, then, that states cannot have it both ways. They can sign the convention which means refusing to recognise sites claimed outside it; or they can sign what Ratiner calls 'an alternative mini-treaty', which effectively rules them out (as states, though not necessarily their companies, which can change nationality) of the system of the convention.

Prospects for the Law of the Sea

The United States announced on 9 July 1982 that it does not intend to sign the convention. Most European Community members have not so far shown their hand. At the time of writing Ireland had decided to sign; the Danish foreign ministry had recommended signature but no decision had been taken either by the government that resigned in September or by its successor; France had indicated that its vote for adoption of the convention did not necessarily imply that it would sign, and that a final decision would depend upon the actual text submitted for signature; and the other member states were also reserving their position.[11] There will no doubt be some attempts, and some willingness, on the part of member countries, to arrive at a common decision, or at least one common to the ocean-mining members. There will also be some attention given to what Japan and the USSR are doing.

The case for signing now, in spite of the US decision not to do so, is strong. The dilemma will become more acute when the question of ratification arises. Not only will all states whose firms comprise a given mining consortium have to ratify before the consortium can be given a contract or a production authorisation to begin exploitation, ratification will also bring into play the obligation, among others, to provide the Enterprise with enough capital to enable it to mine one site, and that is now put at $1.5 billion. The more wealthy states that ratify, the smaller will be the share each is called on to pay. If mining outside of the convention then appears viable for some, it will take a remarkable degree of public spirit, or long-sightedness, for others to ratify and incur their shares of this heavy charge, and also require their companies to bear the heavier obligations that the Sea-bed Authority regime will impose. A consoling thought (for supporters of the common heritage idea) is that mining outside the convention may not prove viable, because of the possible litigation it could involve, and may not attract investors.[12] Thus the convention may in the end prevail because there is no feasible alternative to it. Meanwhile, it has to be kept alive and in this the European mining states, which in the past have not always been noticeably enlightened on ocean questions, might still play a decisive role.

Notes

1   With the significant omission of the word 'present' which might have implied a 'freeze' on further coastal state claims.
2   See 'Polymetallic Sulphides: More Riches from the Sea?', United Nations Division for Economic and Social Information, *FACTS*, March 1982.

3   By a resolution adopted alongside the Convention, UNCLOS III recog-
nised as pioneer investors four states and four private consortia; the
states are France, India, Japan and the USSR; the consortia are:
Kennecott Consortium (unincorporated), consisting of Sohio (USA), Rio
Tinto Zinc (UK), British Petroleum (UK), Noranda Mines (Canada),
Mitsubishi (Japan).
Ocean Mining Associates (registered in the USA): US Steel (USA),
Union Minière (Belgium), Sun (USA), Ente Nazionale Idrocarburi
(Italy).
Ocean Management Incorporated (incorporated in USA): Inco
(Canada), Metallgesellschaft (Germany), Preussag (Germany), Salzgit-
ter (Germany), SEDCO (USA), Deep Ocean Mining (Japan).
Ocean Minerals Company (OMCO) (USA partnership): Standard Oil of
Indiana (USA), Lockheed (USA), Billiton (Netherlands, subsidiary of
Royal Dutch Shell), BKW Ocean Minerals (Netherlands, subsidiary of
Royal Bos Kalis Westminster).
    Other entities may qualify as pioneer investors if they have spent at
least $30 million on sea-bed activities by 1 January 1982, or, if a
developing country, by 1 January 1985. Of this 10% must be specific to a
site.
    Because of its predominant economic interest, as a major land-based
producer and exporter of copper, nickel and cobalt, in restricting rather
than encouraging ocean mining, Canada is not, in what follows, included
among the 'ocean mining states', even though Canadian firms participate
in two of these consortia.
4   Draft United Nations Convention on the International Sea-bed Area, 3
August 1970, United Nations Document A/AC. 138/25 (reproduced in
George A. Doumani, *Ocean Wealth: Policy and Potential,* Spartan
Books, Rochelle Park, New Jersey, 1973, Appendix 17). This draft was
largely devised by Elliott Richardson, who was to lead the American
delegation throughout Carter's presidency. Its generosity lay most
notably in the fact that it provided that every coastal state would transmit
to the International Sea-bed Authority between half and two-thirds of all
revenues it derived from what was called a Trusteeship Zone, which was
to begin at a depth of 200 metres – for most coastlines much closer to
land than the outer edge of the 200-mile wide economic zone, which was
to find well-nigh universal acceptance at Caracas in 1974 and become a
constant in all UNCLOS III texts, including the 1982 Convention. The
outer limit of the Trusteeship Zone was to be the outer edge of the
continental margin. This would, of course, have been in addition to the
Authority's revenues from the Area itself.
5   See 'A Cost Model of Deep Ocean Mining and Associated Regulatory
Issues', Massachusetts Institute of Technology, for a comparison of the
implications of the seven proposals all made in the Spring of 1978.
6   Report of press conference given by Elliot Richardson, 20 July 1977, p. 3.
7   Ratiner had spent the intervening four years working for a law firm
advising one of the ocean mining firms, Kennecott, and had strongly
criticised Richardson's handling of the negotiations. For instance, after
the Geneva part of the Seventh Session, on 26 May 1978, Ratiner sent
Congressmen a copy of a speech by Marne Dubs, the Director of

Kennecott's Ocean Resources Department, attacking UNCLOS III and the role of the US in it. Ratiner's own covering letter commented that the latest UNCLOS text (not yet an official 'revision' of the ICNT) 'shows a few minor improvements [over] and, in some important respects, has become worse [than] the previous . . . text . . . which was characterised by Ambassador Richardson as "fundamentally unacceptable" to the United States last year'.

8 Leigh Ratiner, 'The Law of the Sea: A Crossroads for American Foreign Policy', *Foreign Affairs*, Summer 1982, p. 1009.
9 Ratiner, ibid. p. 1015, lists twelve members of the Group: including Denmark, Ireland and the Netherlands. The group was, however, widely referred to as the Group of Eleven, and when these suggestions were later embodied in a formal amendment (A/CONF.62/L.104 of 13 April 1982) there were only eleven sponsors. The missing one was the Netherlands, the only ocean mining state, apart from Canada, in Ratiner's list, and the only state in that list to abstain on the vote for adoption, rather than vote in favour.
10 Ibid. p. 1016.
11 2 December 1982, the UK announced that it would not sign.
12 And one which Ratiner seems to share, ibid. p. 1017.

5

Export Credit: The Implications of the 1982 Revision for Developing Countries[1]

Joan Pearce

Since the 1950s export credit subsidies have become an important element of competition in exports of capital goods, and one in which some EEC members (as providers of credit) and parts of the Third World (as recipients) figure prominently. Since 1978, the main providers of export credit have operated within a gentlemen's agreement, called the Arrangement, which establishes guidelines on the degree of concessionality that can be offered. In the early 1980s the Arrangement came under increasing strain both because the general rise of world interest rates resulted in an increased subsidy on the permitted export credit rates, and because it regulates only loosely the provision of 'mixed credits', which are a blend of export credits and aid funds. Following protracted and tortuous negotiations, which came to the brink of collapse on several occasions, agreement was reached at the end of June 1982 on several important changes to the Arrangement. Of the 22 countries participating in the Arrangement, those chiefly involved in the negotiations were the USA, Japan and the EEC, which negotiated as a bloc. Their agreement affects the Third World in two ways: it alters the status of and hardens the terms for some of the largest Third World recipients; and it establishes a buffer zone between export credit and mixed credit.

The origins of export credit

Initially official support was given to export credit to prevent export orders being lost through lack of finance. Governments began to guarantee credits against types of risk, such as insolvency, which commercial insurers would normally cover but declined if they regarded the business as too hazardous, too large or too long; and against types of risk not normally covered by commercial insurers, such as transfer risk.

Changes in the international economy during the 1950s brought about changes in the demand for export credit. New markets were opening up in developing countries which, because they were short of capital and foreign exchange, relied heavily on export credit but also entailed greater uncertainty. Capital goods were becoming larger and accounting for a higher proportion of trade and since they were usually sold on credit this implied more and longer credit. The banks were reluctant to take on additional risks and so official support increased. Governments expanded their insurance activities and became more directly involved in the provision of export finance. In some countries an official export bank made direct loans while in others the central bank refinanced export credit advanced by commercial banks.

In response to importers' growing aversion to fluctuating interest rates countries arranged for their commercial banks to offer a fixed interest rate for export credit. Fixed interest rates were intended to remove uncertainty yet not to reduce the cost of credit, but during the 1970s market rates of interest in some countries (notably Britain and France) rose steadily while their fixed rate was adjusted very little, with the result that their governments were substantially subsidising the fixed rate. Since the 1950s financing terms have become an important element in competition for exports of capital goods. Official export credit agencies, besides ensuring that finance was available for these exports, began to match the terms being offered by their opposite numbers in other countries. Although their original function was to remove impediments to exports, credit facilities have increasingly been used to win orders from competitors.

All the OECD countries except Iceland and Turkey offer some measure of official support, and so do some non-OECD countries (including Argentina, Hong Kong, India, Iran, Israel, Korea, Pakistan and South Africa). But the provision of credit is much more concentrated than this list suggests. Some 85% of the export credit supported by OECD countries comes from five countries: France, West Germany, Japan, the UK and the USA; and some 70% is for exports to developing countries. The regional distribution of export credits in two recent years is shown in Table 5.1. There are obviously wide variations between years, but it is clear that middle-income developing countries have been major recipients. In 1977, for example, Latin America received 20% of all the long-term export credits of the five major suppliers, while five North African countries received 12.5%.

Table 5.1 *Regional distribution of official export credits exceeding five years, 1977–78* (Export value in US$m)

	France 1977	France 1978	Germany 1977	Germany 1978	Japan 1977	Japan 1978	Britain 1977	Britain 1978	United States 1977	United States 1978	Total 1977 $m	Total 1977 %	Total 1978 $m	Total 1978 %
Africa/Middle East	2990	1222	822	675	2571	368	790	91	519	781	7692	40	3137	25
(North Africa)[a]	(861)	(595)	(482)	(234)	(798)	(166)	—	—	(269)	(711)				
(Other)	(2129)	(627)	(340)	(441)	(1773)	(202)	(790)	(91)	(250)	(70)				
Asia/Oceania	812	512	144	231	871	631	286	675	599	1652	2712	14	3701	29
(Japan/Australia/New Zealand)	—	—	—	(25)	(61)	—	—	—	(96)	(124)				
(Other)	(812)	(512)	(144)	(206)	(810)	(631)	(286)	(675)	(503)	(1528)				
Europe/Canada	1693	1076	586	1002	1287	717	958	275	588	885	5112	26	3955	31
(Developed W. Europe/Canada)	(34)	—	—	(125)	(648)	(194)	(30)	—	(278)	(683)				
(Developing W. Europe[b])	(14)	(152)	(144)	(21)	(498)	(19)	(38)	(11)	(182)	(106)				
(East Europe)	(1645)	(924)	(442)	(856)	(141)	(504)	(890)	(264)	(128)	(96)				
Latin America	395	276	1727	608	386	433	37	123	1260	564	3805	20	2004	16
Total	5890	3086	3279	2516	5115	2149	2071	1164	2966	3882	19321	100	12797	100

[a] Algeria, Libya, Egypt, Morocco and Tunisia
[b] Cyprus, Portugal and Spain

Source: Export-Import Bank of the United States, *Report to the US Congress on Export Credit Competition and the Export-Import Bank of the United States* Washington DC, January 1980, pp. 13–14.

Export credit policy[2]

Official support for export credit comprises several instruments. Exporting countries have somewhat different arrangements for each of these instruments and offer them in various combinations. At the least, the export credit agency provides an official guarantee for a commercial loan. In addition it may permit an export credit to be advanced at a lower rate of interest or for a longer term than would be available for a commercial loan, either by making a direct loan or by refinancing a commercial loan, or by subsidising the interest rate on a commercial loan. Financing of local costs associated with an export, such as the costs of installing a factory, may also be subsidised.

Some countries also provide mixed credit, in which export credit is supplemented by aid funds (either a grant or a cheap loan). This is the most controversial aspect of official export finance. Until recently they were exclusively a French practice, and so closely are they associated with France that they are frequently referred to by their French name, *crédits mixtes*, even in the context of other countries' export credit policies. By mixing conventional export credit with aid funds it is possible to offer a 'blended' interest rate that undercuts the agreed credit rates. The aid funds are used to cover the down payment or local costs, to lower the rate of interest, to draw out the maturity still further, or to insert a grace period before the repayments have to begin. Other facilities which are sometimes subsidised include insurance premiums, pre-shipment finance, cost-escalation insurance and foreign exchange guarantees.

France takes the view that mixed credit is a channel for development assistance, which has at best a marginal effect on exports. As a rule it is given to the poorest countries (usually to former French colonies) and, within those countries, to public entities. Exceptions have been made, for example in Latin America, in cases where other countries were offering unusual terms which France wished to match. French officials also point out that its importance is exaggerated since it accounts for 4–5% of French exports of capital goods, or about 1% of total exports, and that many other countries provide it.

There has been an increase in the use of mixed credit in recent years. Britain, Japan, Denmark, Belgium and the Netherlands have all begun to take the initiative in its use. For the most part this has been in response to complaints from their exporters that they could not compete if they had to wait until notice had been give by the French authorities before making their own offer of mixed credit. In 1979 the United States also began to provide mixed credit. This innovation was intended to demonstrate its determination to compete more aggressively and, in particular, to persuade France that continued intransigence on mixed credit could prove costly. To drive home the point, the Eximbank arranged a $100m line of credit to Tunisia, comprising two tranches of $50m, one conventional for 10 years at 8%, and the other concessional, for 25 years at 3½%.

There are many differences among exporting countries in the ways they organise and appraise official export credit. The main differences are outlined in the Box. These variations mean that an importer may be offered a diversity of financial terms for a transaction. The proportion of the total financing which receives official support, the insurance premium, the length of the credit, the interest rate and the fees can all vary. In addition, there may be official support for local costs and an aid element may be included. To complicate matters further, the offers are usually in different currencies. The borrower needs to calculate not only the current cost of a credit, but to make a judgment of how exchange rates will move during the period of repayment. A lower interest rate can be more than offset by currency appreciation.

How export credit is organised

In broad terms support can be divided into official insurance or guarantees, entailing a potential cost which varies according to how risky the business is, and official financing, which imposes an actual cost on public expenditure. Policy is administered through specialised export credit agencies, often in close collaboration with commercial banks, but it is formulated in consultation with several government departments. These typically include the ministries of finance, trade, industry, employment, foreign affairs and development, as well as the central bank. They are involved in decisions both on individual export credits and on general policy, such as the introduction of a new facility.

The basic decision is whether to guarantee a particular piece of business. Although export credit agencies take on business that would not be acceptable to commercial insurers, they are generally expected not to make a loss on their activities, which means that they cannot take on unusually risky business. In the case of countries which provide subsidised finance, the granting of a government guarantee automatically gives the borrower access to official finance. Most export credit agencies retain some discretion, however, as to the extent of the subsidy. The predominant policy considerations relate to the impact of an export on the economy of the exporting country, particularly the balance of payments and employment. Some account may be taken of the effect on the importing country if it is a developing country. This aspect may be given more weight in the case of mixed credit.

A further stage of decision-making is to assess what terms are appropriate to meet competition from exporters in other countries. The closer offers are in other respects (price, quality, design, technical specifications, compatibility with existing installations, reputation, compliance with delivery dates, after-sales service), the greater is the pressure to make the financial terms more favourable. Some countries are more prepared than others to intervene in this way.

Importers can seek to turn to their advantage disparities among export-finance packages. They may press an exporter to include in his package a more favourable element being offered by a competitor. The exporter may then try to persuade his export credit agency to improve on the package. However, the extent to which exporters can play off one export credit agency against another is limited by an international agreement on export credit terms and by arrangements for exchange of information between agencies. Moreover, buyers' capacities for appreciating the trade-offs and for taking advantage of them vary widely from one country to another. In developed countries, where buyers are often private companies, much skill and effort are devoted to reaping the maximum benefit. The newly industrialising countries (NICs) are also very competent at weighing up the real cost of borrowing. The importer in one of these countries is often the government or a state entity. The departments responsible for deciding on foreign borrowing are usually well managed and subject to much control. Many of these countries also have a large foreign debt, which makes them all the more exigent when it comes to negotiating terms for new borrowing. In the case of other developing countries, the significance of the currency in which a loan is made is less readily grasped. The importer is almost invariably the government or a state entity, since there are few private companies whose size or creditworthiness qualify them for export credit. In choosing among loans, these importers tend to choose the lowest interest rate, regardless of the currency. In some instances, a low interest rate may be seen as a symbol of prestige; in others, those responsible for negotiating a credit may be aware that a credit bearing a higher interest rate would be cheaper in real terms, but refrain from taking it for fear of being suspected of having accepted a bribe. For the smaller, poorer countries that are virtually excluded from calling on the international capital markets, the cost of credit may seem less important than having access to it.

The renegotiation of the international framework

During the 1970s official export credit was seen by exporting countries as being increasingly wasteful. The growing subsidy was imposing a greater burden on public expenditure, while international demand for capital goods had slackened. The purpose of the subsidy was to promote exports. This meant either increasing total world exports, which was difficult in the prevailing economic climate, or increasing a country's share of the existing market. It was evident that if one country's subsidy was matched by a subsidy from another, they each lost the cost of their respective subsidy but gained nothing because their relative competitive position was unchanged.

In 1974 a gentlemen's agreement on minimal rules for official export credit was signed by the USA, West Germany, France, the UK, Japan, Italy and Canada. This was superseded in 1976 by a more comprehensive international consensus, which was in turn replaced in 1978 by the Arrangement on Guidelines for Officially Supported Export Credits. The Arrangement was essentially the same as the Consensus, but was more formal, more extensive and more stringent. It was signed by all the 22 OECD countries which had facilities for financing or guaranteeing export credit. It set guidelines establishing minimum down payments, maximum repayment periods and minimum interest rates, which varied according to the length of the credit and whether the country of the borrower was classified as relatively rich, relatively poor or intermediate. The terms permitted by the guidelines were most generous for the poorest countries and least generous for the richest countries. Participants undertook either to observe the guidelines or to notify other participants that they intended not to.

Within six months of the Arrangement coming into effect market interest rates in all the major trading countries began to rise steadily. The amount of subsidy implied by the minimum rates fixed in the Arrangement rose commensurately. The United States was particularly concerned at the increased subsidy and pressed for an increase in the minimum rates. A small increase was implemented in July 1980 and a larger one in November 1981. These only partly closed the gap that had opened up between the minimum rates and prevailing market rates so the subsidy remained larger than when the Arrangement had been introduced. A further issue was then sucked into the dispute: subsidised trade with the Soviet bloc.

The negotiations that led up to the June 1982 agreement therefore revolved around two main issues, one economic: the extent to which governments should subsidise the interest rates on credit advanced to finance exports of capital goods, the other political: the amount and terms of credit advanced to the Soviet Union. Because the 10 EEC countries negotiate as a bloc there sometimes appears to be a clear-cut division between the USA and Europe. This is in fact deceptive. On subsidised interest rates West Germany is closer to the US view than to the French view which usually determines the EEC position. But on curbing credit to the Soviet Union the European countries largely concur in an attitude which differs distinctly from that of the USA.

The new system

As a means of raising the interest rates and shortening the repayment period for export credit to some countries the USA proposed that they be graduated from one category to another. Those affected fall into two main groups: the Soviet bloc, and middle-income Third World states. The new criteria are shown in Table 5.2, and were agreed in June 1982 after much deliberation. The yardstick is each country's 1979 GNP per capita. Those over $4,000 are now classified as relatively rich and those below $730 as relatively poor (equivalent to the World Bank's category of least developed countries – see *Survey 2*, Chapter 9); the others are classed as intermediate. This means that one group – including the Soviet Union, Czechoslovakia, East Germany, Israel and Spain – have passed from the intermediate to the relatively rich category, while a second group of some 40 (mainly developing) countries have passed from the relatively poor to the intermediate category (see Box). For this second group, there is a transition period, so that they will not become fully subject to the conditions of the intermediate category until January 1983.

Table 5.2   *The export credit Arrangement: interest rates from 6 July 1982*

Category of borrower	Length of loan (years)		Maximum credit term (years)	Minimum down payment
	2–5	over 5		
Relatively rich	12.15%	12.4%	5*	15%
Intermediate	10.85%	11.35%	8½**	15%
Relatively poor	10.0%	10.0%	10	15%

* 8½ exceptionally
**countries previously in category 3 will continue to be allowed a maximum of 10 years.

Developing countries affected by the new export credit Arrangement

The countries that have moved from the poorest to the intermediate category include: Albania, Algeria, Antigua, Belize, Brazil, Cayman Islands, Chile, Colombia, Costa Rica, Cuba, Dominican Republic, Ecuador, Falkland Islands, Fiji, Guatemala, Ivory Coast, Jamaica, Jordan, Kiribati, North Korea, South Korea, Lebanon, Leeward Islands, Macao, Malaysia, Mauritania, Mexico, Mongolia, Morocco, Nigeria, Papua New Guinea, Paraguay, Peru, St Helena, St Kitts, Seychelles, Suriname, Syria, Taiwan, Tunisia, Turkey, Uruguay and the Windward Islands.

Since countries which have been reclassified will in any case have to pay higher interest rates, the EEC resisted US proposals for a sizeable overall rise in rates. Eventually the participants compromised on increases of 1.15% for rich countries and 0.35% for intermediate countries, to be applied from 6 July 1982, and no change for poor countries. At the same time the USA agreed to cease offering credits with maturities of more than 10 years. A special exception has been made for Japan, where market rates are well below the Arrangement minimum rates. Japan is now able to offer on official export credit an interest rate not less than 0.3% above its long-term prime rate, which is currently about 8.5%.

The minimum rates are now higher than were market rates when the Arrangement began to operate. If market rates descend towards their former levels the subsidy will decline, though there might then be pressure to reduce minimum rates. In the past France has been particularly anxious to subsidise interest rates because it could not match the long maturities offered by the USA. With a 10-year ceiling on US maturities France should be less worried. However, if countries outside the Arrangement continue to subsidise interest rates some participants in the Arrangement will probably want to lower the minimum rates.

Another substantial change, which has direct implications for developing countries, is the establishment of a buffer zone between export credit and mixed credit. Previously there was a continuum of different types of finance ranging from commercial loans through export credit, mixed credit and aid to grants. In future mixed credit with a grant element below 20% will not be permitted. (The grant element measures the extent to which a loan is more concessional than a commercial loan.) Since the grant element of export credit is very much less than 20% this change means there is now a clear break between export credit and mixed credit. The possibility of using mixed credit as a slightly more generous version of export credit will no longer exist; mixed credit will be confined to being an ungenerous form of aid.

Also important is the revision of the prior commitments clause in the Arrangement. This permitted lines of credit agreed before July 1976 to continue to be offered on the same terms until they lapsed. Following each of the subsequent increases in minimum rates existing lines of credit were allowed to continue unchanged. The Arrangement has now been altered, however, so that the terms of prior commitments can apply for only six months after a change in the minimum rates. The overall discipline of the Arrangement has also been made tighter. Whereas before participants were allowed to step outside the guidelines provided they notified other participants and gave them a chance to do likewise, now departures from the guidelines are ruled out altogether. This change, like that on mixed credits, came into effect from 15 October 1982. Whether the closing of loopholes in the Arrangement will result in significantly harder terms for export credit or in increased evasion remains to be seen. It will very much depend on the participants since the Arrangement is a gentlemen's agreement and there are no penalties for infringements.

The impact of the new Arrangement on developing countries is likely to be mixed. As beneficiaries of export subsidies those countries who graduated to category 2 will be adversely affected by the hardening of terms. On the other hand, the creation of a buffer zone may limit the spread of mixed credits which may not be a bad thing, particularly for the poorest countries. To use aid funds to enable developing countries to import capital goods from developed countries more cheaply than they otherwise could may appear attractive. Mixed credit does not, however, increase the total amount of concessional finance. The sums allocated to aid budgets are fixed and when an exporting country provides aid funds for a mixed credit the amount of aid for other purposes is reduced. Experience shows that, as an instrument to promote exports of capital goods, mixed credit tends to be directed to those countries which represent the most attractive markets and where competition is toughest, that is, usually to the better-off developing countries. Developing countries should consider how far it is in their interest that aid funds should be directed towards these products and these countries.

It is important to recognise the distinction between aid policy and export credit policy. Official export credit appears as aid in some statistical series and is seen by a few exporting countries, notably France, as a channel for development assistance. In practice it effects a transfer from a developed to a developing country, and, unlike commercial credit, its terms are more favourable for poorer countries though they are higher credit risks. Nonetheless, whereas aid policy is directed, albeit imperfectly, to the needs of developing countries, export credit policy aims to advance the interests of the exporting country by promoting its exports. Buyers' interests are given a low priority and the policy changes which occur are usually a response to pressure from exporters.

Despite the fact that policy is primarily directed towards developed country exports, there does exist some scope for developing countries to improve the terms of export credit. They should, as in the past, exert influence through exporters to bring about adjustments to policy which they consider desirable but they should also make their increasing market power felt more directly. Export credit agencies are by nature conservative and sometimes operate by rules of thumb which were established under different circumstances from those prevailing today. Early on their function was to support credit advanced by an exporter (supplier credit). Many still prefer to deal solely with the exporter and a bank nominated by him though, especially in the case of long-term credit, much export credit is now advanced by a bank directly to the buyer (buyer credit). A developing country should when appropriate insist that an export credit agency accept the bank which it nominates. This would help to ensure that finance was arranged in a way that suited the buyer and would make export credit agencies more responsive to the interests of developing countries in setting their policy priorities.

Notes

1   Some sections of this paper have already appeared in Joan Pearce, *Policies of Export Credit Agencies in Financing of Training Component in Industrial Projects*, UNIDO/PC. 54, 28 September 1982.
2   For a more detailed explanation of export credit policy, see Joan Pearce, *Subsidized Export Credit*, Royal Institute of International Affairs, London, 1980.

6

Situation Reports on International Negotiations

The UN System and Cancun

Carol Geldart

The second half of 1981 saw three major international conferences of interest to the Third World, one on new and renewable sources of energy, one on the least developed countries, and one on the Brandt initiative at Cancun. None produced any major tangible result. A similar lack of progress has been made on creating a Common Fund and on other elements in the integrated programme for commodities agreed in 1976. These bleak results are, in themselves, an indication of the current state of North–South relations. But, more than this, these international fora provide a window on differences between the EEC and the USA, and between EEC member states. This situation report makes clear these differences. The dual picture that emerges is of the USA apparently out on a limb compared with the EEC which regularly stressed the importance of North–South relations, but also of a consensus by the Atlantic partners on most issues of substance.

UN conference on new and renewable sources of energy

This conference, which stemmed from a 1978 General Assembly resolution, was held in Nairobi from 10–21 August 1981. Its objective was to identify potentially viable new and renewable energy sources and to agree a programme of action to promote their development. Special attention was to be given to current and future energy problems and requirements of developing countries.

The main disagreements were between the Group of 77 (G77) and the USA. The G77 sought additional financial resources for the action programme, and proposed that financial targets be set. Throughout the conference, the USA's general position was that, where possible, it preferred the involvement of private enterprise to multilaterally funded projects, and it considered that it was the responsibility of each country to raise the finance necessary for the development of its own energy resources, assisted where appropriate by international sources of private and public capital. In consequence, governments should ensure that they encouraged investment through appropriate conditions for capital formation, access to capital markets and adequate budgetary support for national programmes. It opposed the creation of a new energy fund and the setting of financial targets, and simply proposed that all governments in a position to do so (not just those of Western industrial countries) and multilateral development institutions should consider giving new and renewable energy sources a higher priority in funding and other activities. It was announced at the conference that the USA would double its bilateral energy aid to developing countries in 1982 by committing an extra $35m, but it was assumed that this would come from funds already allocated to the aid budget.[1]

The EEC Commission took a more interventionist approach. In a communication to the Council prior to the conference,[2] it argued that a significant increase in multilateral funds was essential to promote private flows, and that funds to implement the proposed action programme would be required from all industrialised countries, from developing countries able to contribute and from international financial institutions. It opposed the creation of a new financial agency specifically for activities in new and renewable energy, both on technical grounds and because it considered that machinery for consultations between donor countries should be established and that such a move would make the creation of a new agency unnecessary. But it did favour the creation of an energy affiliate to the World Bank which would help to meet the two criteria it considered essential for financing energy resources in developing countries: a large increase in multilateral finance and OPEC's financial involvement.

The EEC member states – which like the USA were against the G77's proposal for financial targets and earmarked funds – did not make any firm formal commitments at the conference to provide additional finance for the action programme. France, Italy and the United Kingdom along with several other developed countries announced increases in their financial and technical assistance to developing countries for new and renewable energy development, but it was widely assumed that, as with the USA, the extra finance would be taken from existing aid budgets.[3] The member states also lent their support to a World Bank energy affiliate. The USA was the only country to oppose the affiliate proposal outright.

In the end, the conference only agreed that the implementation of the action programme would require 'additional and adequate'[4] international financial resources, both public and private, from all developed countries, from international organisations and from developing countries able to contribute. Following the adoption of the programme however, the USA qualified its support for some of the financial sections, stating that it was not currently in a position to give additional funds to the UN for activities under the action programme. Furthermore, as the US Administration, along with other governments, had adopted a policy of zero net programme growth for the UN for 1982 and 1983, it took the position that any increase in the UN's budget for new and renewable energy must be offset by savings in other areas.

UN conference on the least developed countries

This conference, which took place in Paris in the first half of September 1981, originated from a decision taken at UNCTAD V to launch a special programme of action for least developed countries (lldcs) for the 1980s which would promote structural changes in their economies with a view to assisting economic development and the establishment of more self-sustained growth. Convened as a result of a 1979 General Assembly resolution, it was the first UN conference devoted solely to the 31 designated lldcs (see *Survey 2*, Chapters 8 and 9). Its aim was to finalise, adopt and support a Substantial New Programme of Action (SNPA)[5] for lldcs for the 1980s. It was eventually adopted by consensus but negotiations on finance and trade revealed differences in approach to the problems facing lldcs between the USA on the one hand and the EEC Commission on the other, as well as among EEC member states.

At the conference, the G77 reiterated a proposal previously advanced within the General Assembly that developed countries (which had already agreed at UNCTAD V to double their aid to lldcs 'as soon as possible') should undertake to give at least 0.15% of their GNP to lldcs by 1985 and 0.20% by 1990. It also proposed that the volume of aid to lldcs should have at least quadrupled in real terms by 1990 and that 30% of concessional aid should go to lldcs. Finally it suggested that new mechanisms, such as international taxation, IMF gold sales and the linking of IMF Special Drawing Rights to development assistance could be used to increase financial flows to lldcs.

The developed countries rejected the 1990 and 30% targets and they would only agree that new mechanisms to increase resource transfers merited further study in the appropriate institutions. However their response to the 0.15% target was by no means unanimous. At the outset, the USA, which gives the lowest percentage of its GNP to lldcs in the Western industrialised world (in 1979, it gave 0.02% against an OECD DAC average of 0.06%) took the position that the pace of progress envisaged at the conference was too ambitious. It called on

OPEC countries, other developing countries able to do so, and communist countries, to increase their aid to lldcs but suggested that more aid was being asked for than many donor countries could provide and than recipient countries would be able to absorb. It stressed that national economic policies and budgetary allocations played an important role in determining the economic performance of developing countries and argued that the international support required by lldcs could not substitute for or be effective without appropriate economic policies in those countries. The furthest it was prepared to go at the conference was to undertake to make 'a special effort' to increase its aid and to direct aid increasingly towards lldcs.[6]

The European Commission in its communication to the Council in June 1981[7] took the view that the conference was important in the context of the North–South dialogue and that the 31 countries (22 of which were ACP) would inevitably require sustained external assistance, mainly in the form of concessional aid, to help them develop, because of their inadequate resources, the weakness of their financial institutions and the dramatic decline in their terms of trade. Like the USA, it argued that all parties should contribute to implementing the SNPA, and it also drew attention to the importance of domestic policies in lldcs to the development process, and opposed demands for aid to lldcs to be expressed in terms of GNP or percentages of total aid. It suggested instead that within the context of the commitment already agreed to give 0.7% of GNP in aid to developing countries, developed countries should commit themselves to a realistic target for 1985 of doubling, in nominal terms, the volume of aid given to lldcs in 1979.

Both the Commission and the Council Presidency were represented at the conference and EEC member states sought to adopt joint positions on issues under negotiation. But they were divided for much of the conference over what position to adopt with regard to the demand for a 0.15% GNP aid target. France (which gave 0.06% of GNP in aid to lldcs in 1979), was the first country to undertake to reach the 0.15% target by 1985 and by all accounts played a major role in getting the more reluctant member states – namely the UK, West Germany and, for a time, Italy – to accept the target figure. It also undertook to reach the 0.7% target by 1988. France's approach contrasted strongly with that adopted by the USA. Opening the conference with a major policy statement on relations with developing countries, President Mitterand adopted the Brandt Commission's argument that aiding Third World development would help the industrialised world out of its present crisis and stated that there was a need to find ways of reviving the North–South dialogue.[8] Resistance to the 0.15% target was strongest from the UK (which in 1979 gave 0.12% of its GNP to lldcs) followed by West Germany (with 0.09%). Both countries, in referring to volume targets for aid, emphasised their domestic economic problems. Germany issued a plea for more realistic aid targets and stated that its aid contributions could no longer rise as fast as in recent years. The UK's general position was that lldcs, like other developing countries, should try to provide a favourable climate for private investment, but it did announce that it was setting aside £9m in aid to lldcs for agriculture, population control, water, health and energy. Both the UK and West Germany eventually agreed to commit themselves along with other EEC member states to reach the 0.15% target 'in the coming years'.[9] The Netherlands and Denmark had already surpassed the target in 1979 with 0.23% and 0.22% respectively. Some other member states also committed themselves to target dates: Belgium (0.13% in 1979) agreed to achieve the target by 1985, while Italy (0.023% in 1979) and Ireland agreed to by 1990.

On international trade, the G77 demanded the removal of tariff and non-tariff barriers in developed countries, greater preferential access for lldc goods, as well as further measures to stabilise lldc earnings from exports of primary products and for compensatory financing. There was broad agreement at the conference that action should be taken in the relevant fora to reduce tariff and non-tariff barriers which might be restricting lldcs' exports of major processed goods and that preferential schemes should be simplified and improved. The EEC Commission was known to have advocated the extension of the Generalised System of Preferences (GSP) for lldcs and to have undertaken to study the possibility of extending preferences given to lldcs to cover more agricultural products (see *Survey 2*, Chapter 5).[10] The EEC Council Presidency undertook at the conference that the Community would examine the possibility of further improvements to its GSP scheme. There was less agreement between developed countries however over commodity price stabilisation measures. The United States remained unenthusiastic about international commodity agreements (ICAs) until the end of the conference, although it had been agreed in the SNPA that participants would make renewed efforts to conclude ICAs quickly and to implement the Common Fund Agreement. As for compensatory finance, France and West Germany favoured the creation with other donor countries of income stabilisation mechanisms similar to Stabex (see Chapter 11),[11] but the UK and several other member states were unenthusiastic. The USA opposed new Stabex-type schemes and stated that the IMF was the best forum in which to tackle financial problems resulting from export earnings shortfalls. In the end it was decided simply that developed countries should study ways and means of helping lldcs to offset the damaging effects of fluctuations in commodity export earnings and report their findings.

The Cancun summit and global negotiations

The UK, West Germany, France and the USA were among the eight
industrialised countries represented at the Cancun summit of heads of
state/government of 22 selected countries held on 22–23 October 1981
and formally known as the International Meeting on Co-operation and
Development. The idea for the summit originated from a proposal in
the Brandt Commission Report in 1980 that such a meeting might be
able to give new impetus to the search for solutions to the world's
urgent economic problems. The four countries reacted in different
ways to the proposal for a summit. Germany and France along with
nine other countries agreed to co-sponsor the meeting. The UK took a
more positive attitude than the USA, which under the Carter Administration was hostile to the idea. The new Reagan Administration finally
agreed to attend the summit but only on condition that Cuba, then
chairman of the Non-Aligned Movement, would not be present and
that it was postponed to October from its original date in June.

Prior to the summit, the Foreign Ministers of the 22 countries agreed
that the meeting would not have a formal agenda, would be confined to
an informal exchange of views and would not produce a final communiqué. It was decided that the framework for the discussion would be the
future of international co-operation for development and the reactiva-
tion of the world economy, and that the themes to be covered would
include food security and agricultural development; commodities,
trade and industrialisation; energy; and financial and monetary issues.
After some hesitation on the part of the USA, it was also agreed that
although the summit had no formal link with the proposed UN global
economic negotiations, one of its main aims would be to 'facilitate
agreement' on how to proceed with them.[12] Preparations for the global
negotiations had long been at a standstill due to disagreements between developing and developed countries over parts of the agenda
covering energy and monetary/financial issues and over the competence of the central conference in relation to specialised agencies such
as the IMF, the World Bank and GATT (see *Survey 2*, Chapter 1).

Although the EEC as such was not invited, the Commission had
made its position known in a series of communications to the Council
which endeavoured to establish an EEC policy or negotiating position
on major North–South issues in preparation for various international
meetings including the Ottawa and Cancun summits.[13] (See *Survey 2*,
Chapter 1.) It argued that the question of global negotiations was
inseparable from that of reactivating the North–South dialogue and
stressed that it was important that the EEC was seen to be actively
assisting in the search for an agreement which would enable these
negotiations to be launched quickly. A few days before the summit,
the President of the Commission, Mr Gaston Thorn, criticised the
Reagan Administration's approach to the problems facing developing

countries and the international economic system. He warned that these problems could not be left to market forces alone, that developing countries could not wait until the end of the economic crisis before their problems were tackled and that the decline of developing countries would ultimately threaten the well-being of the West itself.[14]

At the summit, differences in approach were most marked between the USA and the developing countries present. However France, Germany and the UK also adopted different positions to the USA on most of the issues discussed. President Reagan made it clear that the USA considered free enterprise, trade and private investment to be more effective ways of assisting developing countries than increased aid flows. He opposed a fundamental reform of existing international monetary institutions and financial and trading arrangements on the basis that the existing system had served the world well and that it could be further adapted and used to help developing countries. In a five point plan for development he called *inter alia* for a more liberalised trading system, for assistance to developing countries to develop self-sustaining productive activities in food and energy, and for improvements in the climate for private capital flows. No mention was made of the proposed World Bank energy affiliate. On global negotiations, the US Administration had made no major pronouncements since the Ottawa summit at which it had eventually committed itself to participate in preparations for the negotiations 'in circumstances offering the prospect of meaningful progress'.[15] At Cancun, President Reagan specified four conditions under which the USA would be willing to take part in preparations. These were that the talks should cover specific subjects; should respect the role of existing specialised agencies and should not seek to create new institutions; should be orientated towards achieving 'greater levels of mutually beneficial international growth and development, taking into account domestic economic policies';[16] and should take place in a co-operative atmosphere.

The three EEC representatives, Mrs Thatcher, Mr Genscher (substituting for Chancellor Schmidt) and President Mitterand, expressed some common themes. All supported a World Bank energy affiliate or something similar, and a prompt launching of global negotiations, on condition that they did not compromise the effectiveness of the specialised agencies. But there were also differences of approach. In her opening address, Mrs Thatcher emphasised the importance of free enterprise, private investment and trade for a country's development and growth. Mr Genscher defined eliminating hunger and ensuring energy supplies as the most urgent development tasks for the 1980s, and called for national food and energy strategies in developing countries. In a position similar to that of the US Administration, he stressed that the benefits of trade were far more significant than aid flows and stated that the German government considered that maintaining open markets and further liberalising trade was one of the most important development tasks ahead.

France's approach was summed up in a memorandum given to the other participants, in which the government argued that the future course of the North–South dialogue could have implications not just for development but to a certain extent for world peace: the level of interdependence between countries made it in the interests of industrialised countries to promote Third World development, and there was a need to inject some predictability into international economic relations via a system of international agreements and to create a more organised process of development in developing countries. President Mitterand had made it clear that he wanted specific decisions to promote North–South co-operation to emerge from the discussions. Like the USA, the UK and Germany, France considered that global negotiations should not encroach on the competence of the specialised agencies, but it also argued that a degree of flexibility in procedures might contribute towards progress on the negotiations and that the French government did not exclude the possibility that the structure of the financial institutions would eventually have to be altered to fit economic realities. On the other issues before the summit, the French government called for increased aid to developing countries and offered to assist efforts to establish 'self-based' development in industry and agriculture in the Third World.[17]

The concluding summary issued to the press by the summit co-chairmen revealed that there was little agreement on specific ways in which North and South could best co-operate together in the future to tackle major economic problems. On global negotiations, participants drafted a compromise text which made it clear that they could agree only to informal talks within the UN on launching the negotiations and that the same disagreements between developed and developing countries that had blocked further consideration of the issues in the UN had persisted at Cancun. There was no progress towards agreement on the content or purpose of the negotiations or on the role of the negotiating conference in relation to the specialised agencies. In the energy sphere, it was agreed that increased energy investment from private and official sources was required in developing countries and it was suggested that the World Bank should expand lending for this purpose. But the Reagan Administration's opposition to the setting up of a World Bank energy affiliate prevented the proposal from receiving unanimous support. The rapid elimination of hunger was endorsed as an international obligation and as a major priority for international co-operation. However, whilst a number of specific suggestions were put forward, none found general acceptance and it was agreed only that the workings of UN agricultural and food organisations should be reviewed with the aim of avoiding duplication of effort and of improving their efficiency. The only agreement on trade issues was that there was a need to complete procedures for bringing the Common Fund into operation, to improve the GSP and to resist protectionism. On financial and monetary issues, deadlock persisted between developed and developing countries over the question of increasing financial flows to developing countries and over Third World demands for reforms to the role and decision-making process of the major international financial institutions.

Since Cancun, informal consultations within the UN on launching global negotiations have not succeeded in bridging the gap between developing countries and the USA. At the end of March 1982 the G77 put forward a draft resolution to the General Assembly for a UN conference for global negotiations to begin in May. This found general acceptance as a basis for further discussions among EEC member states, but the Reagan Administration did not consider that it provided sufficient guarantees against erosion of the power of the specialised agencies. It also wanted a preliminary conference, separate from the main negotiations, to fix the agenda and structure as well as a time limit for the negotiations. At the Western economic summit at Versailles at the beginning of June 1982, the USA joined the other countries in accepting that the G77 draft would serve as a basis for consultations on global negotiations but subject to several amendments which were agreed to by the heads of government. Two of these amendments were subsequently rejected by the G77. The issue is expected to come before the 37th session of the General Assembly.

Despite the agreement on the Common Fund, progress on bringing it into operation has been slow. By August 1981 all EEC member states had signed the Common Fund agreement (Greece being the last), but they have not yet completed ratification. By the end of August 1982, only the UK, Denmark and Ireland had ratified despite repeated urgings from the Commission. The USA signed under the Carter Administration but had not ratified by August 1982. In April 1982 a US representative to the UN was reported to state that ratification would occur 'at the appropriate time',[18] but the Reagan Administration is known to be unenthusiastic about the whole concept of commodity agreements and is unwilling to ratify until it is clear that the Common Fund will become operational. The deadline for ratification has now been extended to 30 September 1983.

Progress on achieving effective international commodity agreements (ICAs) has also been poor. In March 1981 the Council adopted an arrangement designed to make the EEC an effective participant in commodity negotiations by agreeing that, except for products covered by the CAP, member states would take a common position in a joint delegation with a single spokesman; agreements would be signed by both the Community and member states. In practice, the problems of achieving a united position have been very difficult to surmount so that on occasions the EEC has been unable to participate effectively in discussions. The two extremes tend to be France, which is relatively sympathetic to ICAs, and Germany, which takes a position much more akin to that of the USA. Both Germany and the UK were reluctant to participate in the New Cocoa Agreement (ICCA) due to the absence of Ivory Coast, and in mid-1981 Germany blocked the EEC's provisional support for ICCA for several weeks. Similarly, the two countries dragged their feet on EEC participation in the new tin agreement in early 1982 because of the USA's refusal to join, and because of the operations of the mystery tin buyers at that time. When the EEC does succeed in negotiating as a group, it tends to adopt an intermediate position between the USA and developing countries, as in the case of tea and cotton. On ICAs covering CAP products, notably sugar, the Community has been much less positive, showing great reluctance to accept any limitation on its right to subsidise exports.

Notes

1 *Observer News Service,* 14 August 1981 and *Financial Times,* 26 August 1981.
2 Commission of the European Communities, 'Community Position for the United Nations Conference on New and Renewable Sources of Energy (Nairobi, August 1981)'. COM (81) 381 final, Brussels, 9 July 1981.
3 Jon Tinker, *Nairobi: Promises, Compromises*, Earthscan/UNERG, August 1981.
4 UN Press Release, 'United Nations Conference on New and Renewable Sources of Energy, Nairobi 10–21 August', EN/65, 24 August 1981, p. 11.
5 The SNPA was divided into three chapters covering: the implementation of structural change at the national level in lldcs; measures at the international level in support of the programme; and follow-up and monitoring mechanisms.
6 United Nations, 'Report of the United Nations Conference on Least Developed Countries held in Paris from 1–14 September 1981', A/Conf.104/22, p. 40 and p. 22.
7 Commission of the European Communities, 'The United Nations Conference on the Least Developed Countries, Paris, 1–14 September 1981', Brussels, 19 June 1981, COM (81) 319 final.
8 *Le Monde*, 2 September 1981.
9 United Nations, op. cit., p. 22.
10 Commission of the European Communities, op. cit., para 2.3.
11 *Telex Africa,* 15 September 1981, p. 25.
12 International Meeting on Co-operation and Development, 'Preparatory Meeting of Ministers of Foreign Affairs, Cancun, 1–2 August 1981', IMCD/PM/INF.5, p. 2. In G77 sponsored resolution 34/138 adopted by the General Assembly in 1979, it had been decided to launch global

negotiations within the UN system, that these negotiations should not adversely affect negotiations in other UN fora and that discussions would include issues in the field of raw materials, energy, trade, development and money and finance.

13   'Community Policy for the North–South Dialogue', COM (81) 68 final, 7 May 1981; 'North–South Dialogue', Com (81) 118 final, Brussels, 24 April 1981 and 'North–South Relations' COM (81) 323 final, Brussels, 18 June 1981.

14   *The Times*, 20 October 1981 and *European Report*, 21 October 1981, External Relations, p. 6.

15   *The Times*, 22 July 1981.

16   International Communication Agency, Official Text, 'President Reagan's Statement at the Cancun Summit', 23 October 1981.

17   Ministère des Relations Extérieures, Direction des Services de Presse et d'Information, *International Meeting on Co-operation and Development, Cancun, October 22–23, 1981*, p. 4.

18   *Le Monde*, 2 April 1982.

The Multifibre Arrangement

Betsy Baker, Jim Fitzpatrick, Annette Robert, Christopher Stevens, Jürgen Wiemann*

In December 1981, after much brinkmanship, the EEC reached agreement with the other parties to the Multifibre Arrangement (MFA) for a renewal (the third in the series) to cover the period January 1982 to July 1986.[1] But MFA III was not the end of the hard bargaining; it was just a prelude to the negotiation of bilateral agreements negotiated between each of the main importing and exporting states. At the time of going to press, the EEC's bilateral negotiations had reached an impasse. On 28 September 1982 the Commission announced that it had 'discontinued' talks with nine Third World countries, including the most important exporters of clothing and textiles. The future of the EEC's participation in the MFA was thrown into doubt.

In such a fluid situation it is clearly premature to assess the impact of MFA III and its associated bilateral agreements. The purpose of this 'situation report' is more modest: to outline the positions of the EEC member states and the USA. Although there was never any serious

---

* And additional material from Dr Giovanni Bianchini, J Teunissen and members of the Editorial Board.

doubt that protectionist forces would be in the ascendant, the positions of some parties are of interest. In stark contrast to its position in other international fora described in the preceding section, the initial stance of the Reagan Administration was significantly more sympathetic to the Third World than was that of the EEC, although the US position has since hardened. The position of the UK government, which shares a similar economic philosophy with the Reagan Administration, shifted even more rapidly from a relatively liberal to a heavily protectionist position.

Negotiating MFA III

The EEC experienced some difficulty in establishing its negotiating mandate. The Council of Ministers had to hold three meetings before the start of MFA negotiations in Geneva on 18 November 1981, but they succeeded only in papering over very thinly the deep differences between the member states. During December 1981 considerable doubt was expressed over whether the Community would be able to hammer out a common position in time for the talks to conclude as scheduled on 23 December thereby avoiding a hiatus between MFAs II and III. In the event, a united EEC position was agreed, and a new MFA adopted. But partly as a result of this brinkmanship, the text of MFA III was 'vague enough to have included sops to all the main negotiating groups',[2] and the EEC warned that it might yet withdraw from the arrangement unless it negotiated major cutbacks with the leading exporters. MFA III is in a number of respects more satisfactory for Third World exporters than was its predecessor. The 'reasonable departures' clause introduced for the first time in the MFA II agreement had been dropped. Under it, the importing states were permitted to suspend MFA provisions, and it formed the basis for the more restrictive bilateral pacts negotiated in the wake of MFA II's signature. A second change is that the definition, under the MFA, of 'market disruption' has been tightened; importing countries using this criterion now have to provide specific factual information on the existence or real risk of disruption before safeguard measures can be invoked. At the same time, MFA III is tougher on the Third World in a number of respects. It contains provisions for cutting back the quotas of 'dominant' suppliers and an 'anti-surge' mechanism to deal with sudden increases in imports even when annual quotas are being observed. The relative importance of these 'plus' and 'minus' features of the new Arrangement were left to be fought out in the bilateral negotiations. By September 1982, the EEC had concluded deals with 27 MFA suppliers, but Hong Kong, South Korea and Macao were refusing to accept the cutbacks demanded by the Community. Since these three suppliers plus Taiwan (not an MFA signatory) account for over 40% of the EEC's textile imports from the Third World, the impasse threatens the whole MFA structure.

EEC member state positions.

In the run-up to MFA III, the EEC member states divided into two camps: the hard-liners including France, Italy, UK, Eire and Belgium; and the liberals – Germany, Holland and Denmark. Within the hard-line group, the positions of France, Belgium and Italy were predictable and in keeping with their past attitudes towards trade protectionism in manufactures (see *Survey 2*, Chapter 4). The French tradition has been to emphasise the role of state guidance in industrial affairs, and the notion of 'organised free trade'. Italy's position was strongly influenced by its success in exporting clothing to other EEC states, and its fear that imports from the Third World would threaten this trade. The Belgian attitude was low key and hard-headed, reflecting the interests of its large and politically influential textile industry.

The Irish position is less well-known. The negotiations for MFA III came at a time when the Irish textile and clothing industries were in severe difficulty. Since the signing of the first MFA at the end of 1973, 10,000 jobs, equivalent to a quarter of the 1973 workforce, had disappeared.[3] The full extent of the upheaval in these industries over the 1970s is even greater than these aggregate data suggest. During the decade many new foreign-owned textile and clothing plants were established in Ireland so that this new employment partially counterbalanced much greater gross job losses in older indigenous firms. Ireland had supported a protectionist EEC line at the 1977 MFA renegotiations,[4] and after a slow start the Irish government became a prominent user of the various safeguard mechanisms provided by the subsequent EEC textile trade regime. This existing policy position, together with the immediate economic difficulties, made support for a restrictive EEC approach to MFA III inevitable. The fullest statement of Irish policy on MFA III was made by the Department of Industry and Energy to an Irish Textiles Federation seminar on the MFA in September 1981. This stated that, against the difficult economic background, the Department felt it could not 'contemplate MFA III in a spirit of liberality or even generosity' and it was 'aiming at a new arrangement which will be no less restrictive than the current one'.[5] This position reflected a broad consensus of industry and trade union opinion, both of which had called for a strongly protectionist renewed MFA.[6] The view that low cost competition was a major cause of job losses in the industries and that their survival required protection of both the domestic and the export (ie the EEC) market was largely accepted by the media and those of the general public interested in the issue. There were a few attempts to query the validity and wisdom of this approach, but such attempts were very much the exception.[7]

Possibly the most interesting of the hard line positions was that of the UK's Conservative government, not because it differed substantially from that of its Labour predecessor (it did not) but because it changed from apparent liberalism in the early months of the new administration in 1979 to an ultra hard-line position by the time the MFA negotiations commenced. The government had begun by actively pursuing an anti-interventionist policy with regard to the textile industry as much as to other industries. The then Secretary of State for Trade, John Nott, even went as far as to say the industry had had long enough to adjust to world competition. However, the government's position began to shift rapidly. This was in part due to the active lobbying of the textile industry's trade associations, particularly the British Textile Confederation (BTC) and in part to the Department of Industry. The BTC had begun to make an impression on British government policy as far back as the mid-1970s, when bilateral agreements under the first MFA were being negotiated. During the following seven or eight years, it had become increasingly skilful at co-ordinating with other organisations which shared its aim, from trades unions to civil servants and foreign trade associations to MPs, both those at Westminster and those in the European Assembly. Equally, and possibly even more important, were the worries of Conservative MPs from textile constituencies, particularly in Lancashire and West Yorkshire. Many of these MPs had already been very active in influencing government policy on textile trade under previous governments and they had no intention of losing influence when their own party was in power, particularly since 78,000 jobs were lost in the UK textile industry between June 1979 and June 1980, and in July 1980 another 9,000 disappeared, compared to only 16,400 lost between 1978 and 1979. By 1980 the textile industry and all its various and diverse supporters had some years' experience not only of working with other organisations in the UK but also of using other EEC member states to put pressure on the UK government. Much of their knowledge and skill was acquired by work with and through Comitextil, the EEC-level trade association for the Community's textile industry. During the MFA II renewal negotiations, the British industry and its supporters learned how helpful the French, with their strongly protectionist approach, could be in helping to shift the UK government's view closer to its own by providing external pressure, while the British industry and its domestic supporters took a similar line at home. In addition to pressure from a number of MPs from all four major parties at Westminster, the government had had to take at least some account of the views of the MPs of the European Parliament. The European Democratic Group, made up largely of British Conservative members with a few Danish

Conservatives, took a strong interest in the problems of the textile industry in 1980.

Although the vast majority of pressure on the British government prior to the renewal of the second MFA was protectionist and was exerted by the industry, there were other groups who took a different view. One of these was the British Importers Confederation (BIC) which, although it was willing for the MFA to be extended for a further four years, wanted any renewal agreement to make a commitment to phasing out import restrictions and to be less restrictive than the textile lobby was demanding. In addition, many pro-Third World groups opposed the views of the industry, believing that increased access to EEC markets, and particularly the UK market, was important in helping ldcs develop their exports and thus earn badly needed foreign exchange to pay off international debts and buy oil. Yet despite this pressure, by the time the final internal EEC negotiations began in Brussels, the position of the UK government was close to that of the UK industry, and there was no significant disagreement over the tone to be taken on renewal of the MFA.

Among the liberals, Denmark has been possibly the least ambiguous in opposing protectionism but also the least influential, given the fact that it accounts for only 3% of imports. Danish liberalism applies equally to employers and trade unions. The Federation of Danish Industries is very insistent on its liberal attitudes, and the relevant trade union has not asked for protectionist measures, although it has joined the effort of the European trade unions to influence the MFA. The Danish textile industry experienced heavy restructuring towards the end of the 1970s, leading to a specialisation which has created more stable conditions for the industry, with employment currently 30–35,000. Textiles are the third largest item of Danish exports and increased by 24% in 1980 (in current prices). Sales on the home market and exports (mainly to neighbouring countries) are of roughly equal magnitude and involve the same type of goods, mainly hosiery, carpets, ready-made clothing and piece-goods. Of total consumption approximately 60% is imported.

The Netherlands government formulated the main lines of its policy at the end of 1980, following inter-ministerial discussions between the rather liberal Ministry of Foreign Affairs (covering aid) and the Ministry of Economic Affairs. The latter was split between its liberal orientated foreign economic relations committee and its more protectionist industry division.[8] The policy adopted was therefore a compromise. From a liberal perspective, the government stated its commitment to the original objectives of the MFA (including the enlargement of trade), that the number of import restrictions should be as small as possible, temporary, and show a declining trend; that the ultimate aim should be an international division of labour reflecting comparative advantage; that the application of the 'reasonable departure clause' should be reduced; and that there should be a reduction in the number of bilateral agreements, provided other major importers reciprocate. On the other hand, it also emphasised that there should be 'orderly' developments of trade avoiding 'distortions' in individual markets and products, and that there should be greater differentiation between ldcs. In theory this could help poorer ldcs to develop their exports, but in practice it has rather tended simply to restrict the most competitive exporters. It also called for reciprocity for exporting countries to open their markets to EEC exports and, despite the emphasis that the MFA should be temporary, would not agree to any attempt to block further extensions after MFA III.

The most influential member of the liberal camp is Germany, where the fundamental consensus shared by the government, trade unions and industry that a highly export-orientated country can only maintain its international competitiveness through rapid structural adjustment has not really been challenged, even with the increasing competition from low-cost countries during the 1970s. The recurring demands of the textile trade union for more effective import controls have gained only lukewarm support from the confederation of trade unions, and they have frequently been rejected by the Federal Government on the basis of textbook arguments in favour of the international division of labour. In the absence of any special government support the German firms have followed three main strategies to improve their competitiveness against low-cost imports. First, the textile industry has increased productivity by introducing new technologies so that production is now almost fully automated. Second, the clothing industry transferred the labour intensive parts of standard production to low-wage countries in Eastern Europe, the Mediterranean region, and to some Asian developing countries (see *Survey 2*, Chapter 7). The German textile and clothing industry lost about 320,000 jobs during the 1970s, more than a third of all textile and clothing jobs in 1970. Third, both the textile and the clothing industry have shifted their product mix to higher value-added items. Through this trimming and trading up, the German industry has so far defended its international competitiveness with remarkable success. Today, Germany is both the world's largest importing and leading exporting country of textiles and clothing.

It would be a one-sided view, however, to attribute the profound restructuring of the German textile industry to the free trade policy of the German government alone. The truth is that the German textile industry, no less than any other industry in the EEC, relies on medium-term stability of domestic and world market trends if it is to take the considerable risks in investing for adjustment. Therefore, it has always favoured the MFA concept of 'managed textile trade' and the moderate protectionism of the EEC between 1974 and 1977. The Federal Government has never really challenged this basic concept, yet it has strongly opposed increasing protectionism of other EEC members since 1977. Its general inclination in favour of a liberal trade policy is reinforced by the need to take account of the special interests of those German firms which have transferred production to developing countries in the expectation of secure access for outward processed textiles to the EEC market.

Of course, the protectionism of other EEC governments allows the Federal Republic to cultivate its image as a free trader without having to fear that its principles will ever be really tested. A similar rift between principles and actual policy can be detected in the tacit division of labour between the Federal and the Länder governments in industrial policy. Apart from the comprehensive regional aid schemes which have benefitted the textile and clothing industry, the Länder governments have provided considerable support to ailing firms through public guarantees or direct fiscal measures. These effective but little noted measures relieve the Federal Government of the need to design the sectoral aid schemes for the textile industry common in other EEC countries.

The USA

Like the EEC, the USA has experienced a growing trade deficit in clothing which has more than offset its continuing surplus in textiles. Nonetheless, its overall position on textiles and clothing changed only from a deficit of $2,100mn in 1973 to one of $3,400mn in 1979, which is not a deterioration in real terms, and imports still form a much smaller proportion of total supply than is the case in Europe. In 1979 the overall rate of import penetration was 10.6% by volume and less than 10% by value. In certain sub-sectors, however, rates of penetration were much higher (e.g. sweaters, shirts, coats and trousers). The bulk of imports (81% in 1979) come from controlled suppliers. In 1979, in response to the growth in imports, the Carter Administration issued a policy paper which, *inter alia* pledged global import evaluation, greater control over import surges and understandings with major suppliers regarding tighter controls for the remaining life of the bilateral agreements. Consequently, the USA increased control over its major suppliers and re-opened its bilateral agreements with Hong Kong, Korea and Taiwan, adding further restraints. It also concluded a new bilateral agreement with China.

The US government thus entered the MFA III negotiations from a position of concern with low growth (1.5% p.a.) in domestic consumption of textiles, and rapid growth in imports in some sub-sectors. However, during the negotiations it found itself playing the role of the 'mediator' between the differing positions of the EEC and the ldcs.

Initial US proposals were much closer to those of the ldcs than to those of the EEC.

The reasons for this more liberal position were: the lower market share of US textile imports as compared to EEC imports; a decision by the Reagan Administration to oppose moves by the Community to adopt more restrictive measures against textile imports from the developing countries (it is not clear whether this was primarily a manifestation of Reaganomics or a tactical manoeuvre to deflect attention away from its own protectionism and the problems its exports cause the EEC); and concern about the effects of further import curbs on US cotton sales to South-East Asia – many of the ldc exporters are heavy users of US cotton.

During the final negotiations of MFA III, however, the US position has hardened partly due to pressure from the textile industry and in Congress, and partly in response to the further decline of the textile sector. In negotiating bilateral agreements the government's main aim has been to limit the growth in imports to the rate of growth in US demand. Nonetheless, the US system of bilateral agreements is less extensive and restrictive than the EEC's. New entrants into the textile market are not automatically subject to quotas. Only when imports have reached levels where they might cause market disruption will the USA negotiate a bilateral agreement. At the time of going to press bilateral agreements had been negotiated with Mexico (23 December 1981), Pakistan, Brazil, and Hong Kong (on 9, 31 March and 23 June 1982 respectively). They are very similar to those which were concluded in 1979 under the Carter Administration.

Notes

1   The parties to the MFA, which is a GATT agreement, include most of the industrialised importing states and many of the developing country exporters. Those excluded (but normally covered by similar accords) are non-GATT signatories (notably most communist states) and those countries like the Maghreb and ACP that have association agreements with the EEC.
2   *The Guardian*, 23 December 1981.
3   Data are from the *Industrial Employment, Earnings and Hours Worked* series published by the Central Statistics Office, Dublin.
4   This is noted in C. Farrands, 'Textile diplomacy: the making and implementation of European textile policy 1974–1978', *Journal of Common Market Studies*, 18(1), 1979.
5   J. Hogan, *An Irish View of the MFA*, paper presented at an Irish Textile Federation Seminar, Dublin, September 10–11, 1981.
6   For example Irish Textiles Federation, *Submission to the Irish Government on the Renewal of the Multi-Fibre Arrangement*, September 1980,

and Irish Transport and General Workers' Union, *Submission to the Minister for Industry, Commerce and Tourism on the Future of the Irish Clothing and Textiles Industry*, November 1980.

7   See J. Fitzpatrick, *Industrialisation, Trade and Ireland's Development Co-operation Policy*, Dublin, Advisory Council on Development Co-operation, 1982.

8   Government Printing Office, EG-beleid en Ontwikkelingssamenwerking, Tweede Kamer, zitting 80–81, 16506 no. 1 en 2 and Dokument, Tweede Kamer, zitting 80–81, 16400 nfdst XIII, no. 71.

Part 2
EEC and USA – Regional Conflicts

7

Southern Africa: What Kind of Dialogue? What Chance of Sustained Co-operation?

Reginald Herbold Green[1]

What is important in Lomé is the general inspiration, rather than individual points. It is a contract and thus, a quest for two regional entities, and thus respecting the identity of each . . . development is the logical corollary to independence and that development should be according to your desires . . . In this search for economic independence, you (SADCC) are joining forces. Sixty million Africans recognise their interdependence and seek to organise it practically and solidly . . . In this initiative in regional development, the European Commission is at your side.

Commissioner, Claude Cheysson,[2]
Maputo SADCC, 1980

This conference was convened primarily to fulfil the commitment which the Heads of State and Government made in the (Lusaka SADCC) Declaration . . . to provide a mechanism through which SADCC member states and their partners in the development effort can survey results, evaluate performance, identify strength and weaknesses and agree on future plans.

Blantyre SADCC Chairman Peter S. Mmusi,[3]
1981

It would be a fatal, and historic, mistake for Angola and Mozambique not to learn their lesson . . . and to fail to co-operate with the West, actively, alongside the other ACP states.

Lucien Pagni, *The Courier*[4]
(ACP/EEC) 1982

Our determination to seek a peaceful, non-racial and prosperous region in which our people can have hope for the future develops naturally into a commitment to work together. It was out of this solidarity that SADCC was a plaything for those who desire a larger canvas on which to experiment. Rather, SADCC has grown out of a common awareness of common interests.

SADCC Chairman, Quett K. J. Masire,[5]
Gaborone Summit, 1982

The EEC's relations with Southern Africa present a complex picture of cross-cutting geographical and functional issues. They highlight differences in approach between the EEC as a Community, between its member states, and between Europe and the USA. They cover topics of high politics (East–West security, access to strategic raw materials, the status of Berlin) and low economics (beef and sugar quotas). Many of the issues are related. However, for purposes of analysis it is helpful to consider them in two main categories: relations with SADCC, and with Namibia.

SADCC and the EEC: complementarity or mismatch?

At first glance it appears unlikely that there could be close co-operation between the EEC and the Southern African Development Co-ordination Conference (SADCC) – a body whose basic charter is entitled 'Southern Africa: Toward Economic Liberation' and whose first stated aim is 'the reduction of economic dependence, particularly but not only, on the Republic of South Africa'.[6] The EEC's Third World policy is orientated to preserving access to markets, raw materials and economic influence. This is especially so in respect to its neo-mercantilist fresco of conventions with Third World states and regional groupings.[7]

Similarly, the underlying political economic approaches of the EEC and SADCC would appear to diverge markedly. The EEC is based on the freeing of market forces via a reduction of internal barriers to trade and selective market management, combined with import controls and export subsidies to restrict outsiders who could out-compete EEC producers. Institutionally it is complex, bureaucratic, partly multinational, with some attributes of supranationality. SADCC is based not on trade via free markets but on co-ordinated state action to identify and act on perceived common interests, and on production promotion via state action.[8] It has no elements of supranationality – 'SADCC exists only to the extent that member states breathe life into its common programmes and projects. It does not have an autonomous existence . . .'.[9] Actual project implementation is by co-ordinated national, not joint, action. Institutional minimalism and direct state involvement have been the hallmarks of its internal structure.[10]

Further, the EEC has a reputation for hard sell tactics in respect of its concept of North–South co-operation and to ACP membership, which has been noted as posing potential difficulties.[11] SADCC includes two non-ACP states (Angola and Mozambique) as well as seven ACP members (Botswana, Lesotho, Malawi, Swaziland, Tanzania, Zambia, Zimbabwe) and is firm, if polite, in rejecting attempts to dictate its approaches: 'Of course we are interested in exchanging experience and hearing suggestions . . . But equally obviously the final decisions on appropriate policies and institutions rest with our people'.[12] Angola, Mozambique, Tanzania and Zimbabwe are usually perceived as among the most self-confident and self-reliant – or prickly and stubborn, depending on point of view – of Third World states in their response to external proposals on strategic or major policy issues, and to react negatively to any attempt at a hard sell.

However, from a different perspective the potential for EEC-SADCC cross-regional co-operation in respect to Southern Africa is good. The EEC has a clear desire to develop good relations with Third World economic regional integration/co-ordination bodies which have demonstrable action programmes. As a regional grouping itself it shares with them a common belief in the value to member states of co-ordinated action: 'birds of a feather flock together' is a starting point for dialogue. SADCC has repeatedly expressed and acted on a commitment to enter into dialogue with co-operating governments and institutions.[13] This is arguably partly related to diplomatic public relations and certainly partly to fund-raising, but it also goes beyond that to a genuine desire to listen and to learn so long as that process is seen as a two-way street. Indeed, one of SADCC's major programme clusters – food security and agriculture – resulted from reflecting on suggestions by external participants at the 1981 Arusha SADCC.

THE EEC is operationally interventionist and etatest in many spheres, and not least in its relations with Third World countries and regional groupings. Since the negotiation of Lomé I it has become more used to (if not necessarily more enthusiastic about) the Third World side actually bargaining and not simply accepting. SADCC and its member states are willing to bargain and believe that there are overlapping interests on which bargains can be struck.[14] Because of the EEC's need to maintain access to markets, raw materials and investment, its interests overlap with those of SADCC and its members. Both parties would benefit from a reduction in Southern Africa's economic dependence on South Africa. From SADCC's point of view, an increase in exports (which would reduce dependence on external finance) and a diversification of external economic relations (away from South Africa in order to lessen dependence on any one trade or aid partner) are desirable, and may be furthered *inter alia* via co-operation with the EEC.

The EEC's record to date

Even before SADCC was formed the EEC acted – at least in principle – on its commitment to regional co-operation and to treating
Southern Africa as a region in its own right separate from South Africa
by allocating 70 mn units of account for Southern African regional
projects. Perhaps more daringly, it entered into serious discussions
with the Patriotic Front (ZANU/ZAPU) and SWAPO on the grounds
(already justified in the case of Zimbabwe) that the liberation movements were likely to be major constituents of independent
governments.[15] This does provide credibility to its claim that the EEC is
not on South Africa's side, and a pre-independence habit of contact
facilitated Zimbabwe's accession to the ACP, and is likely to lead to a
similar result with Namibia.[16]

Over 1979 to 1982 the EEC's approach to Southern Africa as a
region has become focused on its relations with SADCC, as the latter
has emerged as a clear, functioning locus of interstate co-ordination at
regional economic level.[17] The EEC has been represented at senior
levels at the Arusha, Maputo and Blantyre SADCCs of 1980, 81 and
82, while SADCC Chairman Masire addressed the European Parliament's Development Committee and the Joint Committee of the
ACP-EEC Consultative Assembly in October 1980. There have been
numerous contacts at official level, including those with SADCC
member states on regional co-operation and on implementation of
projects in the SADCC programme of action.[18]

The EEC has committed itself to, and made initial provision for,
technical assistance in support of SADCC programme studies and
initial research and conference support. One project (Botzam road) in
the SADCC transport programme is being financed from the Southern
Africa regional fund, and special EEC funding is also involved in the
Lobito Bay-Copperbelt railway rehabilitation programme (also a regional project) although this pre-dates SADCC. Projects for the
balance of the regional fund have been identified and are awaiting
approval. The EEC estimates that its total development spending in
support of national and regional projects and programmes will be of
the order of $180–200m annually during the first half of the 1980s. No
doubt some EEC member project and programme support has also
been influenced by, or partially co-ordinated by, the EEC. For
example the West German aid for feasibility studies of projects in the
SADCC transport and communications priority list was offered in
1982 to the Southern Africa Transport and Communications Commission, via Botswana as SADCC Chair State. Similarly the UK pledge at
Zimcord for Zimbabwe–Mozambique rail rehabilitation (the Limpo-
po line to Maputo) is usable on the Mozambican as well as the
Zimbabwean section.

Areas of tension

However, this relatively positive overall pattern of evolution of relationships has been marked by five actual or potential areas of tension.
None has created a crisis in relations, but none can be said, as of late
1982, to have been fully resolved. They are: the question of balance
between ACP and non-ACP external assistance by the EEC; Angolan
and Mozambican relations with the EEC; particular issues of market
access; the EEC's style of relationship with SADCC members; the
relative slowness with which EEC commitments in principle evolve
into actual project pledges, approved projects and disbursements. In
practice, several of the areas of tension interact. For example, the
more relaxed the EEC becomes about assistance to non-ACP states,
the less critical are the issues of Angolan and Mozambican accession to
Lomé and the less likely it is that the rather overstated EEC attempts
to convince them to join will lead to significant irritation at member
state and SADCC level. However, it is probably useful to examine
each area separately with cross-references to major overlaps.

The EEC has been moving, relatively slowly, towards a global aid
programme by increasing the share of its aid going to non-ACP states
and towards regional, as opposed to single country, frames. These are
controversial issues within the EEC, with Germany and the Netherlands usually perceived as championing, and France and Belgium as
opposing, this trend. From a Southern African perspective, more
weight to regional approaches is welcome. So long as Angola and
Mozambique remain outside the ACP, the same is true in respect to a
more global approach. However, these favourable trends have been
offset in the case of Southern Africa by disputes between West
Germany and Angola/Mozambique which have blocked the flow of
non-associates aid (see *Survey 1,* Chapter 1 and *Survey 2,* Chapter 1).
This has been the most evident area of disagreement (while not
formally at regional level on the SADCC side) and has centred on
Mozambique and Angola's unwillingness to accede to the Second
Lomé Convention. The EEC has lobbied hard to encourage them to
join. It has done so directly, via other members, and at SADCC
meetings, and not always in terms or tones likely to be productive. Two
issues have been central in the case of Mozambique: the form of the
'Berlin Clause' that is annexed to Lomé II (i.e. whether Berlin is
referred to as Stadt Berlin or Berlin-West); and whether the most
suitable form of association with the EEC is accession to Lomé II, or a
separate agreement analogous to that which the EEC has with Algeria
(see *Survey 1,* Chapter 4). Unlike Mozambique, Angola has an
ambassador accredited to the EEC and does not appear to have such
serious problems with the 'Berlin Clause'.[19] There are also some
indications that it would accept a special protocol as a way of resolving
the question of accession to Lomé II versus a separate agreement.

However, it has been clear that Angola and Mozambique wish to co-ordinate their negotiations with the EEC, and to reach a common resolution of the disputed issues. Both have expressed a wish in principle to enter into some formal relationship with the EEC.

The 'Berlin Clause' issue turns basically on the disagreement between the two Germanies over the status of Berlin; is it a Federal German state or an Allied Power Occupied Territory? West Germany has insisted on wording referring to 'Stadt Berlin', except for agreements with CMEA members. East Germany resists this approach and often inserts Berlin-West wording (explicitly or implicitly) in its agreements even when the relevance of the status of Berlin to the document in hand is less than self-evident. Some EEC and SADCC member states have viewed this controversy as it affects aid and economic contracts as a somewhat irritating theological distraction. Some SADCC member states sign agreements with West and East Germany with mutually inconsistent wordings on the status of Berlin and related intra-German issues since they do not regard these as functional clauses, or of concern to them. Nonetheless, until 1982, Mozambique refused to accept 'Stadt Berlin' wording on the basis that it was a socialist state, and that West Germany accepted 'Berlin-West' wording in such cases. The result was a deadlock on ACP discussions and on bilateral aid relations and, perhaps more tension-creating, a West German veto on EEC aid to Mozambique, and a general blocking of approval for projects from the Southern African regional allocation. This situation now appears to have shifted. In August 1982 Mozambique signed an agreement on food aid with West Germany including the 'Stadt Berlin' wording. An EEC credit of £4.5m to Mozambique has since been approved in principle and early resolution of the backlog of approving projects out of the regional allocation is anticipated.[20]

The question remains of the form of association. The EEC still has a strong desire for Angola and Mozambique to join the ranks of the ACP, and its initiative in mid-1982 to unblock the flow of aid stressed that this was a temporary measure until they could join the ACP. However, because 'Lomé III' is now under initial discussion/negotiation, the opportunities for a compromise are better than they were. There is now the opportunity to include Mozambique and Angola in formulating the ACP position and in negotiating the new Convention and, perhaps, special protocols (for which there are precedents).

Particular problems on market access have probably been less serious for most SADCC member states than for Third World countries in general. The two key access restricted commodities – sugar and beef – are covered by Lomé II quotas which have not been cut, and are therefore not a current source of substantial disagreement. The running debates on sugar prices primarily affect Swaziland. However, Zimbabwe, with more temperate agricultural products and manufactures in its export mix, has protested against EEC restrictions on ACP exports of wheat, bran, maize, offal, poultry, butter and cocoa which are in derogation of the Lomé Convention.[21] Some SADCC members, notably Tanzania, have suffered from the under-funding of Stabex, which forced cuts of up to 50% in payment of 1981 entitlements and is likely to have a similar impact in 1982 (see Chapter 11). However, there has been surprisingly little sustained criticism to date; a situation which may change during the negotiation of 'Lomé III'.

In the past, the EEC's style has grated on some SADCC member states. The ACP membership issue is a major example, but not the only one. The Community's style is paternalistic, and is not always readily compatible with open dialogue or negotiation. More particularly, Commissioner Cheysson, while accepted by all SADCC member states to be committed to co-operation and development and to economic liberation from South Africa, was felt by some of those with whom he came in contact, to be too pedagogic, too unwilling to accept even secondary criticism of Lomé or DG8, and too little willing to listen and to explore alternatives. His successor, Commissioner Pisani, is considered by some ACP state officials to be a better listener, and less committed to existing ways, means and programmes.

EEC support for SADCC member state projects has been slow in moving from initial commitments to actual disbursements. Part of this problem relates to the fact that the EEC's procedures and internal politics make it notoriously sluggish in reaching disbursement stage.[22] Part of it, however, results from the ACP membership and 'Berlin Clause' disagreements cited above. The effect of the lag is more evident *vis-à-vis* projects in SADCC's programme of action than it is at a purely national level because SADCC was inaugurated only in 1980 and consequently lacks a long pipeline of earlier applications finally reaching disbursement stage.

The USA and SADCC: a certain tentativeness

At first glance the USA has endorsed and indicated willingness to assist the SADCC objectives and programme of action along lines not radically different from the EEC's.[23] If it has a low continuity of interest between the annual SADCC conferences, and if the broad parameters of its pledges are lower than the EEC's, this might simply be seen as a reflection of the generally lower level of US economic aid to the member states. The USAID position for over a decade has been to support practical regional economic co-operation groupings. It had an aid office to the late East African Community and a section of its Harare Office is responsible for regional co-operation in Southern Africa. Pledges of up to $25m a year for two years were made at the 1981 Maputo conference of SADCC, albeit by a lame duck delegation.[24] Support for studies and programme development in manpower development and food security has been, or is being, provided. It has also provided capital assistance to a regional priority project – the Zambia/Zimbabwe highway link reconstruction.

However, on looking more carefully at statements and actions, there seems to be a certain hesitancy, or at least tentativeness, about the USA's relations with SADCC and vice versa. The reasons are multiple: AID's history in respect to approaches to Southern Africa, strained bilateral relations between the USA and two of SADCC's members, the current administration's economic philosophy as adumbrated to SADCC and, most crucially, the USA's attitude to Southern African liberation and to South Africa's economic destabilisation of the SADCC's member states.

Traditionally the USA has seen Southern Africa as a region centred on South Africa. It has been slower than the EEC to shift from this view and in talking of mineral sources still clearly lumps supplies from the Cape through to Lubumbashi as coming from one economic and political region. AID's initial regional study of Southern Africa in 1977 aroused sharp academic criticism (albeit little attention in the region) because it still saw Southern Africa as a natural appendage of the Republic of South Africa. A second AID regional study (1978–79) did treat Southern Africa (SADCC less Angola and Tanzania but including Namibia) as separate from and needing to reduce unilateral dependence on the Republic, and up to a point it sought the involvement of the independent governments in the preparation of the report.[25] This approach of accepting the SADCC region as a reality separate from South Africa, and with a legitimate economic interest in partial disengagement from its overbearing neighbour was reaffirmed at the 1979 Arusha SADCC. What puts the US commitment in question and introduces the hesitancy noted by some listeners is not so much anything AID says or does but the State Department's treatment of Southern Africa/South Africa as one political concern zone (or cold war battlefront). This tendency has been especially marked under the Reagan administration.

The fact that the USA does not have formal relations with Angola, and has strained relations with Mozambique, limits AID's freedom of action in selecting projects to support. (Ironically Angola is the country with which the USA has the largest and, on the company side, most cordial and profitable economic links.[26]) These strained relations make truly regional actions difficult: one regional technical assistance study could only cover seven countries, necessitating a request to Brazil to fill the gap and a long delay in compiling a data base on which to construct an action phase.[27] It was the tone of the USA's presentation at the 1982 Blantyre conference that apparently grated on some ears (and not just the radical ones), perhaps more than its endorsement of the free market and private enterprise. While urbane in tone and welcoming suggestions, Chairman Mmusi's closing speech stressed the reasons that exist for varying private/public sector balances and that 'obviously the final decisions on appropriate policies and institutions rest with our people'.[28]

Important though these constraints are, the greatest cause of hesitancy or tension is the ambivalent US stance towards Southern Africa liberation. Unlike the EEC, AID has not been willing to have preliminary technical level discussions with liberation movements. At the 1979 AID Southern African regional study review conference, Zimbabwe and Namibia were 'represented' by a number of academics only one of whom had any working relationship with the economic secretariat of the relevant liberation movement. This policy is contrasted unfavourably with the EEC's willingness to talk. The general issues of USA–South African relations and the US role in the Western Contact Group in Namibia do not directly affect relations with SADCC. In the regional division of labour they are the business of the Front Line States (FLS) not of SADCC. But there is an area of overlap which, according to some observers, became a source of tension at Blantyre. This is the South African disruption of SADCC economies and, in particular, sabotage attacks on key regional transport links.[29] The EEC, and several of its members, backed SADCC's condemnation of economic destabilisation and transport sabotage. But, reading between the lines, the use in the conference communiqué of the words '*several* invited Governments and Agencies', strongly suggests that not all did.[30] An article, apparently based on conversation with delegates, names the USA, supported by the World Bank and the UK, as the leading dissenters on the grounds that such a condemnation was a political act and therefore not a legitimate concern of a regional development body.[31] This interpretation of the closed session would seem to be borne out by a quote attributed to the head of the US delegation: 'If SADCC becomes more political, our interest in it would have to be re-evaluated'.[32]

The USA, the EEC Contact Group members and Namibia

The EEC as such has had no substantive role in respect to negotiations on the disentanglement of Namibia from South Africa's illegal occupation, even though its development of contacts with SWAPO and encouragement to them to join the ACP after independence is clearly a *de facto* forecast, statement of position and quasi-endorsement which SWAPO has welcomed. The key EEC players on Namibia are the UK, West Germany and France who, with the USA and Canada, make up the Western Contact Group (or 'Gang of Five'). Identifying the divergences between the USA and the EEC members within the

Contact Group is hard. They are not a matter of public record and must be sought in the different emphases of national statements, in off the record remarks (which may be self-serving and are not fully consistent) and in the very evident congruent belief of both South Africa and SWAPO that such differences do indeed exist. In reductionist terms the USA is seen, at least since President Reagan was inaugurated, as 'South Africa's friend' in the Gang, while Canada, West Germany and France, since the inauguration of President Mitterand, are much more sympathetic to SWAPO, with the UK gyrating rather uneasily in the middle. A more nuanced examination can be centred on five issues:
- the nature of the South African presence and what to do about it;
- the election format and results;
- economic interests in Namibia and their direct relevance to Contact Group positions;
- 'linkage' (with Angolan or South African security concerns);
- the relationship with South Africa.

Each of the Contact Group members is agreed that South Africa's presence in Namibia is unlawful. The UK does not accept the UN Mandate Revocation – the International Court of Justice Opinion route to arriving at that position, but is agreed on the illegality. Each also sees it as essential that South Africa withdraw from Namibia after internationally credible elections. None is willing to consider the use of force or mandatory sanctions (under the 'threat to peace' provisions of the UN Charter) to exert pressure on South Africa to agree expeditious arrangements to implement Security Council Resolution 435, which is the nominal justification for creating the Contact Group. While the USA may well be more adamantly opposed to mandatory sanctions than is France, in practice this difference is not operationally significant.

The election format became an issue in 1982 when the USA (acting as a link between South Africa and the Contact Group) secured Group agreement to a 'one man, two votes' combined constituency/proportional list electoral pattern. While the initial form of the proposal was in fact the West German system, nobody has suggested it was their proposal. However the Front Line States and SWAPO flatly rejected 'fancy franchises' in favour of either a proportional list (preferred) or a constituency system (subject to an independent census and registration). Following this rejection, only the USA seems to have thought it worth trying to pursue the issue. It was ultimately put to one side, although South Africa is believed to have agreed privately to accept a 'one man, one vote' system.[33]

There is a fairly general acceptance by Contact Group members, and indeed by the South African government and its proxies, that SWAPO will win a substantial majority in any reasonably fair, internationally supervised, election. The analogy in all evaluations is Zimbabwe. The USA apparently shares South Africa's hopes that SWAPO might not win the two-thirds majority that it needs to enact the independence constitution without having to seek allies or make compromises in the Constitutional Assembly. The three EEC Contact Group members take the view either that this is unrealistic (i.e. that SWAPO will win 70–75% of the votes and seats), or that a SWAPO block of over 60% of the delegates could readily assemble a two-thirds majority without giving much ground, or that an Assembly deadlocked at 65–35 would be an unhelpful result. Fairly clearly the UK, France and West Germany are reconciled to a SWAPO government and perceive delay in reaching the implementation phase of Resolution 435 as more likely to push SWAPO into harder line positions and more radical economic policies than to yield bankable guarantees of moderation. South Africa's establishment is not fully reconciled to a SWAPO government and the Afrikaaner electorate certainly is not. In consequence the government's position seems to be to hope that something may turn up while the talks drag on. The US Administration seems to have a parallel hope that either a significant 'moderate' party might emerge and win a share in the independence government, or that SWAPO might weary of fighting, come to see the USA as the only party capable of 'delivering' South Africa and alter its policies (and perhaps leadership) accordingly. This appears to be a misreading both of the probable effect of prolonging a brutal war of attrition and a negotiating process in which the party internationally named as the illegal occupier makes all the demands and gets all the concessions, and of the degree of resilience, determination and solidarity of SWAPO. However, the USA has a fairly consistent track record of misreading the nature and possible evolution of revolutionary movements and of their response to US pressures.

Economic interests in Namibia vary as does their apparent effect on policy. The USA has significant private investment – the Tsumeb mining and smelting complex – and related trade, but this does not, in practice, seem to be a policy consideration. Certainly the USA is worried about nationalisation in Namibia, but this is mainly because it identifies such actions as characteristic of pro-Soviet governments and woolly-minded states with unsound policies, rather than because it is overly concerned about the Newmont/Amax investments. The UK is concerned both about the future of its uranium oxide import contracts with Rossing Uranium (concluded after South Africa's League of Nations Mandate to administer Namibia was revoked), with RTZ's substantial investment interest in Rossing and probably also with Barclays, Standard Bank, Shell and BP interests.[34] France is apparently more concerned about future trade (including uranium oxide supplies and perhaps investment in a potential mine) than in its nationalised industry's small shareholding in Rossing. West Germany's concerns are uranium oxide supply and the status of Namibians of German origin. After early 1981 the SPD/FDP coalition government came to accept – to South Africa's ill-concealed anger – that SWAPO intends to maintain uranium oxide production, sell it commercially to power industry related buyers, respect personal property and pay compensation if it acquires individuals' productive assets (except land), give full citizenship rights to European residents who seek them and seek to retain European resident professionals, technical civil servants, small businessmen and (in some cases and with a shorter time span) ranchers. This is the one clear case of national economic interests causing what is widely perceived as a significant change of stance (opening toward SWAPO, hardening towards South Africa) in the Contact Group. The EEC as a Community has an economic interest. It seeks to bring Namibia into the ACP and out of the Southern African Customs Union. SWAPO's informal response is that if it gets a satisfactory beef quota (to allow switching exports away from South Africa) both are consistent with its preliminary economic thinking. The EEC views this as reasonably forthcoming and positive.

The idea of linking the UN presence and election run-up in Namibia to the withdrawal of Cuban troops from Angola is apparently of US origin, albeit enthusiastically endorsed by South Africa. The Contact Group fairly obviously is not agreed, but the four other members have been unwilling to argue with the USA in public, although Claude Cheysson has publicly criticised the insistence on linkage. Given that the Cubans came to Angola in force to repulse a South African column and that South Africa is engaged in continual campaigns into and marginal permanent occupation of Angola, the proposal would seem to be a non-starter unless dated after a full South African military withdrawal from Namibia. Further, Resolution 435 (the Contact Group's supposed brief) cannot be read as including this topic. Angola has, in fact, made it clear that once South African forces are out of Namibia it will see no need to retain a major Cuban military presence. But it remains unwilling to negotiate this topic formally, especially in the context of Namibia.[16] The Front Line States and SWAPO back that position and, it appears, France, Canada and West Germany accept it as reasonable and also as probably unshiftable. South Africa seems to have taken up 'linkage' primarily as a way of preventing any agreement unless and until it thinks the time is ripe and only secondarily in hope of increased security, which it can use to justify itself to the Afrikaaner volk. The USA, on the other hand, apparently mistakenly sees the Namibian talks as representing a viable opportunity for formally negotiating the withdrawal of Cuba, which it views as an expansionist Soviet proxy.

In terms of relations with South Africa, the USA stands out as wanting a 'special relationship' with the following elements: helping the Republic out of its Namibian entanglement, restoring it to a semi-respectable international standing, and coaxing economic and political reform, by using as carrots firm US backing in international institutions, trade, credit, and technology transfer. France, West Germany and the UK have no desire to engage in, let alone be seen as engaging in, any such strategic package especially in the ambit of the Contact Group. They are much more cynical (or realistic) both about the pace and meaning of South African internal reform and about the (negligible) chances of restoring the country to a normal status in international affairs. However, this may be more a matter of style than substance. It is hard to see any basic differences in present policy on trade, credit and technology transfer practice – indeed because of the heritage of Ambassador Young actual US practice is probably still marginally more restrictive!

The overall Contact Group approach to negotiations has hardly been one to inspire confidence on the African side. It has identified South Africa (the illegal occupier) as the party needing to be convinced and SWAPO/FLS as reasonable people willing to make concessions. As a result its standard response over the years has been to ask South Africa to state its needs which, usually in a watered down form, are then presented to SWAPO/FLS as 'necessary to make progress'. When they are accepted, South Africa promptly has new concerns, 'justifying' new concessions. The process thus makes the Gang of Five appear to be objectively allies of South Africa. This appearance has worsened over the past year. South Africa is apparently no longer dealing substantively with the Contact Group direct. Via its most senior diplomat, Brand Fourie, now Ambassador to Washington, it has been holding bilateral Namibia negotiations with the USA which has transmitted their agreed positions to the other four for acceptance.

Quite apart from the question of tactical procedures – and their tendency to alter the balance of Resolution 435 implementation in South Africa's favour – the Gang of Five seems collectively to labour under certain misperceptions:
- that when South Africa raises technical issues and demands for reassurance, these can be taken at face value rather than as a stalling device (a point on which the USA seems more ingenuous than the other four but even they seem almost incredibly naive).
- that South Africa really believes that pre-independence pieces of paper can determine post-independence conduct, and therefore that negotiations about them can in any meaningful sense reassure the South African government or reconcile it to a SWAPO electoral victory.
- that Prime Minister P. W. Botha will agree to any settlement acceptable to SWAPO (or international opinion) before he has resolved his own fight for personal and party survival at home.[36] He can only lose support by such an agreement and it would therefore be quite irrational to reach one before he is installed as Executive President complete with tame Council and trifurcated, rubber stamp Parliament.[37]

These differences in approach have had a clear impact on SWAPO attitudes. It distrusts the USA's judgement, tactics, ultimate objectives and motivation almost as much as those of South Africa. Indeed, it probably overestimates the 'closeness' of the special relationship that the Reagan Administration envisages or could sell to Congress and relevant sections of public opinion.[38] the UK's position is also viewed with suspicion – particularly because of the central UK role under both Conservative and Labour governments in RTZ which is seen as *the* symbol of naked exploitation by a South Africa-TNC-Western Government alliance begun after the revocation of the League of Nations Mandate made South Africa's presence illegal. However, SWAPO also perceives that the UK is experienced in decolonisation, tends to accept realities (including in this case a SWAPO electoral victory) and to cut its losses by not hanging on too long. It might, therefore, at some stage be perhaps able and willing to talk South Africa into actual agreement on implementation. This view of the UK position has been strengthened by Zimbabwe's transition. Initial enthusiasm for France's highly public shift of tone on South Africa and Namibia under the Mitterand government has been cooled by the quiet continuity in trade (including atomic sector trade) and the avoidance of a public break with the USA comparable to that on Central America. Ironically, the most favourable image may be that of West Germany because there seems to be both *de facto* agreement on post-independence bilateral relations and a certain low key, low intensity German annoyance with South African obstinacy and prevarication. However, that image may well not survive the fall of the SPD/FDP coalition: the CSU (especially Herr Strauss) and some elements of the CDU are perceived (not entirely unreasonably) as even more pro-South Africa than the present USA administration. Also, any sharp divergence with West Germany recalls the German colonial period of blood and iron in Namibia, a fact to which the SPD and FDP seem far more sensitive than Herr Strauss and his allies.

Toward problem resolution and co-operative consolidation?

In some respects the outlook for resolving several of the areas of tension appears moderately favourable. On others, substantial ambiguity exists, especially because they affect overall EEC-Southern African relationships.

Namibia

SWAPO's perception of the UK, France or West Germany could improve markedly under one of two conditions. First, that they publicly dissociate themselves from linkage and from the bilateral South African–USA 'planning session' approach to Gang of Five operations. Second, that they openly condemn South African time-wasting tactics; insist that 'reassurance' and 'impartiality' are two-way streets with rather more legitimate claims on the Namibian than the South African side; and warn that South African failure to negotiate seriously and agree expeditiously would have negative results.[39]

SWAPO's perception of the EEC is more favourable than that of any of the three EEC Contact Group members. The EEC's image as an institution seriously and constructively committed to political (Namibia) and economic (SADCC) liberation in Southern Africa is likely to continue. By its outreach to the then Patriotic Front and to SWAPO, its statements at SADCC meetings and its initial assistance commitments, the EEC has built up an image distinct from (and in at least two cases distinctly more positive than) that of its member states. As its own goals of access to Southern African markets, raw materials and investment opportunities are served by that image, it can be expected to seek to maintain it.

SADCC

The issues of Namibia and SADCC are closely related. Any tarnishing of the EEC's image in Namibia will tend to weaken its relations with SADCC which will, in any case, be strongly influenced by the forthcoming 'Lomé III' negotiations. The EEC's apparently greater willingness to listen and to consider alternatives will be tested in these negotiations. A repetition of the Lomé II approach, which most ACP states viewed as a rigid determination to yield no ground and to refuse to deal even with evident problems, could rapidly reverse the increased acceptability of EEC style.

Three areas which the EEC is believed to wish to stress in its future co-operation programmes are: food security (going beyond food aid to production, storage and reserves), mining development and support for regional initiatives (see Chapter 13). Given that food security and agriculture are major SADCC priorities, as is mining, all three seem to be shifts which increase the probability of more EEC–SADCC co-operation, although this will depend in part on the exact form of the mineral sector proposals. Angola and Mozambique seem likely, as of late 1982, to participate in negotiations towards 'Lomé III' with a view to seeing whether that Convention (possibly with the addition of special protocols) would be an acceptable vehicle of co-operation. The outcome may rest more on how flexible the EEC is in general than on issues specific to these two states.

Most of the special issues likely to be raised during the negotiations (e.g. beef, citrus and sugar quotas, access for temperate foodstuffs and manufactures, adequate funding for and perhaps partial indexation of

Stabex) are largely a question of global EEC positions rather than of its Southern African relations. However, the beef quotas are an exception since they are of particular concern to Botswana, Swaziland, Zimbabwe and, on independence, Namibia, which will be able to count on the support of their fellow SADCC members in ensuring that the ACP position is fairly firm on this topic.

The poor disbursement record of the EEC is evidently going to be a topic in the current negotiations. What form the dialogue will take is less clear. Some ACP states (including at least one SADCC member) have tentatively suggested that the bulk of 'Lomé III' commitments should be in quick disbursing programmes untied to projects, because the available balance of Lomé I and II allocations will almost certainly be adequate to meet all project disbursements actually made during 'Lomé III', barring a major acceleration in the present review, study, approval and implementation process.

It would seem, therefore, that SADCC/EEC co-operation is likely to continue, and to expand in the 1980s. The EEC's tentative areas of increased emphasis and the current issues in Southern African economic co-operation point in that direction. However, the creeping protectionism which has built up in the EEC since 1980 and any repetition of the stonewalling attitude it displayed toward ACP initiatives during the Lomé II negotiations could lead to a general deterioration of EEC–ACP relations, which would overwhelm the more positive signs. While EEC–ACP co-operation is an area of North–South co-operation with better prospects than most, it is not separable from the growing international economic disorder and the disastrous impact that this is having on many Southern economies (including a majority of SADCC's members) and on North–South relations.

Notes

1 While Professor Green has served as a consultant to, and Liaison Committee member of SADCC and a consultant to SWAPO, this article represents his personal interpretations and evaluations, and is not to be read as a statement by or for SADCC or SWAPO.

2 *SADCC Maputo*, London, SADCC, 1981.

3 *SADCC Blantyre*, Blantyre, SADCC, 1982, p. 66; closing statement by Minister Mmusi to conference.

4 No. 73 – May/June 1982, p. 33.

5 'Opening statement by the Chairman', Gaborone Summit, July 22 1982, Gaborone.

6 *Southern Africa: Toward Economic Liberation*, SADCC, London, 1980.

7 See, for example, Green, R. H., 'The child of Lomé: messiah, monster or mouse', and Ravenhill, J., 'Asymmetrical interdependence: renego-

tiating the Lomé Convention' in F. Long (ed), *The Political Economy of EEC Relations with African, Caribbean and Pacific States,* Pergamon, 1980.

8 See for example Green, R. H., 'Economic co-ordination in Southern Africa: the struggle continues', *Africa Contemporary Record 1980–81;* Green, R. H. 'Co-ordinating common interests in development: SA in retrospect and prospect', Scandinavian Institute for African Studies, *Africa out of Recession Conference,* September 1982 (mimeo); Nsekela, A. J. (ed), *Southern Africa, Africa Toward Economic Liberation* (Arusha SADCC and Lusaka Summit papers with introduction by President Khama), London, Rex Collings, 1981: *SADCC Blantyre,* Blantyre, SADCC, 1982; and 'Opening statement by the Chairman' (Gaborone Summit, July 22 1982) Gaborone.

9 *Ibid.*

10 For example, *Southern Africa: Toward Economic Liberation,* London, SADCC, 1980 and 'Opening statement by the Chairman' (Gaborone Summit, 22 July 1982), Gaborone.

11 Cf. Green, R. H., 'Constellation, association or liberation: economic co-ordination and the struggle for Southern Africa', *Africa Contemporary Record, 1979–80,* Africana, 1981.

12 Chairman Mmusi, *SADCC Blantyre,* Blantyre, SADCC, 1982.

13 *Southern Africa: Toward Economic Liberation,* London, SADCC, 1980; Nsekela, A. J. (ed), *Southern Africa: Africa Toward Economic Liberation* (Arusha SADCC and Lusaka Summit papers with introduction by President Khama), London, Rex Collings, 1981; and *SADCC Blantyre,* Blantyre, SADCC, 1982.

14 Cf, for example, President Machel, *SADCC Maputo,* London, SADCC, 1981.

15 For example, in the autumn of 1982 the EEC met with a SWAPO delegation headed by President Nujoma for wide-ranging talks including future economic strategy and relations with the EEC of an independent Namibia.

16 It may be argued that a lack of comparable pre-independence contacts to built trust and familiarity with Frelimo and MPLA has contributed to the more difficult subsequent interaction of the EEC with Mozambique and Angola.

17 SADCC is a logical economic, as well as political economic, grouping – with Lesotho a rather special case. Tanzanian involvement in transport and potentially in co-ordinated production and trade (as well as its history of involvement in central and Southern African liberation) are compelling reasons for that northward extension of the region. Zaïre is not historically, economically or geographically, part of the region. The remaining occupied territory, Namibia, is perceived as becoming SADCC's tenth member on its independence by SADCC, SWAPO and the EEC.

18 Since SADCC programme project implementation is by the states which are directly concerned, some logical difficulty arises in separating outside contacts/funding into SADCC and member state components.

19 It has bilateral agreements with West Germany which include the same 'Stadt Berlin' wording.

20   See, for example, J. Hanlon, 'Berlin recognition opens way for EEC aid to Mozambique', *Guardian,* 10 August 1982.
21   See, for example, I. Murray, 'Mugabe worried by EEC trade barriers', *The Times,* 28 May 1982.
22   A SADCC programme animal disease control study seems to have been a recent example.
23   See USA speeches in Nsekela, op. cit. *SADCC Maputo*, 1981, *SADCC Blantyre,* 1982.
24   *SADCC Maputo,* 1981.
25   USAID, *Development Needs and Opportunities for Co-operation in Southern Africa,* Washington, 1979.
26   Compare, for example, 'Rockefeller says African Marxism poses no threat to US interests' and 'Shredding a veil of distortions around Angola', *International Herald Tribune,* 3, 11 March 1982.
27   Apparently either AID initially believed that it could allow its consultant – institutionally assigned to the co-ordinating country – to do the field work in all nine countries, or there was a misunderstanding as to what he could do.
28   *SADCC Blantyre,* 1982, p. 66.
29   Referred to in 'Communiqué' (*SADCC Maputo,* 1981) and in even more biting terms in the Ministerial Council 'Statement of Condemnation' (SADCC, Blantyre Council of Ministers, *Record*).
30   Emphasis added.
31   See J. Hanlon's articles in *Guardian,* 24, 27 November 1981.
32   'SADCC balances aspirations with realities', *Africa Economic Digest,* 27 November–3 December 1981.
33   Why South Africa raised this issue is unclear. Reasonable calculations do not suggest it would cost SWAPO or gain South Africa's Turnhalle Alliance more than one or two seats. Perhaps the most likely interpretation is that South Africa proposed it (and let it be known it had done so) precisely because SWAPO was sure to suspect that it was really a carefully calculated way of altering the results and, therefore, to oppose it vigorously. That would – and did – serve to buy South Africa about six months of time without the appearance of refusing to negotiate.
34   Realistically the banking and petroleum interests are much less at risk than RTZ and the uranium oxide supply contracts.
35   Compare for example, *International Herald Tribune,* op.cit.
36   SWAPO at times seems to share this misreading. However, because the centre of SWAPO's worldview is Namibia (unlike either Prime Minister Botha's or the Contact Group's) it is less surprising that they should fail to see that, for Botha, Namibia is secondary to his domestic political problems.
37   Whether the new President Botha would seek an early agreement on implementation of Resolution 435 is unclear. There is some reason to suppose he might do so.
38   See C. Crocker, 'South Africa: strategy for change', *Foreign Affairs,* Winter 1980 for what is probably a reasonable approximation to the main line US Administration position. Compare this with *South Africa: Time Running Out,* (Rockefeller Commission Report), Rockefeller Foundation, New York 1981 for what is basically an 'establishment' view of what

US policy should be. While not able to prevail in the present context, this body of opinion almost certainly could marshall a blocking majority in Congress against any major, overt changes in US relations with South Africa (especially if they involved spending – including lending – money).

39 Exactly what measures is unclear – SWAPO has no illusions that they would include overall trade or oil sanctions. But curtailing export credits, discouraging bank lending, limiting technology transfer and atomic sector sales would be seen as significant measures which might influence South African action, or at least its timing.

8

EEC and US Policies Towards the Caribbean Basin

Lucy Blackburn and Fiona Merry

The traditional involvement of both the EEC and the USA in the Caribbean Basin is deep-rooted and already well documented.[1] EEC interest has concentrated almost entirely on its present and former British, Dutch and French colonies in the Caribbean as shown by the preferential economic status granted by the UK to the Commonwealth and by the EEC to the ACP countries under Lomé I and II. US policy, on the other hand, has focused on Central America as well as the Caribbean and has been based primarily on a continuing desire to defend strategic, political and economic interests in the region rather than on historical ties.

For the USA, the prime objective remains to prevent any spread of 'Soviet influence' in the region. However, the means by which it has attempted to achieve this objective have changed noticeably over the last two years from an initial approach, which sought to tackle the dangers of East–West confrontation by direct intervention in individual countries, to a more indirect approach, which aims to promote political stability through an improvement in the economic welfare of the region. The concept of the Caribbean Basin as a region is in itself an innovation, aptly described by the Jamaican Prime Minister, Mr Edward Seaga, as 'more a term of art than logic'.[2] Previously Central America and the Caribbean island economies had been treated separately, because of differences in their colonial past and economic structures, which are reflected in two distinct associations, the Caribbean Community (Caricom) and the Central American Common Market (CACM). However, in the first half of 1982 both the USA and the EEC launched proposals that treated the Caribbean basin as a unified region. In February 1982 President Reagan unveiled his plans for a Caribbean Basin Initiative (CBI), and a month later the EEC Commission developed an initiative of its own. This chapter examines and compares both proposals, discussing whether either represents a new approach in foreign policy making and analysing their potential effect on the recipient nations.

Table 8.1   *Who belongs to what in the Caribbean Basin*

	CBI	Lomé	EEC initiative	Caricom	CACM	CADC**	OAS
Bahamas		x					x
Barbados		x		x			x
Dominica	x	x		x			x
Dominican Republic	x		x				x
Grenada		x		x			x
Guyana		x		x			
Haiti	x		x				x
Jamaica	x	x		x			x
St Lucia	x	x		x			x
Suriname		x					x
Trinidad & Tobago		x		x			x
Antigua	x	x		x			
Montserrat	x	x*		x			
St Kitts-Nevis-Anguilla	x	x*		x			
St Vincent & the Grenadines	x	x		x			
Cuba							x
Belize	x	x		x			
Costa Rica	x		x		x	x	x
El Salvador	x		x		x	x	x
Guatemala			x		x	x	x
Honduras	x		x		x	x	x
Nicaragua			x			x	
Panama							x

* OCT
** Central American Democratic Community

Both initiatives indicate shifts of policy that go beyond the innovation of treating the Caribbean basin as a unit. No united EEC policy or action towards Central America had been formulated before 1982, though as *The Times* has noted, 'European governments have tended to support the more moderate elements within the opposition forces in the region . . . while the US has tended to opt for a policy of encouraging the forces of moderate change within existing governments'.[3] For the EEC this interest in Central America and non-ACP Caribbean states (Haiti and the Dominican Republic) marks a shift in emphasis from a geographically arbitrary selection of ACP states, into a region which until recently had been regarded almost exclusively as the 'American backyard'.

For the USA, Central America and the Caribbean have always been of much more direct concern. Interest in the region has been justified in terms not just of history and a concern for development, but also of geopolitics. The belief that 'political stability and strongly pro-American governments in the region are essential for US security and well-being'[4] has resulted in the USA maintaining sovereignty over Puerto Rico and the US Virgin Islands as well as, under the 1979 Panama Canal Treaty, the legal right to operate the Panama Canal until the year 2000 and to keep military bases there. Sporadic attempts have also been made to oust potentially left-wing governments in the region, sometimes backed by military intervention: Guatemala 1954, Cuba 1961, Dominican Republic 1975, Nicaragua 1976–79 and Grenada 1980–81. In the case of Grenada US actions included pressure on the EEC to alter the pattern of its assistance to the Bishop government. The CBI marks a change in US tactics. Instead of tackling 'problem countries' as they arise, it attempts to restrain 'communist expansionism' by a programme of regional development, although support for the region is seen in terms of strengthening bilateral links between the individual countries and the USA rather than of strengthening multilateral ties between all countries of the region.

Three main factors have contributed to this recent shift in US policy-making. First, growing domestic opposition within the USA to the previous strategy. President Reagan's policy of singling out target countries in Central America has failed to win Congressional support, except in Honduras where the election of a new civilian President, Dr Julio Suazo Córdova, on 27 January 1982, gave President Reagan a justification for increasing US military aid (see Table 8.2). In Nicaragua, Congress rejected his proposal for military intervention in September 1981, while in El Salvador, US support for the Constituent Assembly elections on 28 March failed to provide a majority for the Christian Democrats. Instead the coalition government dominated by Major Roberto d'Aubuisson, leader of the extreme right Arena party suspended the third stage of the land reform. This did not prevent President Reagan on 27 July certifying an improvement in human rights, but did raise concern in Congress which rejected the President's proposed increase in military aid from $60m to $163m.[5] Secondly, the Falklands crisis created a realignment of relations within Latin America, which undermined the traditional relationship with the USA. Cuba and Nicaragua gained a new respectability within Latin America as a result of their support for Argentina, while the USA temporarily lost its staunchest ally on Central American issues, Argentina. Thirdly, the new policy represented a realisation that the USA no longer has exclusive hegemony in the region, with Venezuela and Mexico (not to mention Germany, Japan and Canada) becoming increasingly important economic actors.

The US initiative

Early in 1981 representatives of the USA, Mexico, Canada and Venezuela met in Nassau, Bahamas, to discuss aid strategy for the Caribbean region. All are major donors and trading partners in the region. Mexico and Venezuela have a joint petroleum assistance fund, the San José agreement, which was signed in August 1980.[6] Mexico has granted concessional credits valued at over $700m p.a., Venezuela has given more than $2.5bn in financial aid since 1977, and Canada is a major aid donor as well as granting duty-free or preferential access for almost 98% of the region's exports to Canada. The meeting stressed the importance of multilateral organisations in any programme and included representatives from the World Bank. Hopes were expressed that other countries, particularly those already active in the region such as Colombia and Brazil, would participate in the final programme.

But this move towards truly regional action failed, resulting only in disagreement over which countries should be included (Mexico and Canada favoured the inclusion of Nicaragua and, possibly, Cuba) and what form the aid should take. The USA decided to act unilaterally when, almost a year later in February 1982, President Reagan announced the Caribbean Basin Initiative to a meeting of the Organisation of American States. Although he made specific reference to co-ordinating programmes with other donors to the region, the CBI revealed an approach to development for the Basin that differed widely from those of other donors. Unlike the Nassau discussions, the US approach is framed within the context of East–West conflict, stressing the need to 'encourage and protect' emerging economies from neighbouring Cuba's influence. In the words of one American official, 'If we do not react promptly and decisively in defence of freedom, new Cubas will arise from the ruins of today's conflicts'.[7] The CBI excludes unsympathetic countries and makes an attempt to use the traditional tools of the West (free trade and private investment) to counter any destabilising effect of Cuban encroachment. It has been described in Congress as 'a program which will combine the democratic capitalist ideals which we hold with the strong desire for freedom and democracy which our neighbours have clearly demonstrated'.[8] Unlike many contemporary aid and development packages, it discourages government participation in the economy and it appears that US direct foreign investment is a more important criterion for assessing benefits than is need. El Salvador, Costa Rica and Jamaica are likely to be the main beneficiaries while Cuba, Nicaragua and Grenada are excluded; Haiti and Honduras, probably the two poorest nations in the region, are awarded an insignificant portion (see Table 8.2).

Table 8.2 US aid to the Caribbean Basin ($m)

Fiscal year (Oct–Sept)	1980 Economic	1981		1982		1982 Supplemental economic (CBI)		1983	
		Economic	Military	Economic	Military	original	amended[4]	Economic	Military
Central America									
Belize	—	—	—	—	—	10.0	10.0	—	0.1
Costa Rica	13.6	13.3	—	51.3	0.1	70.0	70.0	85.0	0.1
El Salvador	58.5	104.5	35.5	104.5	136.0	128.0	75.0	164.9	61.3
Guatemala	11.4	16.7	—	11.8	—	—	10.0	13.0	0.3
Honduras	50.7	36.1	8.9	38.0	10.6	35.0	35.0	63.1	15.3
Nicaragua	37.0	59.6	—	23.1	—	—	—	—	—
Panama	2.1	10.5	0.4	11.2	5.4	—	—	12.3	5.5
Caribbean									
Dominican Republic	54.8	36.8	3.4	45.2	5.4	40.0	41.0	46.8	10.2
Eastern Caribbean	—	—	—	—	5.8	10.0	20.0	—	5.8
Guyana	5.0	1.2	—	2.3	—	—	—	2.7	0.1
Haiti	27.9	34.0	0.4	31.5	0.6	5.0	10.0	34.7	0.7
Jamaica	12.7	69.1	1.7	87.1	2.1	50.0	50.0	112.0	6.7
Suriname	—	—	—	—	—	—	—	1.0	—
Other	—	—	—	—	1.0	—	—	—	—

Regional								
Regional Office for Central America and Panama	4.2	10.6	—	18.0	—	—	25.0[5]	19.0	—
Caribbean Regional	46.1	27.1	—	50.6	—	—	—	60.0	—
Latin American & Carib. Regional Programme	—	—	—	—	2.0	2.0	2.0	50.0	—
Central American Total[1]	177.5	251.3	44.8	257.9	152.0[3]	243.0	200.0	357.3	82.6
Caribbean Total[1]	146.5	168.3	5.5	216.7	14.9	105.0	121.0	257.2	23.5
Caribbean Basin Total[2]	324.0	419.6	50.3	474.6	166.9	350.0	349.0	664.5	106.1

Columns may not add up due to rounding.

[1] Excluding Latin American and Caribbean Regional Programme
[2] Including Latin American and Caribbean Regional Programme
[3] Includes $55m supplementary military aid to El Salvador in February 1982; $25m to replace military equipment and $30m for training
[4] Figure in the 1982 Supplemental Appropriation Bill passed by Congress
[5] Unallocated

Source: US State Department

Box 1
The Caribbean Basin Initiative as announced by President Reagan, 24 February 1982

Trade

This forms the centrepiece of the Initiative. Under the proposals, the USA is to extend duty-free access to virtually all imports (apart from textiles and clothing) from the Caribbean Basin. Under previous arrangements, some 87% of these imports were covered under the GSP.

Investment incentives

There will be major tax advantages for US companies wishing to invest in the Basin countries, for example a five-year domestic tax credit, with possible extension, for up to 10% p.a. of the fixed asset investment. Bilateral investment treaties will be sought covering such areas as profit repatriation assurances, dispute arbitration and equal treatment for foreign and local companies. There is likely to be extended insurance cover for US commercial concerns with the Overseas Private Investment Corporation (OPIC), particularly in countries where the insurance limit has been approached and in poorly covered sectors such as oil and mining. Additionally, private sector insurance schemes and cover via multilateral banks are to be considered.

Aid

Supplementary aid of $350m (excluding military) was announced to bring total aid to the region up to $825m. It will be concentrated largely on the private sector. Beneficiaries were to include El Salvador ($128m), Costa Rica ($70m), Jamaica ($50m), the Dominican Republic ($40m), Honduras ($35m), Eastern Caribbean ($10), Belize ($10m) and Haiti ($5m). The remaining $2m would go to the American Institute for Free Labor Development. The aid is to be distributed via three paths. First, through development assistance which is project-orientated with the emphasis on agriculture, health and population problems. Second, through economic support funds to provide direct balance of payments support and credit for vital imports. Finally, some aid will be directed as food aid.

Technical aid

Training and assistance will be offered to the Caribbean private sector in export promotion and marketing, investment and technology transfer, particularly in the agricultural sector. The Peace Corps and the US private business sector will be involved.

Security

There is no military aid component in the CBI. However, contained in the supplemental Bill alongside CBI aid requirements were provisions for military assistance (see Table 8.2).

Coverage

In his speech, the President did not exclude any Central American or Caribbean state from becoming potential beneficiaries. However, to take advantage of the CBI, two criteria must be met by all nations: first, assistance to any country must serve US national interest, and second, the country must be committed to the concept of private enterprise and have a political climate conducive to private overseas investment. Any country which has 'unlawfully seized' US property will be excluded. This effectively excludes Cuba, Grenada, Nicaragua and possibly Suriname. Although the French colonies of Martinique and Guadeloupe are not included in the package, British colonies are (Anguilla, Cayman Islands, Montserrat, St Kitts-Nevis, Turks and Caicos Islands, British Virgin Islands), as are the Netherlands Antilles.

The Initiative also marks a geographical shift in emphasis. Although the USA is the major trading partner for most Caribbean as well as Central American countries (see Table 8.3), it has previously seen the Caribbean islands more as a European sphere for aid programmes, and so has concentrated its own efforts on Central America and its dependent territories of Puerto Rico and the US Virgin Islands.

The provisions outlined in the CBI and subsequent amendments are covered in Boxes 1 and 2. The original programme comprised three interrelated components:
– Trade: 12-year duty-free access to the US market for all exports except textiles;
– Investment: special arrangements to encourage US firms to invest in the region;
– Finance: an aid package.

Box 2
The Caribbean Basin Initiative and Congress

Congressional attitudes

(a) Congress faced mid-term elections in November 1982 and in a period of recession did not want to appear to be sacrificing the domestic economy. This affects the *trade* aspects of the CBI and the *investment* proposals. Domestic industries and unions have lobbied for a reduction in free trade concessions and against the 10% proposed tax cut for investors in the Caribbean Basin which they claim will cause the export of US jobs. The tax incentives would reduce US government revenue by about $65m in the fiscal year 1983, increasing to $81m in fiscal year 1986.
(b) Liberal members are concerned that the package is simply a ploy to aid El Salvador and are voicing doubts about the human rights record there.
(c) Approval for the package comes from the anti-immigration lobby who sense that a more prosperous Caribbean Basin will stem the flow of both legal and illegal immigration into the US.

The procedure

Every major element of the package must be passed in Congress. The bill first passes through various committees in both Houses. Amendments may be passed at any stage. Since the two may well differ, the leaders of the two Houses hold a conference to draw up a final co-ordinated version. This, if passed by both Houses, then goes to the President for ratification or veto. Following this, appropriation bills must also be passed in both Houses to permit outlays of money for the programme. The direct aid ($350m) component of the bill is part of the 1982 supplemental appropriations bill.

The passage

SENATE
May
Foreign Relations Committee
recommended by a narrow vote of 9:8 that the $350m aid package be disbursed through an international fund, to be overseen by the World Bank, and that it should represent no more than one-third of total funds, which should also be subscribed by other countries, particularly members of the Nassau Group, Colombia and Brazil.

HOUSE OF
REPRESENTATIVES

Sub-committee on Inter-American Affairs recommended that aid to El Salvador should be limited to $75m (previously $128m) and Costa Rica's share should be increased to $75m from $70m. More should be allocated to Haiti and the Eastern Caribbean nations.

Ways and Means Committee:
After pressure from US trade
unions, Puerto Rico and the US
Virgin Islands, Caribbean rum
exports were removed from the
duty-free access list. Leather and
rubber footwear, luggage, gloves,
handbags and other leather goods
were also removed. (Sugar had
practically been removed already,
though CBI members have been
granted larger quotas.) Meat was
also threatened.

*Sub-committee on International
Economic Policy and Trade*
recommended that no single
country should receive more than
$75m and that 25% of funds
should go for infrastructural and
social service development.

June
Foreign Relations Committee
reversed their earlier decision to
make funding available
multilaterally after discussions
with the Jamaican Prime
Minister, Mr Seaga. The World
Bank had expressed itself unable
to administer such a scheme.

July
Foreign Relations Committee
recommended cut in aid to El
Salvador to $100m of which $20m
is to go towards the land reform
programme. $44m is to be
development assistance
(originally all was to be for
balance of payments support).
The $28m should be reallocated
to the Eastern Caribbean and
Haiti, although no aid should go
to the latter until IMF fiscal
targets are met. Guatemala
should be added to the list of
possible beneficiaries from the
CBI. The committee also
recommended that $7.5m should
be used for scholarships for the
region and 20% of the remaining
economic support funds should
be made available to general local
currencies for development.

Foreign Affairs Committee
approved the CBI and passed it to
Senate Foreign Relations
Committee.

Specifically with reference to Haiti, part of the funds ($10m) are to be administered by private voluntary organisations to prevent official corruption. The bill was renamed the Caribbean and Central American Aid Bill.

The Administration voiced hopes that the bill would achieve full congressional approval by end-August, before the end of the current legislative session. However, US budget complications delayed progress somewhat.

The Finance Committee working on the trade and investment provisions within the CBI decided to consider the bill only after it had been passed by the House of Representatives.

House of Representatives: On 29 July after a bipartisan agreement had been made to push the CBI through the House, the bill fell on a procedural point raised by its opponents. Authorising legislation had not yet been passed for allocation of the $350m. The compromise was to have been that the administration would not push for a large separate military aid package of $35m for El Salvador. The main opponents were liberal members concerned for human rights in El Salvador.

August
Senate passed the CBI by 54:42 votes and approved extra military aid of $11m for El Salvador. They also passed an amendment to the bill stating that the US intended to prevent the spread of 'Cuban-style communism' by 'whatever means necessary including the use of arms'.

House of Representatives: On 18 August the CBI was passed by 281 votes to 129, agreeing to add the $350m to a $14.6bn supplemental appropriations bill. The House also approved $27m within the bill for US military aid including $10m for Honduras and $2m for Costa Rica. This was passed by 237 votes to 175. The CBI was then sent to Senate for final approval. The bill contained the following CBI package: some $350 for the Caribbean Basin is to be made available from 15 September 1982 until 31 March 1983 distributed as follows: El Salvador (not more than $75m), Costa Rica (not less than $70m), Jamaica (not less than $50m), Dominican Republic (not less than $41m), Honduras (not less than $35m), Eastern Caribbean (not less than $20m), Belize (not less than $10m), Haiti (not less than $10m) and Guatemala (not more than $10m). Not less than $2m is allocated to the American Institute for Free Labor Development, not less than $2m to the Inter-American Foundation, and $25m remains unallocated.

It included the amendments made by Senate in July with respect to conditions for allocating funds to Haiti, and El Salvador, and in August with respect to Cuban encroachment in the region and also stipulated that only countries co-operating to prevent drugs entering the USA unlawfully could be eligible.

On August 19 Congress passed the CBI as part of the appropriations bill and sent it to the White House. President Reagan vetoed the whole appropriations bill on the grounds that it was a 'budget buster' (including the CBI). By a 60:30 majority Congress overrode the veto on 10 September, just securing the two-thirds majority needed.

Following mid-term Congressional elections, it was hoped that the remainder of the CBI would be passed during the 'lame duck' session in December. However, informed sources put its chance of success at substantially less than 50% – in spite of official confidence.

Trade

The trade provisions extend GSP facilities for 12 years to all imports into the USA from countries in the region. It has been officially recognised however that 87% of imports were already covered under the GSP. Furthermore, about half of the remaining 13% are textiles and clothing, which have been totally excluded, and sugar, which is in any case subject to quantitative restrictions.[9] If rum, leather and rubber footwear and leather goods are excluded, as recommended by the Senate Ways and Means Committee (see Box 2), virtually no new trade will result from these proposals. Moreover, the experience of the Lomé Convention suggests that trade preferences alone have little impact on flows (see Chapter 10). Although it appears from Table 8.2 that the present trade balance is strongly in favour of the Basin countries, if oil exports to the USA are excluded this is no longer the case.

The rules of origin component to qualify for the CBI have yet to be decided. At the time of going to press the Senate was suggesting a minimum of 25% local content, which could be met by an accumulation of inputs from all Basin countries. Clearly, a balance needs to be struck between too high a value-added threshold (which is beyond the reach of the less developed economies) and too low a threshold (which will provide little incentive for the development of local industries). The Senate suggestion is probably on the low side and can be compared with the Lomé threshholds which the ACP claim are at about 60% and too high (see *Survey 1*, Chapter 3).

Investment

Through its emphasis on private investment the CBI reinforces the role of US companies as agents of American influence. The tax incentives and duty-free access for 12 years will benefit the US companies by reducing the risk of investment, but are unlikely to lead to equal benefits for all Caribbean basin countries. Normal commercial criteria such as good labour relations and government attitudes will continue to dominate the choice of suitable locations. Moreover, because of the similar structure of the Basin island economies, countries which have the necessary infrastructure are likely to succeed in gaining a larger share of investment and trade in the limited markets for tourism, agricultural commodities and minerals than those such as the Eastern Caribbean which do not. Regional disparities will tend therefore to widen.

Aid

The aid component of the CBI is highly politicised. Even though the Senate refused to include military aid to El Salvador in the Initiative, it did approve a policy declaration within the CBI which states that the United States will prevent Cuban aggression in the hemisphere by any means including the use of arms. The high level of military aid already allocated by the USA to the Caribbean basin (see Table 8.2) will ensure that this commitment can be fulfilled. Within the CBI, the bilateral provision of economic aid will enable the USA to reward politically sympathetic nations such as Jamaica and exclude those such as Grenada who 'have turned from their American heritage'.[10] This has given rise to the cry that the package is simply a 'trojan horse' in which aid could be sent to El Salvador. The Initiative itself does not exclude absolutely any country within the region, so long as certain criteria laid down by the USA are met, but in practice only a select group will benefit. Moreover the distribution of benefits even among this select group is not balanced. El Salvador, Jamaica and Costa Rica are together earmarked in the original proposal for 71% and in the final version will still receive 56% of the total economic aid.

Such considerations should not lead one to exaggerate the size and potential impact of the aid programme. Though the Initiative will almost double US economic assistance to the region from $420m in 1981 to $825m in 1982, falling to a planned $665m in 1983, the amount is too small to have any major effect. To put this in perspective, the external debt of Costa Rica alone amounted to $3bn in March 1982, more than eight times the direct aid offered in the CBI, while in political terms the 1982 proposed level represents only a notional $20 per capita, compared to the estimated $300 per capita supplied annually by the USSR to Cuba or $700 per capita supplied by the USA to Israel.[11]

The European Initiative

The European interest which has emerged towards Central America (see Box 3) may be interpreted somewhat cynically as a desire to ensure that the EEC does not lose a foothold in the region while the USA, Canada, Venezuela and Mexico increase their stake,[12] or, more idealistically, as a genuine concern for peace and stability in the region and a gesture of support for the CBI. The attitude of EEC member states to Central America has been varied with France, under President Mitterand, being the most vocal in its opposition to US policy, and the UK, under the Thatcher government, being the most sympathetic. France, for example, denounced the elections in El Salvador and sought instead a joint peace initiative with Mexico in February 1982 which recommended negotiations with the FMLN, the leftist umbrella organisation. In contrast the UK, alone in Europe, sent two observers to the country who reported reasonably favourably on their fairness. The European Parliament limited itself to a statement that the elections 'cannot be regarded as free elections as no political liberties have been guaranteed and opposition politicians have to face the possibility of assassination'.[13]

Box 3
Original EEC initiative as outlined by the Commission in May 1982

Amount   70–105m ecus. Minimum 10m ecus per country.
Countries theoretically eligible to receive this aid:
   Central America   El Salvador
                     Costa Rica*
                     Guatemala
                     Honduras*
                     Nicaragua*
   Caribbean   Dominican Republic*
                     Haiti
Conditions   Aid to be conditional upon pursuit of agrarian reform to resolve structural difficulties; for El Salvador and Guatemala an improvement in the political situation.
   * countries likely to fulfill the conditions

Purpose   Balance of payments support to be directed towards:
                         (a) improving equipment of small farmers, supplying agricultural inputs, infrastructure such as irrigation, increasing production of essential food and agricultural credit;
                         (b) immediate aid for products to stimulate production and maintain consumption levels.

Background to the EEC initiative

September 1981   Suggestion by Claude Cheysson at Council of Foreign Ministers in London.
March 1982   EEC Commission outlined proposals for transfer of 70–105 million ecus from savings on budget to non-associates programme for use in Central America and Caribbean.
29/30 March 1982   European Council adopted resolution 'to co-ordinate and .increase European aid in view of Central American and Caribbean development'.
19 July 1982   Council of Foreign Ministers in Brussels postponed action on 70–105 mn ecus aid, following objections by several ministers about funds to Guatemala. Following arguments between the

	EEC members, the amount of aid was reduced to 40 mn ecus and the number of countries to 4: Nicaragua, Costa Rica, Honduras and Dominican Republic.
21 September 1982	Initiative should have been agreed by Council of Ministers, but because of German elections the Germans did not attend. The proposal was therefore not discussed.
13 October 1982	Plan debated by European Parliament at Strasbourg. Signor Pisani, Development Aid Commissioner, described the suggestion by the Council of Ministers to withhold aid to Nicaragua as 'unjustified and clumsy'.
25 October 1982	Initiative scheduled for discussion at Council of Foreign Ministers.

The European initiative grew out of a concern first voiced by Claude Cheysson at the Council of Foreign Ministers in September 1981 and was outlined by the Commission in March 1982. The financial proposals in the Commission's initiative are modest, like those of the CBI, but would bring Central America level with the Caribbean in terms of EEC aid received. The EEC's room for manoeuvre, however, is limited since in its proposals aid would be financed from the non-associates programme which is drawn from the budget and therefore agreed annually. The proportion of the total that can go to any one region is also fixed in the budget and, in the case of Latin America, is currently 20%. A final decision on whether to accept the proposal was scheduled for the Council of Foreign Ministers on 25 October 1982 – after this *Survey* went to press. Because of the divergent views of member states, the proposed aid had already been reduced from 70–100m ecus to 40m ecus, and the number of recipient countries reduced from seven to four (Nicaragua, Costa Rica, Honduras and the Dominican Republic). France and Italy were strongly in favour of the original proposal; as was Germany, which would have liked to extend it to a broad commercial agreement. Denmark, though excluded from the discussion because of holding the Presidency, was also supportive. However, the UK proved obstinate on both budgetary and political grounds. It lobbied for the lower level of total aid, by arguing that existing aid should be subtracted from the total, and was also sensitive about the inclusion of Nicaragua in the package, on account of its vocal backing for Argentina in the Falklands crisis.[14] The Dutch were pragmatic, and appeared prepared to exclude Nicaragua, in order to preserve the Initiative.

Despite the internal disputes within the EEC, the overall European

and US approaches to development in the Caribbean basin appear to
differ in three basic respects. First, the political criteria used by the
EEC are much broader than those of the USA. The precedent set by
ACP recipients under the Lomé Convention, when Grenada and
Suriname were included as was Jamaica under both Manley and Seaga
governments, has been continued. The original EEC initiative on the

Table 8.3   *US and EEC trade with the Caribbean Basin* (1980, $m)

		USA			EEC[a]		
	GDP 1980 estimate	exports to USA	imports from USA	balance	exports to EEC	imports from EEC	balance
Central America							
Belize	165	60	58	+2	34	36	−2
Costa Rica	4847	356	498	−142	258	128	+130
El Salvador	3484	427	273	+154	329	85	+244
Guatemala	7852	435	553	−118	367	181	+186
Honduras	2538	419	379	+40	182	96	+86
Nicaragua	1566	211	250	−39	119	50	+69
Panama	3511	330	699	−369	207	473	−266
Total	23963	2238	2710	−472	1496	1049	+447
Caribbean							
Bahamas	1267	1382	396	+986	892	220	+672
Barbados	815	96	136	−40	36	91	−55
Cayman Islands	na	3	—	+3	3	68	−65
Dominican Rep.	6733	786	795	−9	77	142	−65
Eastern Caribbean[b]	500	37	—	+37	81	123	−42
Guyana	524	120	96	+24	159	95	+64
Haiti	1453	252	311	−59	88	51	+37
Jamaica	2402	383	305	+78	235	130	+105
Netherlands Antilles	1100	2564	448	+2116	592	331	+261
Suriname	109	109	136	−27	270	98	+172
Trinidad & Tobago	6708	2378	680	+1698	388	383	+5
Turks & Caicos	na	3	—	+3	—	1	−1
Total	21611	8113	3303	+4810	2821	1733	+1088
CARIBBEAN BASIN TOTAL	45574	10351	6013	+4338	4317	2782	+1535

[a] figures derived from EEC exports and imports to the region at a rate of conversion
   US$1.00 = 0.7182 ecus
[b] includes Anguilla, Antigua, Dominica, Montserrat, St Kitts-Nevis, St Lucia and St
   Vincent, and for the EEC, the British Virgin Islands

Sources: US State Department: Direction of Trade and Eurostat Cronos.

Caribbean basin, though it did not include Cuba, took in the rest of the mainland and all Caribbean island economies, including Haiti and the Dominican Republic. Moreover, within the EEC Initiative, distribution of aid was non-discriminatory with a flat rate of 10m ecus to each recipient. Secondly, the EEC plan, unlike the CBI, is directed to governments rather than to the private sector. It is also being given wholly in the form of balance of payments support as finance to pay for imports; the recipients are supposed to earmark the resulting counterpart funds for agricultural reform projects, but it is very difficult in practice to ensure that balance of payments support is tied to any particular activity. The European initiative, therefore, bears greater similarities to the Mexican, Venezuelan and Canadian approaches than to the American. The third difference between the EEC and US policies is over their support for existing regional associations. The EEC has recognised in, for example, its negotiations for sugar purchases, the existence of such regional organisations as Caricom and has used their centralised offices; the USA has played down the role of CACM and within the CBI has undermined the importance of the existing regional fora since it encourages bilateral links to strengthen political and economic dependence.

Both packages are too small to have any major economic effect on the region and both have, in their passage (see Boxes), been threatened by reduction, if not total extinction. Domestic considerations both within the USA and between EEC member states have played an increasingly important role in the formulation of foreign policy towards the regions. As a result of mid-term elections the new Congress may be less responsive to President Reagan's proposals. Yet the differences between the two schemes reflect much about US and EEC perceptions of the region. The CBI is a long-term policy and has deep-rooted political objectives, while the EEC approach is a short-term attempt to extend its sphere of development interests and show that it too has a stake in what up to now has been regarded as America's backyard.

Notes

1 See for instance, *Surveys 1* and *2* for the economic involvement of the EEC through Lomé and J. Pearce, *Under the Eagle: US Intervention in Central America and the Caribbean,* Latin American Bureau, updated edition, March 1982, for US policy.
2 *International Herald Tribune,* 26 July 1982.
3 *The Times,* 21 July 1982.
4 See M. D. Hayes, 'The stakes in Central America and US policy responses', in *The Crisis in Central America,* American Enterprise Institute, *Foreign Policy and Defense Review,* vol. 4, no. 2, May 1982.

5 Under the 1981 Foreign Assistance Act, for military aid to be continued, President Reagan must certify an improvement in the human rights situation. Following this Congressional action, the IMF is considering making the remainder due of SDR75m balance of payments assistance, subject to certain conditions.

6 It was withdrawn temporarily in 1981 but renewed for one year from August 1982. Under the agreement, Central American countries, Barbados, Jamaica and the Dominican Republic, pay the prevailing world price for crude oil but receive a credit equivalent to 30% of the total in the form of a loan either for general development projects at 4% annual interest or for energy programmes at 2% annual interest.

7 *International Herald Tribune,* 26 July 1982.

8 *Congressional Record,* 18 August 1982.

9 In May 1982 all CBI sugar provisions were abandoned (duty-free access for 12 years at a level of 110% of the average of the best two out of three years). This was in order to maintain domestic growers' legal support price at US cents 18.5 per lb. following the collapse of sugar prices on the world market. Import quotas were set at 2.7m tonnes for 1981/82 and 2.8m tonnes for 1982/83.

10 *Caribbean Insight,* March 1982.

11 *Economist,* 11 September 1982. These sums include military aid.

12 'Unjustified account has been taken of the US's supposed sphere of influence' according to an External Relations Committee report presented to the European Parliament in October, *The Guardian*, 14 October 1982.

13 *Financial Times,* 12 March 1982.

14 Labour MEPs have been frustrated by the official UK attitude and it has been described as an example of 'how the EEC follows the madness of President Reagan's policies', *The Guardian op. cit.*

15 Relations between the USA and fellow Nassau participant Mexico are also threatened by the CBI proposals as the latter has complained that its own border industries and US–Mexican trade are undermined by the package. The Mexican border industries form a free zone where US firms produce goods for the export sector and benefit from duty-free imports for the industries. Thus jobs are provided within Mexico in the foreign export sector. It is estimated that the 600 US firms within the scheme provide employment for 135,000 Mexicans.

9

The Mediterranean and the Middle East

Stefan A. Musto

The strip of land and sea between the 30th and 40th parallels, extending from the Straits of Gibraltar to the Persian Gulf, was once the cradle of Western civilisation. It has always been an area in which people have met and traded, but also one of conflict and rival power interests. It has frequently tended to become charged with tension, and no power vacuum has lasted for very long. Today it is where the two fields of world political and economic tension meet: the conflicting interests of East and West on the one hand and of North and South on the other.[1]

Political divergences

Western Europe's formal withdrawal from the Mediterranean area and the Middle East after the Second World War was a long but continuous process. It was accomplished in five decisive stages: the renouncement by Britain and France of their mandates over Iraq, Syria, Lebanon and Jordan, or Palestine, the decline of Italian influence in North Africa, the emancipation of Egypt after 1956, the end of French rule in the Maghreb (marked particularly by Algeria's independence) and Britain's withdrawal from Iran and the Gulf region.[2] Europe's 'soft underbelly' (Churchill) became a region of conflict, whose ability to achieve internal and economic order in no way corresponded to its real world economic and and political importance. The power vacuum filled with tension caused, on the one hand, by a tendency for the unstable situation to lead to local wars and disputes, on the other, by the direct confrontation of the two superpowers, the USA and the USSR, in the area.

This instability led both superpowers to become increasingly involved in the region. The Soviet Union attempted, with varying degrees of success, to extend its influence with diplomatic efforts, massive arms supplies and a military presence. Its efforts were favoured by the anti-imperialist ethos of the Arab countries, rivalry within the Arab world and the smouldering Arab–Israeli conflict. On the Western side, the United States, with its Sixth Fleet, an extensive network of military bases and a policy of limited intervention, virtually monopolised the role of ensuring stability in the region and checking Soviet attempts at expansionism. Against the background of these international political developments, Western Europe had to content itself with little more than the role of a spectator.

The field of diplomacy has also been monopolised by the United States. The history of the Middle East crisis is the history of American efforts to mediate, with which are linked the names of Ralph Bunche (1948), Henry Kissinger (1973–74) and Philip Habib (1981–82). Since the Suez crisis (1956) resulted in the first overt conflict of interests between France and Britain on the one hand and the USA on the other, the Europeans and Americans have become so estranged that Washington saw fit to exclude the countries of Western Europe completely from the negotiation of the Camp David Agreement, even though the aims of the USA and the European Community have always been largely identical.

Western Europe is no less interested in the political and economic stability of the region than the United States. Apart from the historical ties and common security interests of the Western Alliance, what is particularly important for Western Europe is that most of its supplies of oil and raw materials originate from or cross the Mediterranean area. The region is also an extremely important market for the European Community: from 1970 to 1976 EEC exports to the Southern and Eastern Mediterranean countries rose by 385%, compared with a 246% increase in their exports to the EEC.[3] Apart from the other countries of Western Europe (EFTA, and the acceding countries of Southern Europe), the only countries with which the EEC has a favourable balance of trade are those of the Mediterranean region and the Near East (excluding OPEC), its surplus in 1980 being 10,400m Ecu (see Table 9.1). The stabilisation of the region is therefore a goal which Western European and North American policy have in common.

The divergences arise when it comes to translating this goal into practical policy. They relate to two problems, the first caused by differing interpretations of the term 'stability', the second by differing views on the instruments that should be used.

A feature of the first problem is that stability in the Mediterranean area and the Near East is seen by the USA mainly in terms of East–West relations, and by Europeans mainly in terms of North–South relations. This divergence of opinion is reflected by differing

Table 9.1   *EEC trade balances 1980[a] (Ecu bn)*

Region	EEC Imports	EEC Exports	Surplus	Deficit
WORLD	269.9	221.1		48.8
EFTA+W. Europe Other	61.9	75.6	13.7	
Mediterranean (excl. OPEC)	22.6	33.0	10.4	
N. America, Japan and Australasia	71.9	43.4		28.5
OPEC	67.2	36.6		30.6
Centrally Planned Economies	21.6	18.7		2.9
Rest of the World	24.7	13.8		10.9

[a] 9 member states.

Source: Eurostat, *Analytical Tables of Foreign Trade,* Nimexe 1980, Series Z, Countries-Products.

assessments of such issues as the Camp David Agreement, the Palestinian question, Libya's role and military rule in Turkey. While the USA has always sided with Israel in the Arab–Israeli conflict and from this position has endeavoured to exert influence on the Arab countries in general, and Egypt in particular, the European Community has adopted the principles of 'a balanced approach', 'equal treatment' and relative political abstinence, as the Declaration of Venice demonstrates.

'A balanced approach' also means that the Community has no interest in seeing the influence of either superpower in the region growing unchecked. Thus, although the Europeans in principle welcomed the Egyptian–Israeli peace process, their joy at the thought of the possible consequences of polarisation within the Arab world was by no means unbounded. The EEC countries have never shared America's belief that Camp David could separate the solution of the Middle East problem from that of the Palestinian question. They are also concerned that growing American influence in the region may prompt greater Soviet involvement. This would increase the risk of further tension and of developments becoming less predictable. The same ambivalence characterises the European attitude towards the USA's strategic commitment to safeguard supplies of oil and raw materials from the Near and Middle East to the industrial countries of the West: although the security of supply routes is a vital interest common to both sides of the Atlantic, there is a growing undercurrent of disquiet in the EEC countries that America's control of oil and raw materials transport operations might change into control of its European allies. This distrust certainly does not have its source in the Mediterranean region and the Near East. It might be said that the reverse is the case: the basic problems of the European–American relationship show themselves in a particularly clear light in this region because of the political and economic explosiveness of conflicting interests there.

The EEC and the USA also disagree on the instruments to be used to achieve stabilisation in this region. While the United States openly and unashamedly demonstrates political and military power in the Mediterranean Basin and the Near East, the weapons chiefly used by the EEC, as a 'civilian power',[4] are economic co-operation and discreet diplomatic influence. Although the difference in these instruments corresponds to the difference in the roles played by the Atlantic partners in world politics and the world economy, they do not always complement each other, there being some conflict in this respect too. Europe is concerned that the instruments of American policy may endanger relations along the dividing line between North and South formed by the Mediterranean area. In contrast, convinced that it is destined to fill a power vacuum in the area, the USA often views the almost neurotic efforts of the Europeans to achieve credibility in the eyes of their Southern neighbours as opportunism. The controversy between the USA and the EEC centres on the co-operation agreements the Community has concluded with the Southern and Eastern Mediterranean countries as part of its global Mediterranean policy. The fine network of the Community's Mediterranean policy[5] is a thorn in the flesh of the United States, which objects principally on economic rather than political grounds.

The commercial issues

Although the United States generally welcomed the establishment of the European Community, it was not in its interests for Community policies, especially in the areas of agriculture and trade, to be overly harmonised. As the framework of the EEC's Mediterranean policy essentially consists of elements of its agricultural and trade policies, it conflicts with all the concepts the United States would like to see accepted as guidelines for the development of world trade in accordance with GATT.[6] (See *Survey 1*, Chapter 4.) The Americans feel that the EEC's agreements with the Southern and Eastern Mediterranean countries contravene the most favoured nation principle of GATT and discriminate against American exports.

Underlying the USA's general objection to the Community's Mediterranean policy is concern on three counts. The Americans fear that it will discriminate against them in the EEC market, to which the Mediterranean countries have been granted preferential access for their agricultural and industrial products; the markets of the Mediterranean countries, and particularly those granting the EEC reverse preferences under association or free trade agreements (Turkey, Cyprus, Malta, Spain, Israel); and third-country markets, where the European Community puts pressure on competing American products with its export refunds. In view of its chronic balance-of-trade deficits, the USA feels this discrimination places a considerable strain on its relations with the Community.

The first of these problem areas, the preferential access to the EEC market enjoyed by the Mediterranean countries, does not in practice seriously affect US external trade, since the range of export products which the USA and the Mediterranean countries vie with each other to sell in the EEC market is extremely limited. Their exports are in fact complementary: while US exports to Western Europe mainly consist of cereals, animal feeding-stuffs, high-quality consumer goods and capital goods, exports from the Mediterranean countries to the Community are largely confined to raw materials, semi-manufactured goods, Mediterranean farm produce and simple consumer goods (e.g. textiles). Among the few exceptions constituting substitutive trade are citrus fruit and processed foodstuffs, although the southward enlargement of the Community, and especially Spain's membership, is likely to result in greater discrimination against American exports than the present Mediterranean policy.[7]

The second problem area, the EEC's preferential access to the markets of the Mediterranean countries, is more serious. In these markets the EEC's Mediterranean policy does indeed have the effect of discriminating against American exports owing, on the one hand, to the reverse preferences some of these countries grant the Community and, on the other, to other indirect measures coming under the heading of economic and technical co-operation (financial protocols, direct investments, etc.), which also affect external trade. As most Mediterranean countries are in the process of industrialising, there is every likelihood that the Community's Mediterranean policy will lead to trade creation and diversion in these countries from which the EEC itself will benefit.[8] US fears that European goods could replace at least some American exports to these countries are not therefore unfounded. From a glance at the trends in imports into the Mediterranean countries from the USA and the EEC from 1975 to 1979 it would indeed appear that this concern is justified (see Table 9.2). The figures show that imports by the Mediterranean countries from the EEC during this period rose far more steeply than their imports from the USA. What is more, in some cases imports from the USA fell by up to 9.5% a year. It is at least doubtful, however, whether this trend is related to the EEC's Mediterranean policy, since the rate of growth in

US exports to the very Mediterranean countries then granting the EEC reverse preferences (Turkey and Israel, for example) was higher, (compared to EEC exports) than was growth in US exports to other countries in the region.

Table 9.2 *Imports of Mediterranean countries from the EEC and the United States 1975–1979, (US $mn)*

| Importing countries | Imports from | | | | Annual percentage change | |
| | EEC-9 | | USA | | | |
	1975	1979	1975	1979	EEC	USA
Israel	1757	2743	961	1488	14.0	14.0
Jordan	259	731	76	145	45.0	23.0
Morocco	1330	1780	196	212	8.5	2.0
Algeria	3723	5752	672	544	14.0	−5.0
Egypt	1354	1559	757	684	3.9	−2.3
Lebanon	847	1237	405	250	11.5	−9.5
Syria	675	1195	109	132	19.0	5.0
Tunisia	941	1773	95	170	22.0	20.0
Turkey	2256	1768	413	358	−5.3	−3.2
Cyprus	139	473	10	55	60.0	112.0

Source: Eurostat, 1981

As the USA's most important market in the Mediterranean area at this time was Spain, and as Spain was granting the EEC reverse preferences (under the free trade agreement of 1970), this country provides the clearest comparison of trends in imports from the Community and the USA. Table 9.3 shows that from 1973 to 1980 Spanish imports from the EEC rose by 109%, while US exports to Spain grew by 187%. A breakdown into the most important categories of products reveals that in the same period the USA increased its exports of agricultural products to Spain by 226% as compared with a 217% rise in EEC exports, while the figures for industrial products were 147% and 137%, again in America's favour. It clearly cannot be concluded from these figures that the free trade agreement between Spain and the Community has had the effect of discriminating against American exports to Spain. How Spanish trade with the USA would have developed if the EEC preference policy had not existed must, however, remain a subject of speculation.

The third problem area, that raised by competition between US and subsidised EEC agricultural products on the world market (including the markets of the Mediterranean countries and of the Near and Middle East), is now placing a serious strain on relations between the USA and the Community. In the last 10 to 12 years the EEC has become one of the USA's major competitors, particularly as a grain

Table 9.3   *Imports of Spain from the EEC and USA 1973 and 1980 (US $mn)*

Imports from	Total imports		SITC 0		SITC 6+7+8	
	1973	1980	1973	1980	1973	1980
EEC	4970	10418	186	591	2790	6621
USA	1535	4410	280	913	632	1462
Total growth of imports 1973–80 from:						
EEC	109%		217%		137%	
USA	187%		226%		147%	

Source: OECD World Trade Statistics, 1981

Notes SITC 0 – Food and live animals
　　　　　6 – Manufactured goods, classified chiefly by material
　　　　　7 – Machinery and transport equipment
　　　　　8 – Miscellaneous manufactured items.

supplier. In this period the Community has doubled its exports of grain to over 14 million tonnes. The EEC's share of the world grain market is 15% (1981) compared with the USA's 44.8%. As the United States finances much of its overall balance-of-trade deficit from its grain exports, it sees this development as a serious threat, putting the blame on the 'excesses of the EEC's common agricultural policy'. This is more than a blow in a regional dispute: it is an attack on one of the pillars of Western European integration.

In 1973 Christopher Soames, EEC Commissioner for External Affairs, and US Under-Secretary of State William Casey signed an agreement in which the USA declared that the European Community's Mediterranean policy was politically in the general interests of the West since the only alternative for some Mediterranean countries was to gear their trade policies to the Eastern bloc. This is still true today. But it does not prevent the USA from seeking to protect its own trade interests by claiming that the EEC's preference policy infringes the most favoured nation clause of GATT. As conflicts of economic interest usually have political repercussions, the European Community's trade policy towards the Mediterranean countries is likely to strain further the already tense relations between Europe and America.

Notes

1   As to the strategic importance of the Mediterranean see W. Hager, 'Das Mittelmeer – Mare Nostrum Europas?' in M. Kohnstamm – W. Hager (eds.): *Zivilmacht Europa – Supermacht oder Partner?*, Frankfurt, 1973;

R. Regul (ed.), *Die Europäischen Gemeinschaften und die Mittelmeer-länder*, Baden Baden, 1977; A. Shlaim, *'The Community and the Mediterranean Basin'*, in K. J. Twichett (ed.), *Europe and the World*, London, 1976.

2 Comp. G. Lenczowski, 'New Dimensions of Big Power Rivalry in the Middle East', to appear in C. Pinkele – A. Pollis (eds.), *Continuity and Change in the Contemporary Mediterranean World*, Praeger, New York, forthcoming.

3 Detailed analysis by S. A. Musto, 'The EEC in Search of a New Mediterranean Policy: A Chance for a More Symmetrical Interdependence?' in C. Pinkele – A. Pollis (eds.), op. cit.

4 See M. Kohnstamm – W. Hager (eds.), op. cit.

5 The network of the Community's Mediterranean Policy consists in Association Agreements with Turkey (1964), Malta (1971) and Cyprus (1973), Free Trade Agreements with Spain (1970) and Israel (1975), and Preferential Trade and Co-operation Agreements with Algeria, Tunisia, Morocco (1976), Egypt, Jordan, Syria, Lebanon (1977) and a special Trade Agreement with Yugoslavia (1980).

6 Detailed analysis by M. E. Kreinin, 'US Trade Interests and the EEC Mediterranean Policy' in A. Shlaim – G. N. Yannopoulos (eds.), *The EEC and the Mediterranean Countries*, London-New York-Melbourne, 1976, p. 33 ff.

7 Concerning US and Spanish competition of citrus exports on the EEC market see FAO, *Agrume – Projections de l'offre, de la demande et du commerce pour 1985*, (Document PROJ – 78/20), Rome, 1979.

8 See M. E. Kreinin, op. cit., pp. 45–46.

Part 3

EEC Development Policy after Lomé

SECTION A: THE EVIDENCE OF THE PAST

10

Trade between the ACP and EEC during Lomé I

Joanna Moss and John Ravenhill

This analysis of trade between the ACP and EEC during the first Lomé Convention belies much of the optimism that was expressed at the time of its signature. Duty-free access to the enlarged European market had been a principal motivation for Commonwealth African countries to enter into the relationship in the hope that it would facilitate market and product diversification and, in particular, would provide a dynamic framework encouraging greater domestic processing of their exports. The results of this study show that, in reality, despite the Convention's provisions, the percentage of ACP exports going to the EEC market declined; the ACP even failed to maintain their share of the EEC market (faring worse than other developing countries), and little diversification in ACP exports was evident. This has implications not only for the EEC and ACP, but also for the USA with its Caribbean Basin Initiative.

The Lomé relationship

These results are not altogether surprising. Similar trade preferences enjoyed by the Yaoundé associates were estimated to have had little or no effect on their trade with the EEC. Moreover, by the time that Lomé was implemented in 1975 the value of tariff preferences accorded by duty-free access to the Community market had diminished as a result of two developments: the rapid extension of the Community's Generalised System of Preferences (GSP); and reductions in the Common External Tariff (CET) in accordance with successive GATT rounds of multilateral tariff negotiations (see *Survey 1* for an examination of the EEC's overall trade policy towards the Third World). Only 7 of the 25 most important ACP exports have enjoyed any tariff advantage whatsoever over imports from Third World countries, and for four of these, the GSP rates were below those of the CET although other provisions of the Convention favourable to the ACP, such as the Stabex scheme, might also influence exports (see Table 10.8, last column). Lomé, in fact, created only a limited number of new preferential relationships since the Yaoundé associates already enjoyed duty-free access to the markets of the six original EEC member states, and Commonwealth countries enjoyed similar privileged access to the British market. Furthermore the trade provisions of Lomé I were not as generous as the Community claimed. Their apparent liberality was circumscribed by a number of significant restrictions, most notably the rules of origin, the existence of a safeguard clause which has been utilised by the Community to pressure ACP states into voluntary export restraints for 'sensitive' products, and the exemption of products covered by the Common Agricultural Policy (CAP) from unrestricted access. The terms of access for agricultural exports of certain ACP countries actually deteriorated since they were now excluded from the British market by virtue of the product being included within the CAP.

In the period 1970–79 the value of ACP exports and imports more than quadrupled.[1] Exports expanded at an average annual rate of 50% and imports at 46%. In those years ACP countries consumed between 2.8% and 3.5% of total world exports (Table 10.1). ACP shares of world exports peaked at 3.5% in 1974, 1975, and 1977, in large part the result of high prices for oil, cocoa and coffee. Although in aggregate there was no decline in the ACP share of world exports, that of non-oil ACP countries steadily decreased during this period. By 1979 only 1.5% of world exports came from the non-oil ACP countries compared to a peak of 2.3% in 1970. Over the decade, the exports of non-oil ACP

Table 10.1 *Developing countries' trade with the world: value and shares of world trade ($'000 mn)*

| | Exports | | | Imports | | |
	1970	1975	1979	1970	1975	1979
ACP: value	8.5	26.1	47.1	8.7	27.1	44.5
: % of world trade	(3.0)	(3.3)	(3.1)	(2.9)	(3.3)	(2.9)
Non-oil ACP: value	6.5	12.7	22.2	6.7	16.3	26.9
: % of world trade	(2.3)	(1.6)	(1.5)	(2.3)	(2.0)	(1.7)
Developing countries excl. major oil exporters: value	36.4	94.1	200.9	46.1	136.6	261.7
: % of world trade	(12.9)	(11.9)	(13.4)	(15.5)	(16.8)	(16.7)
Major oil exporters: value	17.8	105.9	201.9	9.8	51.4	103.8
: % of world trade	(6.3)	(13.4)	(13.4)	(3.3)	(6.3)	(6.6)

countries rose on average by 27% p.a. in contrast to a 34% p.a. increase in imports. In comparison, other non-oil developing countries managed to retain their share of total world exports over the decade.

Aggregate trade between the ACP and the EEC is predominantly determined by a handful of countries. Nigeria alone accounts for over one-quarter of ACP exports to the Community, and over one-third of ACP imports from the EEC. The eight most important ACP exporters (Nigeria, Ivory Coast, Zaire, Cameroon, Kenya, Ghana, Zambia, and Gabon) provide nearly 70% of the Group's exports to the Community; the eight leading importers (in descending order of importance, Nigeria, Ivory Coast, Liberia, Sudan, Gabon, Kenya, Zaire, and Cameroon) together account for a similar percentage of ACP imports from the EEC. Looked at from another angle, over 30 ACP countries together account for less than 1% of ACP–EEC trade while the 24 most important bilateral flows between EEC member states and ACP countries cover over 60% of total trade.[2] A similar concentration is found in terms of the composition of ACP exports. The ten principal products (the composition of which has varied, as will be detailed below) together have accounted on average for close to 80% of ACP exports to the Community during the decade.

Both sides to the Convention have viewed the trade balance between them as a barometer of the effectiveness of the trade provisions. The Community has proudly proclaimed that it ran a balance of trade deficit with the ACP for most of the period of Lomé I. However this is misleading, in that the Community, of course, utilises data which employ c.i.f. values for imports from the ACP, and f.o.b. values for Community exports. If one examines the relationship from the ACP perspective then we find, utilising c.i.f. values for ACP imports and f.o.b. values for ACP exports, that the ACP have run a deficit in their trade with the Community in all years under the Convention except 1979 (Figure 10.1). Transportation and insurance charges are a sufficiently large component of import costs that both groupings can be running a trade deficit at the same time. By contrast, the ACP have run a surplus with the USA in all years (probably due in a large part to oil).

This chapter presents a detailed study of developments in the trade relationship between the EEC and ACP during the course of the first Lomé Convention, first in respect of changes in the EEC's shares in the imports and exports of the ACP (for details of the methodology employed, see Box), and second in relation to the commodity composition of ACP exports. A word of caution is appropriate regarding the interpretation of these results. Since the Convention is but one factor influencing trade between the parties, definitive causal attribution is not possible. Circumspection is particularly necessary when reviewing changes in the exports of countries which are mainly primary producers, given the intervening factors of natural and man-made disasters. Any study of trade developments in the last decade will also inevitably be affected by structural changes in the world economy – most notably the rapid growth of the oil-exporting countries' share of world trade. Nevertheless, the methodology employed in this study has a number of advantages. By examining market shares rather than changes in the volume or rate of growth of export/imports, the results are not biased by large percentage changes which may reflect only a small absolute increase over an even smaller base figure. (The EEC is fond of citing growth figures for certain categories of ACP manufactures – figures which look impressive if not placed in the context of the small absolute quantitites involved.)

Our principal method of analysis – utilising data on ACP exports and imports – has the advantage of 'controlling' for changes in local circumstances, e.g. if the groundnut crop fails then there is no reason to believe that exports to one market will fall disproportionately more than those to another – the data would show that the shares of importing countries remain constant. This methodology thus has an advantage over one which focuses on the ACP share in the EEC market (which 'controls' for local circumstances in the EEC but not for those in the ACP). Implementation of the Stabex scheme in the first

Figure 10.1   *ACP trade balance with the US and the EEC ($'000mn)*

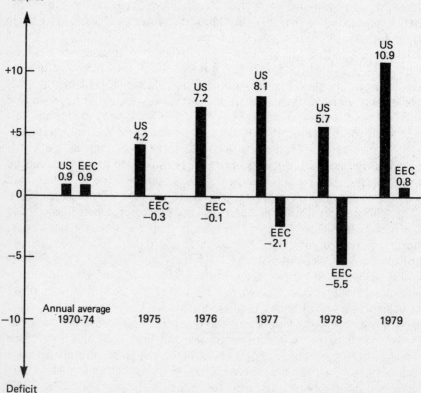

Convention demonstrated clearly that the primary cause of changes in
ACP export earnings during these years was due to local circumstances, rather than developments in the EEC market (see Chapter
11). However, in order to place the ACP performance in the EEC
market in comparative perspective we also examine the changing share
of the ACP in total European imports.

Our methodology also permits us to compare the ACP performance
with that of relevant 'control' groups. Since oil is the predominant
factor in aggregate ACP exports to the Community, and plays a major
role in the imports of non-oil ACP countries, we have compared the
performance for ACP countries as a whole with that of non-oil ACP
states.[3] We have also utilised two other groups for the purposes of
comparison: in the case of EEC share in exports we present data for
non-oil developing countries; and in the discussion of EEC shares in
ACP imports we record data for another major ACP trading partner,
the USA.

Table 10.2 *Statistically significant changes in EEC shares of ACP exports and imports
during Lomé I*

	Exports	Imports
ACP	Downward	None
Non-oil ACP	None	None
Yaoundé ACP	Downward	None
Non-oil Yaoundé ACP	Downward	None
Commonwealth ACP	Downward	None
Non-oil Commonwealth ACP	None	None
PNA ACP*	None	None
Developing Countries (excluding oil exporters)	Downward	Downward
Major oil exporters (including Nigeria)	Downward	None
Latin America	Downward	Downward

* ACP countries not previously enjoying preferential trading arrangements with an
  EEC member state.

EEC shares in ACP exports

In 1970 the EEC accounted for 48.7% of ACP exports, but by 1979 this
share had dropped to 39.7%. During the same period the share of the
USA rose from 16.9% to 32.1% – largely, but not exclusively, due to
increased imports of Nigerian oil – while the share of the rest of the
world dropped from 34.4% to 28.2%. Table 10.2 presents a summary
of the changes in the EEC share in the exports of ACP countries.[4] In
order to place these results in comparative perspective, the Table also
summarises changes in the EEC share of exports from sub-groups of
the ACP, and from other developing countries. The EEC had a

statistically-significant smaller share in the total exports of most developing countries at the end of the decade than at the beginning. Despite the provisions of the Lomé trade regime, this trend also applied to the ACP. One explanation for this is the rapid expansion of ACP oil exports to non-EEC markets, particularly that of the United States, a view that is supported by the finding that the EEC's share of exports from non-oil-exporting ACP states did not decline; it showed no change. Another illuminating comparison is between the experience of the Yaoundé states and the new entrants. Whereas the share of the EEC in the exports of countries previously associated with the Six under the Yaoundé Convention declined, there was no change in the EEC share of exports of those ACP countries which had previously lacked preferential access to any of the markets of the Nine. This difference in the performance of the two groups is particularly interesting. Given that the Lomé trade provisions did not represent a radical departure from existing trade relations for many ACP countries, it is precisely in those relationships where new preferences were created that one would expect to find the greatest impact. In order to examine these it is necessary to breakdown the figures for the Nine as an aggregate into those for its component parts. Summary results are provided in Table 10.3 which records whether or not there was a statistically significant change. Given that the overall trend was for a decline in the EEC's share of exports, those sub-groups that experienced no change were relatively successful (as, of course, were those that experienced an increase).

Table 10.3 *Comparison of statistically significant changes in EEC shares of ACP exports*

	EEC9	EEC6	UK	DK & IR**	US
ACP	Decline	No chg.	Decline	No chg.*	Increase
Non-oil ACP	No chg.	No chg.	Decline	Increase*	No chg.
Commonwealth ACP	Decline	No chg.*	Decline	No chg.*	Increase
Non-oil Commonw. ACP	No chg.	Increase*	No chg.	Increase*	Increase
PNA ACP†	No chg.*	No chg.*	Decline*	Increase*	No chg.
Yaoundé ACP	Decline	Decline	No chg.*	No chg.*	Increase
Non-oil Yaoundé	Decline	Decline	No chg.*	Increase*	No chg.
Other non-oil LDCs	Decline	No chg.	Decline	No chg.	No chg.

* Denotes relationships where Lomé created new trade preferences for the entire sub-grouping.
** DK: Denmark; IR: Ireland.
† ACP countries not previously enjoying preferential trading arrangements with an EEC Member State.

The two most important new preferential relationships created by the Convention were between Commonwealth countries and the original Six EEC members, and between the former Yaoundé associates and the United Kingdom. In the first case, the share of the original Six in the exports of Commonwealth countries increased slightly, but not sufficiently to be statistically significant. For non-oil Commonwealth countries, however, the share of the Six did increase significantly. It is impossible to say whether this occurred at the expense of previously associated African states which lost their preferential margins over the newcomers, but it is of interest that the Six's share of the exports of both the Yaoundé group and its non-oil sub-group declined. In the case of the second new preferential relationship, Britain's share of ACP and non-oil ACP total exports declined (column 3 of Table 10.3). The decline was less marked for the non-oil ACP group, a trend which can be explained largely by Britain's transition from being an oil importer to self-sufficiency. This shift in Britain's oil position had a particularly marked effect on the Commonwealth sub-group. Exports from the Commonwealth as a whole declined (because of the fall in Nigerian oil exports to Britain) but the British market retained its significance for non-oil Commonwealth countries. For the beneficiaries of new preferences in the British market, the previously non-associated states and the Yaoundé group, the record was mixed. New preferences did not prevent a decline in the share of Britain in the exports of the former, but there was no statistically significant change in Britain's share in the exports of either the Yaoundé group or its non-oil sub-group.

In addition to these two new preferential relationships, there are the cases of Denmark and Ireland, which were the only countries that had no special trading relationships with any ACP state prior to the signature of the Lomé Convention. Because of this it is interesting to examine the changes that have occurred in their shares of ACP exports since the implementation of the Convention (despite the fact that the total trade involved is extremely small).[5] The new preferences might have been expected to lead to an increase in their share of ACP exports. This expectation was borne out in the case of the non-oil ACP. For the other sub-groups there was no change in the Danish and Irish share of exports which, as noted above, indicates a more positive experience than that of the EEC group as a whole, although hardly one that indicates great dynamism.

In general it appears that the Convention has had a positive impact on the trading relationships of countries which previously had not been linked in preferential agreements. In reading across Table 10.3, one finds that the share of the Six, and of Denmark/Ireland in Commonwealth ACP exports registered no change, whereas for Britain, where they previously enjoyed preferences, there was a decline. Similarly the Yaoundé group experienced no change in the share of their exports going to the new member states, but a decline in their share in the Six where they had previously enjoyed preferences. This points to a diversification of ACP trading partners within the EEC, which certainly would be perceived by most ACP states as a positive result of the Convention. This finding is elaborated in Table 10.4 which presents data on the share of ACP exports to the EEC going to each member state. Its most prominent feature is the marked decline in the UK's share: from being the leading European importer of ACP products, the UK fell to fourth position, behind France, Germany and the Netherlands, which were the three countries experiencing the largest increases in their share. These changes are in accord with the differing economic performance of the member states over the last decade. Diversification within the EEC market was reflected in a decline in the concentration of trading partners, measured by a Hirschman index.[6]

Table 10.4   *EEC member states' shares in ACP exports to the Community (%)*

	Exports			Imports		
	1970	1975	1979	1970	1975	1979
Belgium/Luxemburg	10.4	6.8	10.0	6.7	5.8	6.4
Denmark	0.7	1.4	1.0	1.3	1.4	1.6
France	19.6	24.4	23.5	25.1	27.8	32.6
Germany	13.3	14.7	23.8	15.8	18.6	17.0
Ireland	0.2	0.3	0.1	0.3	0.3	0.6
Italy	10.6	8.0	9.7	8.5	9.1	8.7
Netherlands	12.8	16.1	16.4	7.0	6.7	8.8
UK	32.4	28.3	15.0	35.5	30.3	25.5
Hirschman index of concentration	44.7	44.5	42.5	48.0	46.9	46.9

EEC shares in ACP imports

The terms of the Lomé Convention itself provided no grounds for predicting that it would result in an increase in the share of the Community in ACP imports. The ACP were not required to offer reciprocal trade preferences; their only obligation was to provide the EEC with most favoured industrialised nation treatment. Since the most favoured trade partner of many ACP states was an EEC member, the only significant change that might have been anticipated would have been a multilateralisation of treatment among the member states; for example Commonwealth countries would be obliged to give as favourable treatment to imports from Denmark, Ireland and the Six, as they accorded to imports from the UK. Moreover, since the non-oil ACP experienced dramatic increases in the costs of their energy imports in the period since 1973, it would be reasonable to anticipate that the share of the EEC would fall (except in those cases where ACP countries imported refined petroleum from the EEC).

Table 10.5 presents data to assess whether these expectations were borne out in reality. It is a summary of the statistically significant changes in the shares of total ACP imports originating in the Community as a whole and in each member state. The share of the Community as a whole in the imports of the ACP (and of all its sub-groups) registered no change over the period. This is in marked contrast to the performance of the EEC in the markets of other developing countries where, with the exception of major oil exporters, the EEC share of total imports declined significantly. Only two of the EEC sub-groups performed less well than the group as a whole and registered significant declines in their share of ACP imports. These were the original Six whose share of Yaoundé imports fell, and the UK which saw a decline in its share of non-oil ACP imports. The experience of the original Six appears to confirm the prediction that the Convention would lead to a diversification of sources within the EEC as a result of the multi-lateralisation of mfn treatment, particularly since the Six also increased their share of Commonwealth imports. Once again, Denmark and Ireland, the only countries that had previously received no preferential treatment from ACP states, registered either an increase or, in the case of some sub-groups, no change in their share. Reading across the columns of Table 10.5, one finds that, as in the case of ACP exports, the statistically significant increases all occurred in relationships where, prior to Lomé, there had been no special economic ties between the ACP sub-grouping and the relevant EEC member states.

Table 10.5 *Comparison of statistically significant changes in EEC shares of ACP imports*

	EEC9	EEC6	UK	DK & IR**	US
ACP	No chg.	No chg.	No chg.	Increase*	Decline
Non-oil ACP	No chg.	No chg.	Decline	No chg.*	No chg.
Commonwealth ACP	No chg.	Increase*	No chg.	Increase*	Decline
Non-oil Commonw. ACP	No chg.	No chg.*	No chg.	Increase*	No chg.
PNA ACP	No chg.*	No chg.*	No chg.*	No chg.*	No chg.
Yaoundé ACP	No chg.	Decline	No chg.*	No chg.*	No chg.
Non-oil Yaoundé	No chg.	No chg.	No chg.*	No chg.*	No chg.
Other non-oil LDCs	Decline	Decline	Decline	Decline	Decline

* Denotes relationships where Lomé created new trade preferences for the entire sub-grouping.
** DK: Denmark; IR: Ireland.

A number of factors can be cited which might account for the success of the EEC in maintaining its share of ACP markets. Among those which are not specifically related to the Convention are traditional trading links, including membership in currency areas (especially the franc zone) and the presence in ACP states of EEC commercial firms, shipping lines, etc., language ties, geographical proximity, and the procurement-tying of bilateral European aid. In addition, there are factors specific to the Convention itself, such as the rules of origin, which encourage ACP countries to purchase inputs from Community suppliers, the most favoured industrialised nation treatment which ACP countries are obliged to extend to the Community, the procurement-tying of EDF aid, and the possibility that the Convention might have created a 'climate' that was favourable to the expansion of EEC exports to the ACP.

Some diversification of sources of imports from the Community did occur during the decade 1970–79, but very little during the implementation of the Lomé Convention. In those years it was not so much a matter of a reduction in the overall concentration of trading partners, but of France replacing the UK as the dominant source of imports from the Community (see Table 10.4). A Hirschman index of partner concentration registers only a very small decline during the lifetime of the Convention (in contrast to the five years preceding Lomé). The EEC's share of ACP imports fell from 44.2% in 1970, to 39.1% in 1975, but then rose to 40.2% by 1979. By comparison, the USA's share fell over the decade from 15.8% to 9.4%, largely as a result of its inability to make inroads into the expanding Nigerian market. The share of the rest of the world rose from 40.0% to 50.3%, which presumably can be attributed to the growth in the value of oil imports.

ACP share in the EEC market

A third facet of the impact of Lomé is the ACP share of total EEC imports. A decrease in the share of ACP exports directed to the European Community could be interpreted as a desirable market diversification, but such a trend would have been welcome to the ACP only if it was not accompanied by a decline in their share of the European market. For one of the advantages that the ACP hoped to gain from the Convention was a guarantee that their primary products would at least maintain their share of European imports. In general this has not been the case. Table 10.6 shows that the ACP share in total EEC imports fell dramatically during the 1970s despite Lomé's preferences. In itself, however, this figure can be misleading owing to the increase in price of EEC imports of oil and manufactured goods. It is more relevant to compare the performance of the ACP with that of other developing countries, particularly non-oil exporting ldcs. Even on this comparison, the ACP fared badly. Their share of ldc exports to the EEC dropped precipitously, as did the share of non-oil-exporting ACP states in the exports of the non-major oil-exporting ldcs. As Table 10.7 shows, the ACP countries fared much worse in their share of the EEC market over the decade than other ldcs despite the preferences that they enjoyed via the Lomé Convention.

Table 10.6 *Developing countries' shares of EEC imports (%)*

	1970	1971	1972	1973	1974	1975	1976	1977	1978	1979
ACP	8.2	7.5	8.0	7.8	8.7	6.9	7.2	7.5	6.6	6.6
Non-oil ACP	6.4	5.1	5.4	5.0	4.6	3.6	4.1	4.8	4.2	3.7
Developing Countries (DCs)	36.5	37.4	37.1	37.2	47.2	43.4	49.5	43.5	39.8	40.4
NODC*	20.9	19.1	19.2	19.5	17.9	17.1	17.6	19.3	18.7	18.5
Non-ACP NODC	14.1	13.5	13.3	14.0	12.7	12.3	13.0	14.0	14.0	14.1
ACP share of EEC imports from DCs	22.5	19.1	21.5	20.9	18.4	15.9	14.5	17.2	16.6	16.4
NOACP** share of EEC imp. from NODC	30.4	26.8	28.2	25.7	25.5	21.3	23.3	24.7	22.6	20.2

*   Non oil-exporting Developing Countries (including ACPs).
** Non oil-exporting ACP Countries.

Table 10.7 *Changes in developing countries' shares of EEC imports (%)*

	1970–1974 Average	1975–1979 Average	Statistically significant change
Developing Countries	39.1	43.3	Increase
NODC*	19.3	18.2	No change
Non-ACP NODC	13.5	13.5	No change
ACP	8.0	7.0	Decline
Non oil-exporting ACP	5.3	4.1	Decline

* Non oil-exporting Developing Countries (including ACPs).

Aggregate figures can be misleading. More definitive conclusions can be drawn if this aggregate analysis is supplemented by a review of the performance in those commodities in which the ACP have a particular interest. Table 10.8 presents data on the ACP share in EEC imports for the 25 most valuable (mean 1976–79) ACP commodities

Table 10.8 ACP share in EEC imports of the 25 most valuable ACP exports 1973–1979 (%)

	1973	1974	1975	1976	1977	1978	1979	Total* Share	CET 1/1/80
Crude Petroleum	7.0	10.4	8.8	7.4	7.6	8.1	10.7	29.2	0
Coffee	31.7	37.8	36.2	42.0	44.7	39.6	38.6	11.7	5 A
Coffee Beans	92.0	85.8	87.5	91.1	85.5	90.7	88.0	9.7	3
Refined Copper	42.0	44.4	40.9	38.3	39.8	31.5	32.7	5.1	0
Non-Coniferous Wood	75.7	74.3	75.4	70.0	70.9	72.2	72.9	3.8	0
Sugar	N.A.	36.0	49.3	59.3	67.1	72.5	71.2	3.2	L
Petroleum Derivatives	N.A.	N.A.	3.5	6.0	7.6	9.3	8.4	3.1	0
Iron Ore	21.5	21.1	19.4	17.8	19.7	18.0	16.9	2.9	0
Cotton	19.2	18.4	18.2	17.6	22.9	18.5	22.4	1.4	0
Blister Copper	43.0	45.0	37.1	40.0	42.2	40.3	43.4	1.4	0
Tea	N.A.	24.7	25.9	27.0	33.8	41.6	39.1	1.2	B
Groundnut Oil	60.2	61.9	83.7	80.0	79.9	53.4	53.0	1.1	10 C
Thorium and Uranium Ores	96.9	95.6	97.7	98.7	96.2	82.5	95.7	1.0	0
Aluminium Ore	33.6	39.0	46.1	58.8	59.1	61.6	54.5	0.93	0
Aluminium Oxide	N.A.	70.0	70.6	55.2	53.1	65.2	79.3	0.93	5.5D
Fresh Bananas	18.7	18.5	19.7	19.0	19.4	19.0	20.0	0.87	20 E
Wood simply worked	N.A.	2.7	3.7	3.4	3.0	3.3	2.9	0.85	0
Raw Tobacco	6.9	7.6	8.6	8.9	8.4	11.2	8.7	0.85	23 LF
Copper Ore	46.3	31.4	58.7	51.1	46.6	46.3	45.0	0.70	0
Calcium Phosphate	21.7	24.9	19.8	18.0	19.1	19.4	19.9	0.69	0
Groundnuts	N.A.	46.2	50.9	56.9	41.6	27.1	9.5	0.67	0
Diamonds	N.A.	15.8	12.9	4.4	4.8	7.1	3.1	0.66	0
Raw Skins	N.A.	14.6	13.0	11.0	10.5	11.4	11.4	0.55	0
Groundnut Cake	N.A.	58.4	67.3	48.5	43.9	42.4	34.7	0.53	0
Natural Rubber	12.3	12.1	12.6	11.6	10.9	11.4	11.3	0.53	0

* Product share in total EEC imports from ACP; average 1976–79.

A GSP rate for coffee is 0 for designated 'least developed' beneficiaries.

B If package in containers of over 3 kilograms. Tea packaged in containers of under 3 kilograms is subject to a CET rate of 5%; the GSP rate is 0.

C GSP rate for palm oil (a competitive subsitute) is 7%.

D GSP rate for aluminium oxide is 0.

E An annual quota of bananas enjoying exemption from the CET is negotiated each year for Germany.

F GSP rate for tobacco is 6% plus reduced levy.

L Product subject to CAP variable levies.

Sources: Data on ACP shares in EEC imports of products from Commission des Communautés Européennes, *Evolution des échanges commerciaux entre la Communauté et les états ACP*, (VIII/378/78-F) (3 April 1978); and *Importations CEE des principaux produits en provenance des états ACP*, (VIII/820/80) (19 August 1980). CET rates from 'Preferential tariff treatment applied by the Community (position as on 1 January 1980)', Official Journal of the European Communities Vol. 23, C88 (10 April 1980). GSP rates from Commission of the European Communities, *The European Communities Generalized Tariff Preferences Scheme for 1980* (COM(79) 348 final) (12 July 1979).

exported to the Community. These 25 commodities may conveniently be divided into three categories: those where the ACP experienced a sustained increase in market shares; those where the ACP share registered a sustained loss; and those where the ACP share fluctuated around the mean with no obvious movement in one direction or another. Five commodities – coffee, tea, aluminium ore, sugar, and petroleum derivatives – fall into the first category, with ACP exporters sustaining an increasing share of extra-European imports. For a sixth product – bananas – the ACP share of EEC imports remained constant. Three of these products were among those enjoying tariff advantages and three – coffee, tea and bananas – are covered by the Stabex scheme. Almost certainly more important in the case of sugar and bananas, however, are the special regimes established by the Convention. For sugar, the Community guarantees to buy a specific quota of ACP sugar at a price within the range prevailing in the Community (see *Survey 2*, Chapter 2). In the case of bananas there is no Community-wide policy; rather a variety of national policies are enforced which in France, Italy and the UK utilise licensing and other means to favour traditional suppliers from among their former colonies.

The second category includes six other commodities – refined copper, iron ore, diamonds, groundnuts, groundnut oil, and groundnut cake – with ACP exporters experiencing a deterioration in their share of extra-EEC imports. Only one of these products, groundnut oil, enjoyed a tariff preference under Lomé. In the case of the three groundnut products, this result was due to a succession of poor harvests in West Africa which caused a marked decline in total ACP groundnut exports – the index of quantity (1975 = 100) fell to 16.9 by 1979. This illustrates the caution with which all these figures must be interpreted, given the predominance in ACP exports of primary products which are particularly susceptible to both natural and man-made disasters.

One cannot of course adequately test the counterfactual; it might have been the case that the ACP performance relative to that of other ldcs would have been even worse in the absence of Lomé. But there is little in these results to suggest that the Convention had a major impact on trade flows. Certainly, it failed to guarantee the ACP group's share in the EEC market.

Changes in the commodity composition of ACP exports

One of the expectations of the ACP in entering the Lomé relationship was that it would provide a means through which they could increase their exports of processed primary products. This idea has also figured prominently in the EEC's promotion of Lomé. The Community has argued that the secure access to its market resulting from the 'contractual' nature of the Lomé relationship encourages investment in local processing. Once again, the pattern of trade during the first Convention has done little to sustain these expectations.

On the contrary, exports in 1979 were more concentrated than in 1975. A Hirschman index of commodity concentration shows a rise from 36.05 to 37.81 during the period. This can be attributed in large part to the increase in the share of petroleum in ACP exports, resulting both from increases in the quantities exported and in the unit values. Over the period of the first Convention the share of minerals as a group in ACP exports increased (see Table 10.9). In 1975 they accounted for 11 and in 1979 for 13 of the 25 most valuable ACP exports, and their share of ACP exports rose from 51 to 53%. Petroleum remained the most valuable ACP export, its share of total ACP earnings never

Table 10.9 *Shares of the 25 most important commodities in ACP exports to the EEC 1975 and 1979*

1975	Value 000 EUA	Share %	1979	Value 000 EUA	Share %
1 Petroleum	2 890 012	33.17	1 Petroleum	5 126 980	34.56
2 Cocoa	599 888	6.88	2 Coffee	1 340 455	9.04
3 Refined Copper	582 468	6.68	3 Cocoa	1 313 122	8.85
4 Sugar	488 303	5.60	4 Refined Copper	674 112	4.54
5 Coffee	479 941	5.50	5 Oil Derivatives	625 075	4.21
6 Iron Ore	327 251	3.75	6 Wood	525 161	3.54
7 Wood	300 914	3.45	7 Sugar	387 697	2.61
8 Blister Copper	148 104	1.70	8 Iron Ore	359 772	2.43
9 Calcium Phosph.	122 496	1.40	9 Blister Copper	182 104	1.23
10 Groundnut Oil	121 800	1.39	10 Cotton	169 817	1.14
11 Oil Derivatives	118 390	1.35	11 Thorium, Uranium	166 194	1.12
12 Cotton	116 981	1.34	12 Tea	153 631	1.04
13 Groundnuts	103 065	1.18	13 Uranium & Comp.	148 150	1.00
14 Bananas	95 461	1.10	14 Aluminium Oxide	136 448	0.92
15 Copper Ore	94 710	1.08	15 Groundnut Oil	123 220	0.83
16 Palm Oil	86 984	0.99	16 Sawn Wood	121 836	0.82
17 Tobacco	74 547	0.85	17 Bananas	117 145	0.77
18 Tea	73 560	0.84	18 Aluminium Ore	114 937	0.75
19 Sawn Wood	68 261	0.78	19 Tobacco	100 806	0.68
20 Aluminium Ore	64 138	0.73	20 Raw Skins	92 595	0.62
21 Aluminium Oxide	62 260	0.71	21 Diamonds	88 502	0.60
22 Raw Skins	56 333	0.64	22 Copper Ore	84 965	0.57
23 Thorium, Uranium	52 831	0.60	23 Calcium Phosph.	83 527	0.56
24 Groundnut Cake	49 125	0.56	24 Cobalt	81 808	0.55
25 Manganese Ore	43 663	0.50	25 Natural Rubber	78 825	0.53
Cumulative Percentage		82.77	Cumulative Percentage		83.55

Sources: Same as Table 10.8

falling below 25%. The share of oil derivatives in total earnings more than tripled in the period, a result of increases in both the quantity exported and the unit value.[7] ACP exports of thorium and uranium ores declined in volume but escalated sharply in unit value. The share of minerals in total ACP earnings was also boosted by the rapid expansion of exports of natural uranium. The first EEC imports of this commodity from the ACP were not recorded until 1977; in the subsequent three years the imports quadrupled so that by 1979 it had become the thirteenth most valuable ACP export.

The inability of the ACP group to diversify its exports to the Community is seen clearly in an examination of the group's manufactured exports. Table 10.10 presents data on all manufactured products which constituted at least 0.05% of total ACP exports to the Community. Although ACP exports of manufactures increased by 106% in

Table 10.10 *ACP exports of manufactured goods to the EEC 1973–1979 (values in thousand EUA)*

	1973	1974	1975	1976	1977	1978	1979
Aluminium Oxide	64012	77474	89126	80883	102551	143056	136448
	(70.0)	(70.6)	(55.2)	(53.1)	(65.2)	(79.3)	
Uranium	—	—	—	2897	25252	35756	148150
				(—)	(3.1)	(3.1)	(9.5)
Clothing	2582	8338	19769	31396	45911	49107	55330
	(—)	(—)	(0.6)	(0.7)	(1,0)	(1.1)	(1.0)
Leather	—	16185	18002	38577	30414	34900	64298
	(—)	(5.4)	(6.0)	(7.6)	(5.5)	(6.3)	(7.0)
Cotton Fabrics	—	—	13901	25344	31167	27285	32790
	(—)	(—)	(2.3)	(2.7)	(3.4)	(2.9)	(2.6)
Veneers & Plyw.	26009	24792	15576	21132	15113	18478	24292
	(6.3)	(7.1)	(3.3)	(4.3)	(3.1)	(3.3)	(3.4)
Veg. Alkaloids	—	—	—	14461	14668	12001	7018
	(—)	(—)	(—)	(9.4)	(9.2)	(6.7)	(4.9)
Other Chemicals	—	—	—	15521	12958	6817	5180
	(—)	(—)	(—)	(5.7)	(5.8)	(2.8)	(1.7)
Essential Oils	7128	9253	4.351	9302	8393	8960	9635
	(—)	(—)	(5.2)	(7.0)	(6.1)	(6.7)	(6.9)
Nat'l Hormones	—	—	—	8666	7193	10481	9554
	(—)	(—)	(—)	(11.4)	(9.9)	(13.9)	(13.5)
Ropes and Cords	—	—	—	1343	7636	8793	15281
	(—)	(—)	(—)	(5.4)	(17.9)	(18.9)	(25.6)

Note: Figures in parentheses indicate the percentage of the ACP in total EEC imports of that good.

Sources: Calculated from data in: Commission des Communautés Européenes, *Evolution des échanges commerciaux entre la Communauté et les états ACP* (VIII/373/78-F) (3 April 1978); and *Importation CEE des principaux produits en provenance des états ACP* (VIII/820/80) (19 August 1980).

value over the five years of the Convention, over half of this increase was accounted for by natural uranium and its composites, which the EEC misleadingly classifies as a manufactured product. A further one-fifth of the increase was derived from another mineral – aluminium oxide. Apart from these two products, only ropes and cords experienced a substantial increase in market share. Modest gains (from a very low base) were registered in clothing, leather, textiles, essential oils, and natural hormones; but a loss was experienced by veneers, plywood, vegetable alkaloids and other chemicals.

Conclusions for the EEC and USA

Our analysis of trade between the ACP and the EEC during the period covered by the first Lomé Convention lends further support to the argument that trade preferences in the contemporary international economic system will have only a marginal impact in the short term on the exports of developing countries. Since the Lomé Convention was but one factor influencing trade between the parties, no definitive causal attribution can be made. All that can be said with certainty is that despite the Convention's provisions the ACP failed to maintain their shares of Community imports of primary products, and failed to diversify their exports. Over the last decade the EEC has become a less important market for the ACP. In contrast, the EEC's economic performance in ACP markets during the Convention was better than its performance in the markets of other developing countries.

This apparently negligible impact has obvious implications for the Reagan Administration's Caribbean Basin Initiative (CBI) which, as explained in Chapter 8, has as its centrepiece a Lomé-style one-way free trade arrangement.

Traditionally, the USA has been hostile to the EEC's penchant for constructing regional preferential trading arrangements. US predilection for multilateralism in international trade has deep philosophical roots, e.g. in its opposition to the closed trading arrangements of the Commonwealth in the inter-war period. Subsequent US hostility towards EEC preferential arrangements with the Mediterranean countries and the Yaoundé Associates was based not only on this philosophical stance but also on the perceptions that such arrangements threatened tangible US interests: reverse preferences would exclude the USA from the markets of countries associated with the EEC (particularly those in the Mediterranean region); the preferences offered to competitors threatened US agricultural exports to the EEC either directly, as in the case of citrus fruits, or indirectly in the case of possible substitutes, e.g. groundnut oil versus US exports of soya beans; EEC preferences for other developing countries might have adverse affects on the exports of Latin America to the Community. Angered by the Community's renewal of the Yaoundé Agreement, Washington at one stage threatened to construct a similar preferential trading area with Latin America. Its decision to exclude any country which offered reverse preferences to its industrialised competitors from its GSP undoubtedly helped the ACP in the negotiations for the first Lomé Convention when they sought to end such preferences.

Yet Washington's reaction to the Lomé Convention was muted in comparison to its objections to its predecessors. Not only had the requirement for reverse preferences been dropped, but the introduction of the Community's GSP scheme had eroded the tariff advantages which would be enjoyed by the ACP over other developing countries; meanwhile, the major Latin American countries had demonstrated clearly that they could compete effectively in the EEC market despite the tariff preferences enjoyed by some of their competitors. Although Washington remained opposed in principle to regional arrangements such as Lomé, there was considerable admiration for the Convention in policy circles, especially in the aid community. In particular, officials were interested in the comprehensiveness of the Lomé package, with its linking of aid, trade, and investment provisions, and there was a perception that the Community, at least initially, had scored a major public relations success at a relatively small cost. Therefore it was not surprising that Washington should choose to model its CBI on the Lomé arrangements.

As explained in Chapter 8 political rather than economic objectives were the principal motivation underlying the CBI although there is some competition between the USA and the EEC in the Caribbean. There was little perception in Washington that Lomé would threaten US trade interests in the region, which in any event are small in comparison to total US trade with the Third World; the Caribbean accounts for under 5% of USA imports from ldcs. This sanguine approach has been justified by the trade pattern during Lomé I. The EEC fared no better than the USA in its share of the imports of Caribbean ACP countries nor is there any indication that the share of

Table 10.11   *Statistically significant changes in the USA and EEC shares of Caribbean ACP exports and imports during Lomé I*

	EXPORTS		IMPORTS	
	To USA	*To EEC*	*From USA*	*From EEC*
Caribbean ACP	no change*	no change	downward	downward
Oil Caribbean ACP	no change	no change	downward	downward
Non-oil Caribbean ACP	no change	no change	downward	downward
Jamaica	downward	no change	no change	downward

* Increase at 7.5% significance level.

the EEC in Caribbean exports increased at the expense of the USA (Table 10.11). If the USA had any misgivings regarding the impact of Lomé on its Caribbean interests, then these were in relation to its encouragement to European investment, especially in the mineral sector under Lomé II (Sysmin and extra finance from the EIB – see *Survey 1*, Chapter 3). It was not surprising therefore that a principal emphasis of the CBI was on the encouragement of US investment in the region.

In principle, the CBI might be perceived as divisive on two counts: it benefits only one part of the ACP group (not even all of the Caribbean countries) and provides nothing for the African and Pacific states, and it offers advantages to US investors which might pose a threat to EEC interests. In reality, neither argument is convincing. Most members of the ACP group enjoy duty-free access to the USA market for the vast majority of their exports courtesy of the GSP. As noted in Chapter 8, the impact of the CBI trade provisions will be marginal, and it is unlikely that other members of the ACP group will be concerned. The EEC appreciates this marginality, so its concern with economic stability in the region overrides any fears it might have that the initiative will adversely affect its interests.

Notes

1 This includes intra-ACP trade, but this is an extremely small part of total ACP trade. From 1975 to 1978 intra-ACP exports as a percentage of total ACP exports fell from 5.65% to 4.66%; in the same period intra-ACP imports as a percentage of total ACP imports fell from 6.13% to 4.93%.

2 See the special edition of *The Courier*, No. 52 (November–December 1978).

3 A list of ACP countries and the sub-groupings employed in this study is provided in the Annexe on p. 239.

4 These results are presented in greater detail in Joanna Moss and John Ravenhill, 'Trade developments under the Lomé Convention', *World Development* (October 1982).

5 There is also the major problem that a significant proportion of Irish imports are shipped via the UK.

6 The Hirschman index is calculated by squaring the percentage shares of each country, adding them, and then taking the square root of the total. If the eight member states (counting Belgium/Luxembourg as a single unit) had shared equally in EEC imports from the ACP then the Hirschman index would have been the square root of $8 \times (12.5$ squared), i.e. 35.36. Albert Hirschman, *National Power and the Structure of Foreign Trade*, (Berkeley, University of California Press, 1980).

7 In 1979 quantity = 257.3, unit value = 206.3, base 100 in 1975. Using the same 1975 = 100 base, thorium and uranium ores fell in quantity to 77.1 and rose in value to 408.0 in 1979.

11

Stabex: Analysing the Effectiveness of an Innovation

Adrian Hewitt

All of the rather limited evaluations undertaken to date on the Lomé Conventions' export earnings stabilisation and mining support facilities, Stabex and Sysmin, and on the comparable IMF compensatory financing facility, have focused on their success in compensating punctually for adverse earnings fluctuations.[1] The pattern is familiar. The schemes invariably fail to stabilise earnings aggregates at the time and place for which they are designed. This chapter concentrates instead on what happened to Stabex transfers and their contribution to development. It draws upon evaluative research conducted by the author and other ODI staff in 1981 for the EEC Commission at the request of the European Parliament and the ACP Assembly, and in 1982 for UNCTAD.[2]

The need for a wider knowledge of the impact of Stabex is clear. The Commission has raised the possibility of joining forces with other industrialised countries to extend the Stabex system to all the least developed countries; UNCTAD is now considering implementing another compensatory scheme, the complementary financing facility; Japan is toying with the idea of introducing a regional Stabex-type scheme in east and south Asia; the French government promised at the Paris conference on the least developed countries (lldcs) to extend Stabex to the lldcs outside the ACP group; and Stabex itself is due for a replenishment and possibly a restructuring, given that in the first two years of Lomé II, 1981 and 1982, it managed to pay out only 53% and 40% respectively of the legitimate claims by the ACP.

The origins and ideas behind Stabex

The mechanics of Stabex were described in *Survey 1* (Chapter 3), and the transfers to date by country and product are given in the Statistical Appendix (Tables 14 and 15). The bare bones of the scheme are sketched in the box. The purpose of this section is to place Stabex in its context.

The mechanics of Stabex

Funding for Stabex is drawn from the European Development Fund, the quinquennial aid component of the Lomé Convention. Eua 375m was allocated to Stabex under Lomé I, for 1975–79, and Eua 550m was allocated for the second Stabex (1980–84) under Lomé II. The Stabex component thus represents just over 12% of the financial resources of each EDF (although a much higher proportion in terms of annual disbursements). The products covered are mainly agricultural, including raw materials and some processed agricultural goods, but Stabex coverage is also extended to rough timber and some fisheries products. Under Lomé I iron ore was the only mineral included; this is being phased out of Stabex in Lomé II, although Stabex II covers exports from pre-existing workings of iron ore until 1984. Copper (although in the original EEC proposals) and all minerals other than iron ore, are not covered by Stabex. However, a Sysmin scheme allocating project loan funds against involuntary mining production fluctuations was introduced in Lomé II. Four main agricultural exports, sugar, beef, citrus fruits and tobacco, are also not covered. Sugar and beef from the ACP have specific preferential arrangements under the Lomé conventions however. For some crops, such as the groundnut, all the processed products up to the stage of manufactured and packaged goods are covered, but for others, such as sisal and cotton, only the raw material is covered.

The scheme is based on fluctuations in export earnings on trade with the EEC and not with third countries (nor in practice with other ACP countries). However, thirteen ACP states are granted Stabex coverage for shortfalls in their exports of a given product to all destinations, in theory because their export trade is almost exclusively with non-EEC countries. A shortfall is defined as a fall in export earnings, by product, in current prices against the average annual earnings (price × volume) on sales to the EEC over the previous four years. The difference when checked and approved normally represents the amount of the Stabex transfer. Transfers are 'normally' made as loans repayable under certain conditions (i.e. when the market recovers both in terms of price and export output) but since transfers are given as grants for the EEC's Lomé list of 35 'least developed' ACP countries and since many of the others have not been required to reimburse their transfers or have not fulfilled the conditions for reimbursement, grant-like transfers tend in fact to be the rule for Stabex.

Justification of an application for a Stabex transfer however requires that the product's exports meet predetermined dependence and fluctuation thresholds. These are lower if the ACP country is classed in Lomé as least developed, island or landlocked. A further complication is that the thresholds are different in Lomé I and Lomé II. The *dependence threshold* is a measure of exports of the product in proportion to total exports, worldwide in the previous year. To qualify, under Lomé I, the ACP export sector in question had to represent at least 7.5% of total merchandise export earnings, or 5% if the product is sisal, or 2.5% for the least developed, landlocked and island countries. For Lomé II, these dependence thresholds were revised down to 6.5%, 5% and 2% respectively. *Fluctuation thresholds* are based, like the actual claims in normal cases, on exports only to the EEC. To qualify, the downward change in export earnings against the reference period had to be at least 7.5%, or 2.5% for the least developed, island and landlocked countries in Lomé I (6.5% and 2% respectively in Lomé II). As part of a partnership and co-operation treaty, all decisions to approve, modify and reject transfers are formally made jointly by EEC and ACP. But in practice there are numerous grounds for the EEC's rejection or reduction of Stabex claims. Applications for advances on Stabex transfers can be made based on comparative monthly export earnings statistics, and can be sent on a six-monthly basis before the end of the calendar year for which Stabex transfers normally apply. Relatively few ACP countries have so far been able to use this advance facility.

The Stabex allocation in the EDF is divided into five annual instalments. Unspent balances can be carried forward and up to 20% can be 'borrowed', to satisfy legitimate claims on the allocation for the following year. In addition, the small amount of Stabex reimbursements from ACP states can be used to supplement funding.

A 'mutual insurance scheme' of international compensatory finance for alleviating the temporary export earnings instability of developing countries was mooted in the UN as early as 1953. The IMF's Compensatory Financing Facility (CFF) began in a small way in 1963 and applies to all IMF members, developed and developing alike. During its first three years of operation it made loans worth $87m, but in 1966 the system was liberalised, with the result that total drawings over the period 1966–71 amounted to $375m. In 1975, its size and scope were extended again, and in 1976 alone it lent $2,700m. Further liberalisation and expansion occurred after 1979. The CFF is purely a loan scheme and operates on the basis of changes in total export earnings (from 1980 onwards changes in food imports can also be taken into account) rather than the product basis of Stabex.

The Stabex scheme began in 1975 as part of the first Lomé Convention between the EEC and 46 (now 64) African, Caribbean and Pacific (ACP) countries. A precursor of the scheme can however be seen in the system of 'Aid to production and diversification' which operated under the second five-year Yaoundé Convention (signed in 1969).[3] Stabex was designed by the EEC (in collaboration with the ACP) as a means of providing compensatory payments to ACP governments for export earnings shortfalls on trade with the EEC on a product-by-product basis, without intervening directly in the market, and thereby to help stabilise the incomes of export producers. It can be assumed that it was devised also as a means of demonstrating good will (backed by concessionary financial resources) to the favoured ACP developing country commodity exporters while awaiting more concrete progress on international commodity agreements and in particular UNCTAD's integrated programme for commodities.

Chief among the scheme's underlying aims as originally conceived by the EEC was the idea that it could develop as an effective way of channelling financial support to producers of export commodities by using aid money to offset the effects (rather than eradicate the causes) of producer *income* instability. The obligation to use transfers in this way was lost during the Lomé negotiations, but the aim itself is open to differing interpretations. The principle of using the transfers in the affected sector may appear laudable, so long as one thinks of production in terms of the classic West African cash crops – cocoa, coffee, cotton, groundnuts – where a large or dominant share is attributable to peasant producers and where sectoral stabilisation measures can be equated with supporting the rural sector. But some Stabex products are not, or not mainly, produced by peasants (e.g. iron ore, timber, and all the processed products) and many of them are not exported as primary commodities. The producers in question may be relatively privileged urban wage earners or foreign-owned companies. Under these conditions the most stabilising influence of an official flow to the government to offset a shortfall primarily attributable to the private sector may not be achieved by boosting incomes in the export producing sector. Moreover, since Stabex transfers are provided as untied foreign exchange without specific end-use conditionality, they cannot necessarily be expected to provide sectoral stability if the recipient government identifies more pressing claims on their use. There are no formal conditions constraining the government's use of the funds transferred, other than the supply of an *ex post* declaration on use (Lomé I) supplemented in Lomé II by an *ex ante* declaration of intent.

The last two years of Stabex have seen severe financial and funding problems. In the Convention, the EEC's commitment to provide Stabex compensatory finance is circumscribed by a resource ceiling, although ACP states wish to interpret the goodwill contained in the Convention more favourably. In 1981 (for export earnings shortfalls in 1980), the EDF could pay only 52.84% of legitimate ACP claims.

Differential treatment was awarded in favour of least developed states, which received 59.51% of their claims, while the others received only 47.36%. Claims of below Ecu1m were paid in full. In 1982 (for export earnings shortfalls in 1981) 40.4% of the claims could be funded. Some claimants had their Lomé I outstanding Stabex loan-based transfers offset against current claims, and the rest was paid to the tune of 41.9% for the normal countries and 46.5% for the least developed, with claims under Ecu1m being met in full. Only Ecu142m of the total Ecu183m payments in 1982 could however be funded from Stabex resources and as Stabex transfers. The rest would be supplied later as project aid, being drawn from the accrued interest of previous EDF balances. The ACP still regard the unpaid balances as due to them eventually (though without interest).

Use of Stabex transfers

Unlike virtually all schemes of development assistance and concessionary finance, Stabex alone has no specifically prescribed end-use; nor does it come attached with formal conditionality on use or on economic policy whether sectoral or macroeconomic, other than the obligation to repay under certain circumstances for some ACP countries. The Commission in fact introduced in July 1982 the obligation on ACP states to use the additional Ecu40m for projects, but mainstream Stabex transfers are not constrained in this way. Little was known until recently about the real use, or the contribution to stabilisation and development of Stabex transfers. Recipient governments merely had to declare a use for the transfers. The Commission sometimes received no notification at all, and sometimes had merely to accept incomplete official statements. No proper procedure for regular and systematic evaluation of use has yet been instituted, although in some cases the amounts transferred are considerable, particularly in relation to the size of certain national economies. The European Court of Auditors has the task of auditing all Community spending but cannot in practice engage in much more than a financial audit.

The research on which this chapter is based involved investigations into Stabex transfers (totalling Ecu206m) under Lomé I to ten countries which together represented over 50% of the total Stabex transfers made under Lomé I, and included the main recipients (Senegal, Sudan, Mauritania, Niger and Tanzania), countries where Stabex inflows were very large in relation to their economy (Comoros, Western Samoa and Gambia), and two where Stabex transfers were relatively and absolutely quite insignificant (Cameroon and Fiji). Thirty-nine distinct Stabex transfers were followed through, and twelve different commodities were involved, with groundnuts dominating the sample, accounting for 64% of the volume of transfers triggered. There were cases of 'all destinations' coverage, advances, and reimbursements, as well as the more normal type of transactions. The experience of this sample can be divided into three main areas: Stabex as a contribution to public finance; more general balance of payments effects; and the influence of the Stabex system, its guarantees, and transfers from drawings on the scheme on the production and exporting sector which triggered off Stabex.

Stabex and public finance

As regards public finance, the overall picture of fiscal shortfalls attributed to products which attracted Stabex transfers is quite mixed: the incidence was larger for those countries (Gambia, Senegal, Mauritania) where a key export, and one sold mainly to the EEC, suffered the export earnings shortfall and attracted the transfer. Where the product was a minor export (e.g. Fiji's coconut oil, Cameroon's cocoa paste) the incidence of the shortfall was very slight. Where the product was just one of a range of Stabex products which regularly attracted transfers (e.g. in the Comoros), the overall incidence of the shortfall was also slight, as increased revenue from the other products tended to compensate for the shortfall identified for that year's Stabex product. In the case of products only partly exported to the EEC (e.g. Tanzania's cotton) the fiscal shortfall on export earnings losses could be large, though Stabex would only operate on a small portion of the shortfall. But in all cases the incidence of the direct (i.e. export) tax shortfall depends on the importance of the product's export taxes in total budget revenue.

The general picture is that falling export taxes related to Stabex products rarely accounted for more than a 5% drop (on an annual basis) in the government's budget revenue. In most cases, import duties were a much more important source of revenue than export duties. For instance, for Fiji, export duties as a whole raised less than 2% of government revenue. There was no export tax at all on coconut oil. Even in the iron ore-dependent economy of Mauritania, export taxes and royalties lost were only a small portion of budgetary revenue, below 10% in normal years. If the indirect influence on other revenue categories is included (decreased tax base as a result of declining sectoral economic activity and lowered effective demand for goods and services, falling import capacity and hence lower import tax revenues, etc.), the fiscal loss attributable to earnings shortfalls in Stabex products is amplified, but it was rarely identified as a major item on the revenue side of the budget; hence the reflection by some observers that it is paradoxical that the government, which itself bears only a small part of the shortfall attributable to the earnings fluctuation, should be the recipient of the whole of the transfer.

However, it is useful to look at the fiscal shortfall in the light of the serious budgetary position of most of the states in the sample. With the exception of Western Samoa (which often had budget surpluses simultaneous with Stabex operations) and Cameroon (which usually ran a balanced budget), the ACP countries in the sample were generally running serious and increasing budgetary deficits. Thus the loss of Stabex product-related revenues compared with expected levels of revenue aggravated a difficult fiscal position. In most cases, this meant that Stabex transfers were bound to have a positive effect on the budget, though they could not be expected to stabilise an imbalance which had many other causes. In the sample there was very rarely any direct budget stabilisation effect, but there were many partial contributions to budget equilibrium.

There was rarely a direct correlation between the amount of the foregone export tax revenue and the Stabex inflow, not only because of the inevitable lag in payment if the advance mechanism was not used, but also because private non-tax shortfalls were included in the Stabex calculations. In Sudan and the Comoros Stabex probably provided more government revenue than the related export tax losses. In one year, Stabex provided an additional 18% to export tax revenues for Tanzania. There could be no substitution of lost export tax revenue in the case of Fiji because the product concerned (coconut oil) paid none, and in the case of Western Samoa not only were export taxes not important (for cocoa and copra they represented less than 3% of revenue) but their yield was constantly increasing after 1977. Thus the government was receiving Stabex payments in addition to higher export tax revenues and was running a considerable surplus on the recurrent budget. Only in the case of Mauritania, where the first Stabex transfer was supplemented by an advance on the next, did the amount approximately match the royalties left unpaid by the mining company, SNIM, though even here there were offsetting tax transfers and liabilities between the corporation and the state which destroy the symmetry one would otherwise see in the substitution of unrequited government transfers for missing ore production tax revenue. Moreover, a much larger Stabex payment came a little later, when tax revenues from the commodity were rising again. In the Senegal case, it was found that Stabex provided as an advance had a budget stabilising function, while normal Stabex transfers, rather than being neutral, actually tended to destabilise.

In quantitative terms, the impact on budgetary shortfalls was very varied. Sometimes the transfers provided more government revenue than the related loss of export duties and indirect taxes, and even added to government revenues when the budget was showing a surplus. Sometimes they helped finance a budget deficit which had arisen from problems largely unrelated to revenue fluctuations from the Stabex product. What they did consistently was to provide additional untied finance to government, sometimes on a significant scale. For 1977, Stabex accounted for no less than 23% of Western Samoa's appropriated receipts and 10% of development expenditure (four-fifths of which is financed by foreign aid); for the Comoros, in one year, Stabex accounted for 31% of the development budget even though this was exclusively financed out of foreign aid. For some other countries, the impact as a financial contribution was more modest. Cameroon's larger Stabex transfer increased budgetary revenue by only 1%, and for Tanzania, Stabex was never more than 1.3% of recurrent revenue or 1.7% of development budget expenditures. Even Fiji's relatively large *repayments* had only a small budgetary impact, representing 1% of current expenditure. Stabex's significance as an incremental public flow shows up most clearly when compared with other aid flows, particularly EEC aid. Due to the relatively rapid disbursement procedures of the Stabex portion of the EDF, Stabex transfers were much larger than the total disbursements of EDF IV project aid over the Lomé I period in six cases (Sudan, Mauritania, Senegal, Gambia, Comoros and probably W. Samoa) and on a similar scale in two other cases (Niger and Tanzania). Even comparisons with the indicative programmes under Lomé I show Stabex in a very favourable light as an aid transfer mechanism: Stabex payments more than doubled the original EDF aid pledge under the indicative programme in two cases – Senegal and Mauritania.

The general conclusion is therefore that Stabex provided, in the majority of cases under study, significant budget support, usually in unconditional fashion, thus allowing increased flexibility in the government's development policy by financing marginal expenditure. But its effectiveness as a short-term *stabilisation measure* providing prompt relief commensurate with specific and very partial fiscal distortions was almost nowhere traceable.

Did the receipt of Stabex transfers help shift government spending towards development investments, particularly in the agricultural sector when the Stabex product was an agricultural one? Some countries rigorously allocated the transfers to the development budget (e.g. Tanzania and Fiji) and submitted the spending projects for Parliamentary approval. Here the partial budget revenue stabilisation effect was lost because the timing of the arrival of Stabex funds required the preparation and approval of supplementary estimates. Others did not enter the Stabex inflows into the budget at all. The Niger economic affairs ministry controlled the funds and ran a separate Stabex account for the domestic stabilisation fund, which even made loans to other parastatals. The Gambian government failed to specify any budgetary use: transfers were deposited with the Central Bank to compensate for 'the enormous sums borrowed by the government from this bank to finance current expenses'. Between these two extremes there were a number of other variations. Cameroon put the transfers into extra-budgetary accounts, but repaid one Stabex transfer out of the recurrent budget. Western Samoa entered only three of the five Stabex transfers in the budget. For the Sudan it was impossible to discover whether some transfers were booked in the budget or not.

Whether or not Stabex transfers were formally included in central government expenditure plans and used as appropriated receipts, the findings were consistent on two points. There was always a positive impact on government finances, though a very minor one when Stabex had to be treated as a short-term loan. This is a fairly obvious point since Stabex was not only an unrequited but also an untied financial transfer to the government. This did mean, however, that it could be used just as easily for recurrent expenditures and government consumption as for development expenditure. For instance, Niger's Stabex receipts were consistently more than the state's total development investments in agriculture, while for the Gambia they were almost equally distributed between current and development expenditure. In other words, the Stabex transfers financed the marginal items of government expenditure, sometimes in the affected export sector, sometimes as diversification, but often for public investments in infrastructure (including the financing of the local costs component of aid projects) or for current public consumption. In a few cases – Mauritania in 1978–79, and probably Western Samoa in the case of two of the transfers – the marginal item of public expenditure had to be the servicing of public external debt, which in its absence would have provoked a default. In such cases there would be no release of funds for domestic public spending operations, and the stabilisation influence of Stabex would be concentrated on the balance of payments.

Stabex and the balance of payments

The balance of payments effects of usually untied unreimbursable foreign exchange were more obvious. Stabex inflows invariably helped to strengthen the balance of payments, though in many cases the effect was quite marginal. But Stabex never had a full stabilising function. Its coverage of the balance of payments aggregates is too partial, and the normal delays of the Stabex machinery usually meant that a return towards equilibrium (if it occurred over the short term) preceded receipt of the Stabex transfers. Advances were more likely to assist stabilisation than the normal payments procedure, yet advances were not used, and the facility barely acknowledged by many countries in the sample. Most of the countries in the sample experienced large and worsening trade deficits, so external balance of payments support measures or adjustments in demand management would remain necessary. The two countries, Cameroon and Niger, which appeared to be moving towards a satisfactory balance of payments equilibrium without severe retrenchment in domestic demand, were achieving this not as a result of Stabex support but due to favourable developments in non-Stabex exports (oil and uranium). Mauritania was still far from reaching an acceptable payments position, but Stabex had made a major and timely contribution to settling certain payment arrears and hence directing the economy on the path towards equilibrium. For Senegal and Sudan, the Stabex contribution had been large, but even more wide-ranging new adjustment measures and allied balance of payments support (both outside the scope of the Stabex mechanism) were only with some difficulty beginning to restore economic stability.

Stabex and the afflicted sector

The effect of Stabex on the afflicted sector depends fundamentally on how appropriate the remedy offered by the scheme is to the causes of the sector's problems. The sectoral problem most prevalent was declining output of an export crop (in a few cases, declining exports only) rather than earnings fluctuations as a result of short-term price or quantity shifts. Aside from this, a great variety of sub-problems were diagnosed, not surprisingly as the range of products covered went from timber via groundnuts to ylang-ylang. But a fairly common cause of the declining output was the diminishing attractiveness of export products in terms of producer revenue, prices offered by state buying monopolies and support and subsidies given by the state to export producers when compared either with the recent past or with alternative crops, notably food for the domestic market. Other factors such as poor weather helped to depress output but this was almost never felt to be the chief cause either of the sector's problems or of the Stabex intervention. Poor world market prices and deficient European demand was the key problem in a minority of cases, particularly for iron ore and timber, but only as a contributory factor in most of the cases.[4]

Given the rules governing Stabex payments, the 'remedy' it provided would be more commensurate with the 'problem' in those cases where product exports to the EEC dominate; where raw materials only were exported and none was consumed or processed locally (except for groundnuts); and where Stabex payments were made rapidly, particularly in the form of six monthly advances. These criteria put the Senegal and Gambia groundnuts sector transfers and the Mauritania iron ore transfers high up the list of appropriateness. At the other extreme would be, say, Tanzania's cotton transfer, where exports to the EEC represented only a small share of cotton exports and where no advance payments were requested or made, or the same country's sisal transfers for a sector also producing processed products for export not covered by Stabex guarantees.

Having established the appropriateness of the scale of the transfer in relation to the sectoral problem, the next question to ask concerns the effectiveness of the use of the transfer in curing the sector's problems. Our conclusions are that where the extent of Stabex coverage was substantial and the transfer prompt the scheme would be very valuable for sectoral stabilisation, even when used only indirectly for the sector (e.g. Mauritania's iron ore). The fact of channelling Stabex through a national stabilisation fund (Senegal, Niger) or a product marketing board (Gambia) did not guarantee efficient use. In many cases the organisation of the parastatal in question was at the root of the sector's inefficiency. Where sectoral policy remains inadequate, Stabex transfers to underpin that policy obviously will not help. But if product stabilisation funds were to perform the function of ensuring steady and appropriate remuneration for farmers in real terms, they could be a suitable recipient of Stabex transfers for losses on export crops. Some cases in Western Samoa where product boards did not operate effectively show that a stricter application of Stabex funds could have been used to promote these aims, if only in a small way.

In cases where the transfers were used exclusively, or almost exclusively, outside the triggering sector – for instance, Tanzania, most of the Comoros transfers, Fiji (in terms of capital spending) and Sudan – the uses are so diverse that it is impossible to generalise about effective use. These nominal uses included road infrastructure, public debt payments, maize production and storage projects, and Stabex payments for copra used partly to promote vanilla production. At best we can say that the governments regarded the transfers as untied to the sector, and they used them for the marginal items of public spending which they considered a priority. In some cases they wished to diversify actively out of a declining export sector. Moreover, in many cases the transfer covered only a fraction of the earnings shortfall, and this, when added to the fact that the sector's earnings performance had often recovered by the time the transfer was received, meant that there were good reasons to endorse the ACP government's assessment of the most efficient use of the transfer. This was particularly true for those governments liable to repay the transfers which thus had notionally to generate a short-term return on the use to which the transfer was put. In conclusion, we recall that there were 39 different Stabex transactions in our sample covering sectors as diverse as groundnuts (partly consumed locally and across borders), and cloves (exported only in raw form); from agricultural crops to timber and iron ore; some 20 products in all (by country). In view of this variety there was no *ideal* Stabex use to be identified at the sectoral level.

What form should Stabex III take?

There will certainly be a Stabex-type scheme in the successor to the Lomé II convention. The main areas for treatment and adaptation are the funding situation, the constraints on use of the transfers, particularly in the agricultural production sector, and the methods for channelling the transfers to ensure they cannot be used as general budgetary expenditure. But as in the spirit of past Lomé conventions, the ways these adaptations will be made will be determined by the joint negotiating process.

The most pressing current problem is the inadequacy of Stabex funding to meet legitimate claims. In 1976–80, declining production and export volume was the main cause of claims, but in the last two years severe falls in virtually all commodity prices have been the important triggering factor. This may continue during the remaining three years of Lomé II Stabex if commodity prices continue to fall (although the reference values and hence the margins of compensation would themselves also decline). Extra funding, let alone a normal replenishment, will not be easy to come by, as the experience in 1982 shows when no fresh funds could be raised and old interest and principal payments had to be recycled to part-rescue the scheme. Some member states, notably the UK, are hostile to any extra funding of the scheme so long as it pays out in untied cash, and even the ACP now recognise that any additional Stabex allocation will tend to be deducted from their project aid allocation.

Stabex financial terms are generally very liberal. But given that Stabex resources (and all aid resources) are scarce, multiple compensation is a problem. Due to the product by product approach, a country may receive large Stabex transfers for shortfalls on product X, while earnings on product Y are booming. It may receive Stabex and CFF drawings at or around the same time. As an aid transfer mechanism, Stabex operates with commendable speed. But its distribution between ACP countries is highly inequitable. Senegal alone has received about a quarter of transfers to date, and has not yet reimbursed, while a dozen ACP countries, some with acute export shortfalls, have received none. Indeed, were Senegal obliged to reimburse, there would be a strong risk of the Stabex mechanism destabilising the economy.

The Commission's discretion in awarding some transfers, rejecting others, and devising new reasons for reducing other applications needs to be regularised. Much play was made in the early days of Stabex as an incentive to export raw materials to Europe. This is only partly correct, and only a very residual feature of Stabex operations. Far more important is the fact that the scheme provided free foreign exchange, for which it is highly appreciated by nearly every ACP government. But there are elements of this 'hewers of wood and drawers of water' argument which still present problems. because article 27 (Lomé II) allowing for the use of Stabex to deal with shortfalls in trade between ACP countries has not been implemented, it does not help to develop such trade, or to reduce trade dependency on the EEC. Discretionary calculation of eligible shortfalls tends to end up as a disincentive both to local processing (whether for export to Europe or for internal or regional trade) and to local consumption, even of food products (like groundnuts).

The link between the financial transfer and the needy production sector (and specifically incomes of producers in that sector) has yet to be properly established. The ACP countries are almost universally favourable to the scheme, and wish it to be continued with a minimum of constraints but with an expansion of the product list and with the coverage to be extended to non-merchandise export earnings, tourism, and even migrants' remittances. For its part, the EEC wishes to tighten up the conditions and use of funds and place Stabex on a securer, if in real terms more modest, financial footing. Moreover, there are substantial differences in attitudes between EEC member governments. France, for instance, wishes the scheme to continue in expanded form, but with transfers channelled through national product stabilisation funds and with control over domestic pricing policy; the UK wishes to limit the scope of the scheme, feels it compares unfavourably in development assistance terms with project aid and that it duplicates the CFF, distorts resource allocation to a relatively small group of countries, and leaves the EEC fulfilling a role which is better filled by the IMF with its stand-by arrangements and the World Bank with structural adjustment lending.

It would be an overstatement to suggest that the Stabex scheme too contributes to the Atlantic rift. This last feature – seeing the EEC scheme as a duplication of the activities of the Washington institutions – is so far only a minor irritant. Exasperation at yet another facility is tinged with envy that a novel scheme formulated elsewhere has had some measure of success. Much more important for the American administration is their perception of Stabex as a scheme which directly *subsidises* African raw material producers exporting to a protected EEC market, with friction becoming acute in the area of oilseeds. As this chapter shows, a proper evaluation of Stabex operations reveals that in practice the scheme has rarely done anything of the sort, at least directly. This does not however prevent Stabex from being the main element (since the abolition of reverse preferences in 1975) of the Lomé Convention about which the US government harbours suspicions strong enough to prevent it fully endorsing the EEC-ACP special arrangements within the GATT framework.

Notes

1   The best examples are: J. M. Finger and Dean A. Derosa, 'The Compensatory Finance Facility and Export Instability', *Journal of World Trade Law*, Jan/Feb 1980; C. Green and C. Kirkpatrick, 'The IMF's Food Financing Facility', *Journal of World Trade Law*, May/June 1982; Roland Herrman, 'On the Economic Evaluation of the Stabex System', *Inter-Economics*, Jan/Feb 1982.

2   The study analysed the use to which Stabex transfers were put in four case studies. Each case study has resulted in a monograph, and, together with six others (between them covering over 50% of all Stabex transfers under Lomé I) have formed the basis for an overall evaluation of Stabex operations during the five years of Lomé I. The case study reports and the overall evaluation are: *Stabex: The Islamic Republic of Mauritania,* by Adrian Hewitt and Mary Sutton, ODI, London, 1981, confidential; *Stabex: The United Republic of Cameroon,* by Adrian Hewitt and Clare Oxby, ODI, London, 1981, confidential; *Stabex: The United Republic of Tanzania,* by Adrian Hewitt and Ann Weston, ODI, London, 1981, confidential; *Stabex: La Republic Fédérale Islamique des Comores*, by Adrian Hewitt, ODI, London, 1981, confidential; *Synthesis Report on the Overall Impact of Stabex Operations 1975–79,* by Adrian Hewitt, EEC Commission DG VIII, Brussels, restricted. Details of two of the other case studies (on Senegal and the Gambia) are referred to in *Prix rélatifs des produits primaires et développement*, ed. Patrick Guillaumont, Centre Nationale de la Recherche Scientifique, Paris, 1982.

3   Under this scheme the EEC-Six allocated part of the third European Development Fund to a type of programme aid for agricultural producers (of export crops). The scheme was not used purely for commodity earnings stabilisation by product: as its title suggests, it could also be used for diversification out of a given export product.

4   The picture is, of course, quite different for the first two years of Lomé II when depressed world prices for, and over-supply of cocoa and coffee have been the main trigger of Stabex transfers.

SECTION B: FUTURE PROSPECTS

12

Forum on Development Policy after 1985

In September 1982 the Commission adopted a major statement of its strategy towards the Third World, which will form the foundation of its development policy in the second half of this decade. The Documentary Appendix is devoted entirely to excerpts from this very important document. But the EEC's actual development policy is not solely (or even largely) a reflection of Commission views. The member states are a considerable influence, and of course policy is also modified during negotiations with the Third World. In what ways are pressures from these directions likely to shape the EEC's policy? In this chapter six eminent political and academic figures give their views on the directions that Europe should take. Although some of them currently hold senior positions in governmental and international organisations, each writes in his personal capacity.

The range of views expressed is wide, even among the contributors from the EEC. It is obvious that there is not yet a clear consensus within the EEC on the scope and direction of the Community's development programme, or even over whether there should be a Community-level programme. Hessel argues for greater co-ordination between the programmes of the member states because he wants the 'Community to be seen henceforth as a group of countries united in their approach . . .'. Hofmann admits that harmonisation is desirable but questions whether it is realistic until 'the EEC can achieve fuller integration in other fields'. Svendsen asks whether it is even desirable. He reports the majority view of a recent Danish report on development assistance that calls for a real reduction in EEC aid to free aid resources to be disbursed through other channels. Views also differ over the focus of EEC policy. Hessel and Hofmann both argue the case for continued emphasis on Africa. Pronk considers the merits of this focus, but also advances the case for a broader policy encompassing all developing countries. Saxena also argues strongly in favour of a broader approach and Persaud, while underlining the positive features of the Lomé Convention, takes the view that its potentially divisive features must be overcome. Not surprisingly, Saxena, Persaud and Pronk emphasise the need for more resources. Hofmann questions the feasibility of this, and Hessel points to the need to improve the quality of aid.

All in all, the debate over the new Commission strategy in 1983 and the treatment it receives in the Lomé III negotiations will reveal a great deal about the current state and future direction of EEC–Third World relations.

Europe and Africa: Hard and Soft Options for the 1980s

Jan P. Pronk

The present international economic crisis is creating many victims. Of these, African countries are perhaps faring the worst; most of them are among the poorest countries in the world and have few resources. Their development potential in the 1960s and 1970s was modest and consequently they had little to fall back upon when the international economic climate deteriorated.

Recently the Economic Commission for Africa summed up development as follows:

'In addition to sagging and sluggish economic growth, escalating inflation and growing unemployment and mass poverty, the African continent continued to face four devastating and debilitating problems in 1980: chronic food deficits; pernicious drought; the impact of inexorably rising costs of imported energy; and deteriorating terms of trade, chronic balance-of-payments deficits and mounting external debt . . . Many African countries are today on the verge of economic bankruptcy, while a few others are simply trotting along.'[1]

However, not all long-term trends in the two to three decades since decolonisation have been negative. Most African governments rightly focused on political consolidation, on laying down basic infrastructure and on the development of human resources. In these fields, economically and politically, quite a few African countries did remarkably well, considering their deprivation during the colonial era and the need to attain some minimum degree of stability before embarking upon a development path. But at the same time, both the initial disadvantages and the inadequate domestic policies, together with an unfavourable international climate have delayed real development in many African countries, leading to dualism and the creation of new instabilities.

The present question of concern in the European Community is 'what about Africa in Lomé III?' It is an important question, yet the European Community should not attempt to answer it too soon. There are underlying fundamental questions which should be addressed by the African people themselves: in which direction and to what extent should African countries review their national and international policies and adjust them to the changed circumstances of the 1980s?; what are the main problems in Africa now and how should they be dealt with? The move from the first to the second generation after independence is a major opportunity for examining these questions.

The early 1980s have seen global North–South relations in deadlock. However, there are now some indications that this deadlock is leading to a reappraisal of those relations. It is too early to judge whether this reappraisal will result either in a joint effort to overcome common problems or in a fragmentation of the international community. But any effort to change relations is preferable to the present stalemate, which has paralysed all the actors on the international scene since 1975. Even the efforts of the US government to restore the framework of international relations which became obsolete in the 1960s might be applauded because it forces others to reappraise and react.

Two strategies for African development

Such a reassessment of policies has also begun in Africa. Heads of States and Governments of the Organisation of African Unity held an extraordinary summit in Lagos in April 1980, devoted exclusively to the economic development problems of Africa, and adopted the Lagos Plan of Action for the Economic Development of Africa, 1980–2000. It consistently serves as a yardstick for the economic policies of African countries and institutions. A year earlier, the African Governors of the World Bank and the International Monetary Fund had requested the Bank to prepare a special paper on the economic development problems of Sub-Saharan African countries and an appropriate programme for helping them. The result was the World Bank report 'Accelerated Development in Sub-Saharan Africa: an Agenda for Action', which was published in 1981 and gave rise to heated discussion because many African policy-makers felt it was inconsistent with the Lagos Plan of Action. In the same period new initiatives (such as the West African economic community ECOWAS and the Preferential Trade Area for Eastern and Southern Africa) were launched to intensify economic co-operation amongst African countries; some of these new initiatives hold more promise than those made previously.

This reappraisal of the development options for Africa should be supported and should not be frustrated by decisions made outside the continent, as too often has been the case in the past. Decisions on relations between Europe and Africa fall into this category; they should not unduly diminish African options. The options available depend on the diagnosis of current problems, but at the moment there is no agreement on this. The World Bank report states that Africa's disappointing economic performance during the past two decades reflects both external and internal structural factors. The latter evolved from historical circumstances or from the physical environment – such as underdeveloped human resources, the economic disruption accompanying decolonisation and post-colonial consolidation, climatic and geographic factors hostile to development, and rapidly growing population – whilst the external factors are notably adverse trends in the international economy, stagflation in the industrialised countries, higher energy prices, relatively slow growth of trade in primary products and adverse terms of trade. The Bank's report goes on to argue that all these factors impeding African economic growth have been exacerbated by inadequate domestic policies, such as a bias in favour of industry as opposed to agriculture, in trade, prices, tax and exchange rate policies and an over-extension of the public sector. From this analysis the Report recommends an 'agriculture-based and export-orientated development strategy . . . for the 1980s (as) an essential beginning to a process of long-term transformation, a prelude to industrialization. It is not a permanent course for any country but one that in Africa generates resources more quickly than any alternative and benefits more people.'[2]

The Lagos Plan of Action has a somewhat different perspective. Like the World Bank Report, it has been drafted with the awareness that external factors are not the only impediment to development and that a change in domestic policies is also necessary if the objectives of self-reliance and a better distribution of the benefits of economic development are to be achieved. However, it gives the industrial sector equal importance with the food and agriculture sector, because both should provide each other with inputs and markets. It also emphasises production for the African market (import-substitution rather than export promotion) and internalisation of the sources of supply of factor inputs (capital, equipment, raw materials, energy and high-level skills). It therefore makes a plea for the development of internal demand stimuli, for Africanisation at all levels and for strengthening economic co-operation and integration within the continent.

Of course the two models are not wholly in opposition. Both are integral approaches in which all factors and sectors have a place. In fact a recent assessment by some African secretariats stated that the 'two documents have a lot in common',[3] but at the same time concluded that the 'goals, objectives and characteristics contained in the (World Bank) Report are in many ways inconsistent with those of the Lagos Plan of Action'.[4] That conclusion is correct, especially when the scarcity of available resources and the necessity to decide on a time path is taken into account. The two strategies necessarily lead to different time paths and different priorities.

To conclude that there is inconsistency between the two strategies does not in itself imply a choice for one or the other. Criticism of the World Bank Report hangs on two assertions. First, it would be doubtful, even if African countries were to implement the recommended reforms, increase exports to markets outside Africa, and receive more external assistance, whether the combined effects would cover current account deficits and provide the external inputs needed to accelerate development. Second, the approach recommended would make Africa too dependent on external markets and resources, and this would be contrary to principles of self-reliance and self-sustaining development.[5] The way in which these criticisms have been presented on many recent occasions, though not unanimously, has been, in my view, rather harsh (partly due to the presentation of the Report itself). Even though the criticisms are not unjustified, they can be answered, the first one by the assertion that it is equally doubtful whether an approach based on internal markets and resources would lead to a timely and adequate acceleration in economic growth, and the second by pointing to a specific time path: a temporary outward orientation could perhaps provide the resources necessary for long-term self-sustainability. But these assertions in turn would have to be proven, which could only be done by putting one strategy or the other into practice. Which of the two is the right approach? It all boils down to a matter of political choice and implementation.

A soft and a hard option

It seems that Africa has in fact already made a choice; namely in favour of the model contained in the Lagos Plan of Action. Taking this decision was important, even if there are some deficiencies in the strategy chosen, because the strength of determination behind it will increase the chances for successful implementation. This determination to implement the Lagos Plan of Action, evident in the vehement African criticism of the alternative approach, should not be overlooked by countries and agencies outside Africa.

In the present international, economic and political climate this choice seems to be rather logical. After all, what chances are there for a substantial improvement in African terms of trade and assistance to this continent? A very interesting analysis of the policy options was recently presented by Adebayo Adedeji, the present Executive Secretary of the Economic Commission for Africa. In his opening address to the ECA Conference of Ministers of Economic Planning, held in Tripoli in April 1982, he stressed the necessity for the African countries to choose one of two options: a so-called soft option or a hard one.[6] In his view, the soft option would imply an emphasis on aid, access to markets and commodity price stabilisation. The hard one would be orientated towards national and collective self-reliance based on the mobilisation of all domestic resources and would imply temporary partial delinking from the outside economy.

Adedeji argued that the soft option would have three disadvantages:
– it would be based on the understanding that the present international economic crisis is a temporary one; however, in the long run African countries would also be confronted with a scarcity of aid, high capital costs, sluggish world demand, protectionism and bad terms of trade;
– it would be based on the belief that external factors are more dominant in the development process than internal ones;
– it would make Africa more dependent on the outside world than it already is.

Since this approach would eventually lead to a decrease in the standard of living, Adedeji advocated a choice for the hard option: 'purposeful development-orientated austerity'. The aim of collective self-reliance would be reached by, amongst other measures, giving priority to production for the African market, restricting imports of non-essentials, and by intra-African co-operation and trade (trade preferences, the establishment of an African Monetary Fund and African multinational companies, and the promotion of Afro-Arab co-operation).

When hopes for a quick recovery of the world economy are fading and concepts like the North–South Dialogue, the new round of Global Negotiations, and the New International Economic Order are hardly mentioned any more, this philosophy seems to offer the only consistent option. On the one hand it assumes that the world economic crisis will continue for a very long period, although this may be too pessimistic, while on the other, policies aimed at more self-reliance and the establishment of priorities for the utilisation of scarce resources are commendable in themselves and, in particular, for a period of transition towards world economic recovery.

Whether the poorest and least developed countries in Africa would benefit from such a policy is questionable. It is hardly possible for them to cut consumption and imports any further. However, so far the 'soft' option has not benefitted them much. The United Nations Conference on the Least Developed Countries, held in Paris in September 1981, produced some inadequate promises in the substantial new programme of action (see Chapter 6i), and even these are not being kept.[7]

It remains to be seen to what extent the policy advocated – commendable or not – would be politically feasible. The attractions of the 'soft' option may make it very difficult to choose and implement the 'hard' one, especially given the already existing strong economic and political ties of Africa with the world outside, and in particular Europe. Moreover, there are great ideological differences between African states themselves, which would make it very difficult for Africa to make an effective choice for a common inward-looking policy.

So it seems that the 'hard' option is based both on realism (e.g. the expectations with regard to developments in the world outside Africa) and on a lack of it (e.g. the optimism concerning possibilities for collective self-reliance and industrialisation). But if it is chosen, within a framework such as the Lagos Plan of Action, it deserves a chance.

A challenge for Europe

What should be Europe's reaction to these proposals within, for instance, the framework of Lomé III? It could be argued that the 'hard' option for Africa is the 'soft' one for Europe, but this assumes that only African forces would determine Europe's policies *vis à vis* developing countries. However, there are other forces: those exerted by non-African ACP countries, by all other developing countries, by other rich countries like the USA and Japan, and forces within the Community itself. These also must be taken into account when considering the alternative European reactions.

One option for Europe, next to the 'soft' option of not offering any substantial additional assistance to African development, could be really to improve aid and trade relations with Africa (including those countries which are not yet associated with the Community), and the other ACP member countries. The participation of the latter, although welcome, has not so far effectively broadened the original Europe–Africa development axis into a more worldwide co-operation. On the contrary, the participation of the Caribbean and Pacific in Lomé has enabled the EEC to intensify its orientation towards Africa without it becoming either absolute or too costly.

This second option for Europe implies a further intensification of relations with Africa, but with more resources. This would imply major quantitative and qualitative improvements in both the European Development Fund and in Stabex, and perhaps the introduction of some new elements, such as industrial and monetary co-operation. It would also undermine some of the assumptions on which the African continent's plea for the 'hard' option is based. It might even frustrate African determination to choose collective self-reliance and to implement the Lagos Plan of Action. In my view, there would have to be a very substantial improvement of the European offer, made during the negotiations for Lomé III, for Africa to benefit from renouncing some of its determination. This improvement should at least compensate for the additional negative effects on Africa of further deterioration in the present international economic situation.

There is, however, a third possible European reaction. This would be the broadening of its development co-operation policy to all developing countries and the intensification of these relations. It could be differentiated by country or group of countries, depending on their different stages of economic development, but it should imply substantial improvements for all of them. This too would undermine certain assumptions even more than would the second option, because it would not only be a major signal to African and other developing countries that external assistance in the form of trade support and financial resources would be forthcoming, but it would also be an important contribution in the fight against the world economic recession.

To be politically credible and economically effective, such an approach must be ambitious. However, let us be realistic at the same time: given the present political climate and economic crisis in Europe, we simply cannot expect a sudden and complete reversal of present practices. But we can demand a major policy decision in 1983 to change the hitherto self-centred co-operation into a system based upon mutual interests between Europe and the Third World, to be implemented, say, within a period of five to seven years, to coincide more or less with the duration of Lomé III and the period between UNCTAD VI and UNCTAD VIII.

Such a strategy could consist of the following elements:
- The launching of an emergency programme, possibly with other rich countries, to cover the needs of the poorest and most seriously affected developing countries in the areas of food, energy and balance-of-payments deficits.[8]
- A European initiative, again possibly with others, for instance at UNCTAD VI, to break through the present stalemate in the North–South dialogue in the fields of trade, industrialisation, and money and finance in general.
- A substantial improvement in the offer to the ACP countries during the forthcoming Lomé III negotiations with regard to aid, trade and other forms of co-operation.
- Simultaneously with the above, an offer to make available the resources of a substantially increased European Development Fund to all least developed countries, and an invitation to other rich countries which are in a position to increase their aid levels (such as Japan, Canada, Australia and Switzerland) to participate in such a scheme.

- A similar two-pronged offer with regard to Stabex, together with the announcement of the willingness to renegotiate its character and provisions within the framework of the Integrated Programme for Commodities.[9]
- A pledge by all individual member states of the Community to reach the development assistance expenditure target of 0.7% of GNP before the end of the decade. (An increase, for example, in the development budget of the European Community from the present 0.05% to 0.1% of the joint GNP, without increasing total oda of the Ten, would have no meaning.)
- A European growth, industrial restructuring and employment plan for the rest of the decade, based on a general stimulation of the economy (together with the Keynesian injection in the world economy provided by the other programme elements), selective sectoral support, creating as well as redistributing employment, and reduction of trade barriers.[10]
- An announcement of the willingness to enter into international negotiations with a view to abolishing the protectionist elements of the present Common Agricultural Policy.[11]

This is a rough sketch of a programme which combines some quick, substantial improvements in the present practice of European development co-operation with political commitments for further improvements during the decade. It combines some unilateral action with steps conditional upon similar actions being taken by others, along with suggestions of European offers for negotiation. All of this is necessary in order to be ambitious and feasible, credible and effective.

Elsewhere I have recently argued for an initiative towards a world recovery and development programme and am of the opinion that, despite the disappointing European performance so far, such an initiative could come only from Europe.[12] European interests, both economic and political, in restructuring world economic relations with a view to stimulating development, are different from those of other Northern countries, both in the West and in the East. They are also greater. Europe is not one of the superpowers attempting to strengthen and increase its sphere of influence merely for political reasons. It is more dependent than many other countries in the Northern hemisphere on imports of raw materials, and on foreign markets, for its industrial products. Its economy is more diversified and has recently been less renewed than that of others. In short, Europe is a microcosm: because of its integrated character, anything which is happening elsewhere in the world will affect some part of it.

The present international economic crisis demands such an initiative and Europe is in a position to take it. Recent history has shown that many others may follow. It would be worthwhile, even if the United States were to opt out for a while. Europe has been somewhat hesitant to launch worldwide initiatives due to its special ties with Africa.

However, present options for Africa also challenge Europe to be bold, to their mutual interest and that of the rest of the world.

Notes

1   Economic Commission for Africa, 'Survey of Economic and Social Conditions in Africa 1980–1981', E/ECA/CM.8/17, p. 4.

2   World Bank, 'Accelerated Development in Sub-Saharan Africa: An Agenda for Action', Washington, 1981, p. 6.

3   Economic Commission for Africa: 'Accelerated Development in Sub-Saharan Africa: An Assessment by the OAU, ECA and ADB Secretariats', E/ECA/CM.8/16, para. 24.

4   *Ibid.* para. 137.

5   *Ibid.* see Chapter V.

6   Appendix to Report of ECA Conference of Ministers, E/ECA/CM.8/32; Tripoli, April 1982.

7   In his report to the United Nations Conference of the Least Developed Countries ('The Least Developed Countries in the 1980s', A/Conf.104/2 and Add. 1–3) the Secretary-General of the Conference estimated that the flow of real resources to these countries should be doubled by 1985 and trebled by 1990 in order to at least continue the historically rather low growth rates. The outcome of the Conference falls far short of this: the agreement reached in the Special New Programme of Action for the Least Developed Countries together with the announcements made by donor countries means an increase in real resources of no more than 30–60% in 1985. On the basis of aid commitments made since then, it is even uncertain whether there will be any increase in real resources.

8   See also Dragoslav Avramovic: 'The Developing Countries after Cancun: The Financial Problem and Related Issues', *Journal of World Trade Law,* Vol. 16, No. 1, January/February 1982.

9   See for some suggestions the UNCTAD study: 'Complementary Facility for Commodity-related Shortfalls in Export Earnings', TD/B/C.1/222, 1981.

10 See also J. Tinbergen, J. N. den Uyl, J. P. Pronk and W. Kok: 'A World Employment Plan', *Development and Peace,* Vol. 2, No. 1, Spring 1981, pp. 10–20.

11 See also Alexander J. Yeats: 'Agricultural Protectionism: An Analysis of its International Economic Effects and Options for Institutional Reform', *Trade and Development: An UNCTAD Review,* Winter 1981, pp. 1–30.

12 See J. P. Pronk: 'A European Initiative for a World Recovery and Development Programme', *NOVIB Report of the Symposium on the Development Policy of the European Community,* The Hague, 1982.

A French View

S. Hessel

The geographical focus of policy

There can be no doubt that the French government attaches greater importance than most of its partners in the Community to a renewed approach to development in Africa, the Caribbean and the Pacific (ACP). Our links with many of the countries of these areas are strong and mutually binding. It is not only trade or even language: it goes to the roots of French feelings of solidarity and responsibility.

We may well see advantages in creating stronger bonds of co-operation with Asia or Latin America and measures have been taken to give substance to such co-operation. But as far as we are concerned, the area of prime responsibility, not only for France but also for Western Europe, is Africa: the continent that found its new shape, politically and sociologically twenty-five years ago when it emerged on the international scene, broken up into some fifty independent states.

This period may have seemed long to those who worked strenuously to meet the day-to-day challenges of hunger, poverty, lack of trained manpower, political unrest and many others. But in terms of the shaping of a new society it is a very short period indeed. During this time we have witnessed a vast number of attempts at efficient co-operation: many failures, several significant successes. A network of inventions and interventions which it would take volumes to analyse and to evaluate, but where the critical observer detects side by side masses of good will and huge amounts of unfulfilled expectations.

In terms of economic security and growth, the African continent is today in a worse position than before. Much of what has been transferred in recent decades by way of equipment, training, technology and financial flows has been under-utilised, not to say wasted. The responsibility for this state of affairs must be shared: by the leaders of the new nations and their advisers who have had difficulty identifying from among the many short-term imperatives those decisions which would bear fruit in the longer term and promote the development of their people; by the donor countries and international organisations with their widely diversified and all too frequently reluctant or inadequate approaches to aid and to co-operation.

Characteristics of the Lomé relationship

Amidst so many attempts at establishing significant programmes, a number of which have led to disappointing results, the conventions linking the EEC and the ACP have a number of characteristics that single them out for special attention. It is, I believe, fair to say that they have enjoyed the full support of the French government and have foreshadowed in many ways the principles of the new development policy pursued by the Mauroy government.

What are these features as we find them shaping up in the Yaoundé agreements and gaining strength in the first and second Lomé Conventions? First, joint administration. The terms 'donor' and 'beneficiary' are discarded in favour of a concept of mutual interest and common definition of objectives and resources. How difficult it is to put such a true partnership into practice only those who have experienced the daily life of these programmes know. It requires not only tact and understanding on all sides, but the sharing of a vision that gives meaning to the various components of the relationship and firmness in carrying out its commitments.

Secondly, predictability. Breaking with the habit in donor/beneficiary relations of a project-by-project approach, the Lomé Convention provides a high degree of continuity in each of the fields it covers: programmes are negotiated over several years and trade commitments as well as other forms of transfers are pursued over a sufficiently long period not to create the shock of sudden withdrawals. Here again the degree of continuity achieved constitutes a great step forward when compared with other programmes. Developed nations and multilateral organisations are very reluctant to be committed over a period of several years even though developing countries naturally attach great importance to this aspect of the relationship. It is therefore the French view that more must be done in future to give the dimension of continuity and predictability to the EEC/ACP partnership. How this can best be achieved deserves careful consideration. In a time of crisis, when no nation is immune from sudden and unforeseen shocks to its economy, ways must be found to ensure a special status for mutual commitments to our closest partners in the field of development.

Another important feature of the Lomé Conventions is their wide coverage of development needs from project aid and technical assistance, through programme support and food aid, trade preferences and industrial co-operation, to the stabilisation of export earnings and the exploitation of mineral resources. In each of these fields instruments have been set up by the partners which have to be watched carefully and adapted to changing needs. Experience shows that flexible management is necessary to integrate their contributions into ACP strategy, given that many ACP states are still weak in the fields of public administration, and of economic and social planning.

Future emphasis

These are the areas on which France would wish to place special emphasis in the future, in order to prepare for further decades of mutually beneficial partnership. As the capacity of our African and other partners to ensure their self-sufficiency grows, as they set up their own democratic institutions and economic and social controls, the relationship with Europe should in no way decrease or deteriorate. On the contrary, it may become more meaningful, more reciprocal, more important, as a crucial element of the North–South balance.

The EEC/ACP conventions are significant in bringing together developed, developing and least developed countries and thus embracing the whole range of development concerns. Some ACP populations are still spread rather thinly across their eco-systems, but all face crucial problems as a result of their demographic growth rates. Foresight and regional co-operation are therefore indispensable to avoid the most dramatic effects of rapid degradation. France is particularly anxious to alleviate the plight of the least developed countries. Twenty-two out of the thirty-three listed by the United Nations are in the ACP region. We are all still groping to find a suitable answer to the question of how to help them overcome their handicaps. But one thing seems certain to the French leaders of today: private investment or trade liberalisation will not do the trick. It is essential first that we understand their attempts to combine tradition, based on a profound knowledge of the environment, and modernity, as sought by all men and women of our century. Only then can they consider us as standing by their side in their efforts, not as imposing our superior wisdom or directing them along paths in which we ourselves no longer have full confidence.

To conclude, I would argue that the most unsatisfactory feature of the relationship between the Community and its partners in the ACP is the lack of co-ordination between the Community programmes and the various aid programmes of its member states. Each European country still pursues what it considers its own national interests in its bilateral development co-operation. Each African country tends to deal separately with its European partners in order to play one against another. These attitudes are the legacy of years of mutual mistrust and imperial rivalries, decades of economic exploitation and domination of the periphery by the centre. They must be overcome.

We want the Community to be seen henceforth as a group of countries united in their approach to one of the most central problems of the end of this century: the problem of equitable development of the African continent. By putting together the efforts of all, bilateral and multilateral, over a sufficiently long period and in a sufficiently large but clearly defined geographical framework, the Ten would lead the way, probably the only available way, out of the present predicaments of the world economy and towards a more humane, less unbalanced and therefore less precarious world order.

A German Perspective

Michael Hofmann

The impasse in North–South relations persists at a time when urgent action for recovery in both developing and industrialised countries is needed. Unfortunately, the long recession has reinforced the unwillingness of countries to compromise in international fora just as it has weakened the spirit of compromise within countries. With unprecedented levels of unemployment, bankruptcies and indebtedness, both private and public, at home, industrialised countries seem unable to address North–South relations, which Willy Brandt described as 'the great social challenge of our time'. The United States obstructs IDA and the EEC member countries are reluctant to step in and to mobilise additional funds to meet Lomé II requirements.

The West German attitude is no exception to this rule since the economic success story of the post-war period is under strain. Protectionist measures and publicly guaranteed credit schemes are in high demand. There is growing scepticism about whether recovery is on the horizon, and sluggish growth has become a self-fulfilling prophecy. The means of structural adjustment – accelerated technological change irrespective of its repercussions on employment and the natural environment – create irritations; budget cuts in social security could threaten the consensus of West German society. German development policy is in the process of adjusting to these pressures. Although development philosophy was reformulated after the publication of the Brandt report, the concept of reflating Western economies via massive transfers to developing countries was never really accepted. Despite good intentions, development aid is stagnating (in real terms), considerations of tying aid to German deliveries are in the air, bilateralism is in vogue again, and surveys show declining popular support for development assistance. While development-minded parliamentarians and 'aid lobbies' do their best to prevent major setbacks, official policy is one of benign neglect for North–South issues.

Budget constraints are common to all EEC countries, and so governments have to have priorities. Their first priorities are the more pressing problems at home, the formidable task of integrating the semi-industrialised Southern European countries into the EEC and the need to accommodate the Mediterranean countries. These considerations may explain why enlightened concepts of worldwide 'redistribution with growth' are in jeopardy. Due to financial limitations the EEC's Development Commissioner, too, will find little scope to match the demands of the developing countries with the EEC member countries' preparedness to pay.

Meanwhile, as is commonly acknowledged, African states are among the hardest hit, with many of them, like the once hailed models of Tanzania and Kenya, being virtually on the brink of collapse. Economic crisis may be followed by political chaos and what Edgard Pisani has called the 'temptation of nihilism'. This could easily be exploited by the superpowers thus making more parts of Africa a battlefield for East–West competition. The gloomy outlook for this continent in the late 1980s should stimulate Europe above all to concentrate its development co-operation on Africa. Despite its financial constraints the EEC should recognise that there are mutual interests at stake and that its historic and moral obligations are especially pressing at a time of crisis. Furthermore, regardless of whether high growth rates can be regained in the industrialised countries – which may never happen during the 1980s – there are many reasons to predict that African states, as latecomers, will have fewer opportunities in the world economy and EEC markets than others:

– Apart perhaps from Nigeria, with its vast resource endowment and large internal market, none of the African countries belongs to the group of 15 to 20 'key countries' in the Third World with brighter development prospects or prime importance for European countries as trading partners entitling them to privileged treatment by major EEC members, private banks and investors.

– Commodity prices will presumably not revive to their former peaks because the present trough is not only the result of OECD countries' recession but also of profound technological innovations that reduce reliance on raw materials. The trend is towards delinking output growth from consumption of raw materials. Even a relaxation by the EEC of import restrictions on agricultural commodities would bring few gains to the ACP since the new EEC entrants and other Mediterranean countries will benefit first. Thus further specialisation on raw material exports, as recommended by the World Bank's sub-Saharan Africa Report, could be self-defeating for the Lomé partners. Stabex was a remarkable attempt to accommodate the EEC's need for secure supplies of raw materials and the ACP countries' need for secure demand, but it is only a partial solution. Despite the fact that it is still selective, not covering processed goods nor indexed against inflation, it is under heavy strain since groundnuts and coffee have by themselves absorbed almost all the available funds. Obviously Stabex and Minex are no substitute for comprehensive producer–consumer arrangements. It would therefore be preferable if UNCTAD's Common Fund and the IMF's Compensatory Financing Facility (which sets off Stabex payments against ACP countries' drawings) could fulfill this function. Otherwise the Stabex scheme may endanger the whole Lomé concept, given that there is no control over the use to which funds are put by the recipient state.

– The competitive situation in the EEC suggests that manufactured goods from the ACP will not find a promising export outlet in Western Europe. As we have already seen with textiles, latecomers will find considerable difficulty in penetrating EEC markets for sensitive products despite political declarations that protectionism should be rolled back. To enter the markets for more sophisticated products, where protectionism is less harsh, seems to be beyond the reach of most ACP countries, due to inadequate knowledge and skilled manpower. It will take considerable time to build up indigenous technological capabilities and human infrastructure in order to overcome these barriers.

There are two main lessons to be drawn. First, outward looking strategies will become even more risky than in the past and any attempt to orientate ACP development strategy towards EEC markets may lead to further frustrations. For too long vested interests have biased development paths towards exportable cash crops or minerals in order to import highly complex and energy-consuming goods. The positive effects of international trade on the general development of poor ACP countries has surely been overestimated. African states as well as other latecomers would do better if instead they concentrated on the promotion of the internal division of labour, regional interchange and selective South–South co-operation. Such a new approach is imperative in view of the substantial distortions that have resulted from over-ambitious or simply selfish policies. Big cities are subsidised by unfavourable terms of trade for farmers, and lame-duck industries are supported while agriculture is neglected. Industry-biased fiscal and exchange rate policies are further features of the malaise in most African countries, generally aggravated by rapid population growth. Integrated programmes for broad development of African countries have to focus on agriculture. History shows that successful development started with rural change as a pre-requisite for industrial development. The agreements reached so far between the EEC Commission and three African states, which support national food production programmes and restrict European agricultural exports to emergencies, can therefore only be welcomed. A joint declaration by all parties in the German Bundestag, similar resolutions by the European Parliament (see *Survey 2*) and the 1980 report by the European Court of Auditors all point in the same direction: substitute prestige projects for effective programmes to overcome hunger. Lomé III should follow up this approach by outlining in general terms the framework and commitments, while more precise plans can be included in the country programmes.

Secondly, fundamental changes in development strategies can only be expected if long-term concessional funds are provided. Domestic funds will be in short supply even if imports are reduced to essentials, both because of poor export prospects and above all because the current exploitation by the state of the agricultural sector will be halted. There is a growing awareness that the short-term adjustment programmes of the IMF are neither politically feasible nor theoretically appropriate for the poorest countries. Commercial finance is not available in view of these countries' poor risk rating, and would only increase the danger that more countries fall into the debt trap.

Proposed additional funds for Africa by the World Bank hang on the uncertain replenishment of IDA. In any case European countries should be willing to ensure that projects and programmes that have already been prepared can be implemented. Since numerous bilateral donors, such as West Germany and the Arab Funds, perceive Africa as a regional priority of their development assistance, there should be scope for EEC co-financing with sliding scales of conditionality. Moreover, the EEC could play the role of co-ordinator of suitable programmes. There is also a need for more appropriate instruments for project identification, improved absorptive capacity and evaluation to raise the standard of the EEC's aid. Encouragement should be given to regional programmes where finance is provided for overall plans.

The institutionalised political dialogue provided by the Lomé arrangement and by the EEC delegations on the spot provide a unique opportunity to discuss development strategies. They also give the EEC the opportunity to back reform-orientated elites in order to avoid the danger that projects may be undermined by an unhealthy political or economic environment. This dialogue cannot be a one-way affair, and should include on the agenda unfavourable developments in the EEC, especially those related to the EEC enlargement. Furthermore, the success of inward-looking strategies in ACP countries requires self-restraint by EEC exporters and TNCs so that they do not flood the ACP markets. In this respect the Lomé concept of non-reciprocity is a major asset for the ACP. The overriding goal must be to reach a level of partnership that breaks away from neo-colonial strings.

The centrepiece of the EEC Development Commissioner's difficult task should be an attempt to consolidate the EEC's traditional relations with the ACP on a long-term basis and to focus on the poorest

African states. This does not preclude assistance to other parts of the Third World with similar problems. It is often suggested that the divergent development concepts and procedures of the EEC member countries should be harmonised or that a European Bank for Development should be established. These are desirable goals, but seem unrealistic unless the EEC can achieve fuller integration in other fields. In our period of uncertainty, progress in that direction depends more upon member countries' willingness to compromise than on the abilities of the EEC Commission or pressure from the European Parliament.

The View From Denmark

Knud Erik Svendsen

The debate over Danish attitudes to the EEC's role in international development co-operation is likely to be particularly intense during the final months of 1982 and in 1983. The impetus will come from a report of a committee set up by the Danish government in December 1980 to review the principles of Denmark's assistance to the developing countries. The report of this committee was published in September 1982 covering all aspects of Danish development co-operation, including its contributions to international and regional organisations like the EEC.

Hopefully this report will herald a new phase in the debate over Danish participation in EEC development assistance. So far the debate has been heavily influenced by the split in Danish society over whether to join the EEC and, later on, whether to remain a member. This has often meant that general or detailed criticism of the EEC's co-operation with developing countries has been assumed to reflect general opposition to Denmark's membership of the EEC. The reverse has operated for any defence of the EEC's development work.

The EEC as a multilateral agency

These hangovers may not disappear easily, since they are underpinned by the continuing opposition to Danish membership of the EEC of a section of opinion. Nevertheless, they may have less impact on the public debate on development assistance in the future not only because of the aid report, but also because the debate can increasingly be related to the EEC's actual performance in providing development assistance over the years since Danish entry.

A large part of Danish official development assistance (oda) – between 45% and 50% – has over the years been channelled through international organisations. The contributions to the EEC have been entered under this multilateral heading, even though the EEC is a regional organisation of industrialised countries and not an international association like the UN, the World Bank, etc. The increase in Danish contributions to the EEC has primarily been at the expense of payments to the United Nations Development Programme (UNDP). As may be seen from Table 12.1, Danish payments to the UNDP have fallen from 39.8% of the total Danish contributions to multilateral organisations in 1970/71 to 27.4% in 1981. Contributions to the EEC development assistance, including the EDF, have gone up from nil to 18.7% in 1981. As support to the UN has been one of the cornerstones of Danish foreign policy and, therefore, of its development policy, this reduction of payments to the UNDP has attracted a lot of attention in recent years.

Table 12.1 *The contribution of Denmark to multilateral organisations in the fiscal years 1970/71 and 1981 (%)*

	1970/71	1980
UNDP	39.8	27.4
Other international organisations	8.4	13.9
Multi-bi projects and courses	8.1	5.9
Multilateral humanitarian assistance	4.3	8.1
IDA	16.7	12.1
IBRD	1.9	1.3
Regional development funds	—	2.0
Regional development banks	1.0	0.6
EEC's development assistance, incl. EDF	—	18.7
World Food Programme	19.9	10.0
Total per cent	100.0	100.0
Danish krone million	188.5	1198.1

Another factor influencing opinion is the fairly general view in Denmark that (as expressed in the review report) 'the quality of the project assistance of the EEC cannot be said to differ from the assistance from most other aid organisations. However, this assistance is rather expensive, as the projects in many cases apply advanced technologies and employ experts, who are considerably more expensive than Danish bilateral experts, and even UN experts.'

Views of the Danish development review committee

The government committee was divided in its conclusions on future Danish contributions to the EEC. A majority felt that a further increase in the EEC's share of Danish assistance should be avoided, and that Denmark should argue against a further strengthening of the EEC's development assistance – in order to ensure that such an increase does not undermine the other parts of the international system of assistance. As a consequence it recommends that Denmark should work in the forthcoming negotiations on the renewal of the Lomé Convention for a real reduction in EEC assistance to the ACP countries and for a curtailment of EEC assistance to the non-associated countries.

A minority of the committee held the opposite view and advocated the inclusion of more developing countries under the ACP umbrella and a strengthening of the special mechanisms under the Lomé Convention (e.g. Stabex). This minority also recommended an increase in EEC assistance to non-associated countries in order to reach a more reasonable balance between these countries and the ACP states. Otherwise the committee agreed that Denmark should support a policy of channelling aid to non-associated countries through regional development banks and funds in order to strengthen these organisations and to avoid further duplication of aid organisations. It also agreed that in respect of all multilateral assistance, not just the EEC, the Danish aid organisation Danida should have greater opportunities to study and monitor the implementation of aid.

It is not clear whether the majority or the minority view will prevail. The outcome may depend on the position of the new Danish government formed in September 1982, which is expected to be more positive towards the EEC than was the outgoing Social Democratic government. The Danish Federation of Industries has also over the years advocated stronger support for the EEC development programme. Indeed, at one stage it recommended that Denmark should pull out of UNDP. This attitude was influenced partly by the easier access of Danish business to EEC organisations and committees, for example the Centre for Industrial Development, and partly by expectations of larger contracts from the EEC than from the UNDP. On this last score, it is true that the EEC aid programme returns more orders to Danish industry than does the UNDP, mainly because of the different nature of the two programmes, but it is also true that the World Bank has the best record in this respect.

All members of the Danish government committee were united in the view that 'the question of Danish supplies under the multilateral programmes should not enter into a consideration of the magnitude of the Danish contribution to the various organisations'. Instead the guiding principle in this matter should be the degree of correspondence between the various programmes and the Danish aid objectives. It is obvious, however, that given the financial difficulties of both UNDP and IDA, due to the policy of the Reagan Administration, the Danish contribution to the EEC development programme may come under pressure. Indeed, it has been strongly argued that aid funds through the EEC are not additional, i.e. that they do not increase total aid. This is true for Denmark and probably for all EEC member countries, after the recent changes in Italy's aid programme.

The experience of EEC aid

It can hardly be said that the EEC aid programme has produced any innovations in the international aid process. There are even doubts about the comparative efficiency of the EEC programme during its short existence. This could change, of course, if greater efforts were made to monitor and evaluate EEC aid projects etc., but this would require a substantial expansion of these activities inside the EEC. In these respects, the EEC is far behind most other major aid programmes. Stabex is undoubtedly an innovation, and it is going to be a difficult choice between strengthening it, which would require substantial increases in funding, and efforts to promote a fully international stabilisation programme under the UN.

On the question of the EEC's food aid, the Danish committee was not divided. It recommended that Denmark should support a reduction of this programme, in favour of a further strengthening of the World Food Programme. The committee also recommended that an increasing share of EEC food aid should be channelled through the WFP, and that EEC food aid should be based on multi-year commitments.

The work of the Danish aid review committee is expected to lead to changes in the legislation on development co-operation. Decisions of detail, like the contributions to various international organisations, views on the future Lomé Convention, etc., are not a part of this legislation, but are taken by the government after certain public consultations. Whatever the general outcome of this, it can be expected that the work of the EEC in the aid field will be studied with greater care in Denmark in the coming years. All seem to agree on two rather obvious points: that further adaptation to the needs of the recipient country is desirable, (e.g. through an increase in programme rather than project aid), and that the efficiency with which EEC aid is implemented should be improved – whatever the size of the EEC programme in the future.

An ACP Approach

B. Persaud

Negotiations for Lomé III will begin in September 1983 and preparatory work has already been started. In the case of the EEC this work is
already well advanced, largely due to the comprehensive review and
reconsideration of its development policy initiated by Edgard Pisani,
the new Development Commissioner (see Chapter 13). Thus, proposals by the Commission for a revised development policy, which would
provide the framework within which specific EEC ideas for Lomé III
could be formulated, have already taken shape. This reconsideration
of its development policy by the EEC is to be welcomed. To date, EEC
policy has not achieved any notable relative success in contributing to
economic development, whether viewed in relation to bilateral relations between the EEC and the Third World or in relation to its
contribution to progress in the North–South dialogue. The development contribution of the Lomé Convention has been poor. A major
test of the Convention is the effect of the trade preferences and other
trade and production support policies on the export performance of
the ACP in the EEC market and this shows a worse performance
compared to other groups of Third World countries (see Chapter 10).
Also, no ACP country has emerged as a newly industrialising country,
or is on the verge of doing so, and the growth rate of sub-Saharan
Africa, which comprises the bulk of the population of the ACP, has
been lower than other parts of the Third World in recent years.

The opportunities and constraints in negotiating Lomé III

The EEC's reconsideration of its development strategy is a departure
from the policies of consolidation and conservatism adopted during
the negotiations to establish Lomé II. It provides an opportunity for
innovations not only by the EEC but also by the ACP. But if this
opportunity is not to be missed, the ACP must start their basic
rethinking now. The EEC is already setting the pace and the danger
exists of a repeat of the situation in the Lomé II negotiations, where the
ACP largely played a reactive role to the EEC's proposals, even
though these were minimal and largely reflected the EEC's own
interests. The ACP should, however, be under no illusion that a new

development policy would provide it with much greater economic opportunities. The new policy is taking shape at a most unpropitious time for the emergence of bold and imaginative proposals. Ideas of large-scale resource transfers to assist economic development and world recovery, which had influential advocates in the Commission itself, have not emerged with any prominence. And in the major areas, notably concessional resource flows and market access, the current mood is not conducive to liberal approaches.

In trade policy, Europe has become more protectionist in relation to the Third World. The ACP have not escaped from this and the threat of safeguard action from the EEC has been used to encourage a 'voluntary' export restraint arrangement with one large primary exporting ldc which had begun to diversify into a first stage export manufacturing product, clothing. Superficially, access appears largely free but restrictive origin rules, the use of quantitative restraints against some products and, more potently, the threat of safeguard action against products in which ACP countries have a strong potential export interest, remain great impediments. In resource transfers, the Commission is advocating a doubling of aid channelled through the Community; but the prospects for such an increase do not appear bright. Attitudes to overall levels of aid by individual EEC countries and a renewed preference in recent years for bilateral provision on the part of major donors are obstacles which may prevent the Commission realising its objective. It was probably in recognition of this difficulty that the Commission's proposal has been couched in modest terms; it talks of a target, but one without a time-scale.

In the light of these considerations, the new policy is likely to be concerned more with a change in priorities and emphasis, than with providing more liberal measures. The aim would be to increase impact but through increased efficiency rather than by doing more. There is a great danger that the revised development policy in relation to the Lomé Conventions will be long on rhetoric and short on specifics. ACP countries must be realistic about the possibilities, otherwise they will be swayed by the rhetoric and expect too much. They may also find themselves unwittingly contributing to the continuation of the myths and extravagant claims that have become associated with the Convention.

A strategy for the ACP

One positive aspect of the situation is that the actual negotiations will not take place for some time yet and by that time world economic recovery may well be on the way. Significant changes may therefore be possible especially in the light of a more open attitude to change on the part of the EEC. The ACP must exploit this attitude and must adopt as its strategy the exposure of the extravagant claims being made for the Convention by the EEC. In relation to the contribution of the major co-operation arrangements in the Convention – increased utilisable market access, additionality in resource transfers and the levels of resources being provided through Stabex and Sysmin – the extent of the benefits provided is much more modest than is claimed by the EEC. The Convention is strong on institutional arrangements for co-operation, and is much more advanced in this area than other North–South co-operation arrangements. But in substantive terms the use made of these institutional structures remains limited.

A strong case against the Lomé Convention is that for the Third World generally, it could be divisive. It could inhibit progress towards favourable arrangements for Third World countries based on development needs rather than on geographical and historical considerations. Its continuation could encourage similar arrangements by other developed countries which could lead to a world in which special regional preferential economic arrangements again abound. The recent tendency towards a decline in multilateralism in economic arrangements and an increase in bilateralism is conducive to this possibility. These considerations do not rule out justification for the Convention. In this connection its origin in, firstly, the need to prevent an abrupt break in production structures built up by historical preferential arrangements, secondly the possibility of using such close historical connections to pioneer an advanced form of economic co-operation arrangement, and thirdly the large involvement of countries with special development needs in its membership, is still relevant. But justification does not depend on these considerations alone. The particular instruments and forms of co-operation are also pertinent. This raises the important question of whether the Convention as it is evolving, will continue to justify its existence. This question should be borne very much in mind by the parties involved in their approach to Lomé III. It requires an evolution which seeks to develop the positive aspects and to reduce in significance those unjustified discriminatory aspects which are divisive and unhelpful to economic development and the liberalisation of development policies when viewed from the standpoint of the Third World as a whole.

The evolution of the Lomé Convention along these lines points to some special requirements. Most ACP countries have been severely affected by world recession. The situation today in sub-Saharan Africa points to the urgent need for increased aid and other resource transfers. While on grounds of burden-sharing the EEC alone could not be expected to provide substantial alleviation, the fact that most of these countries belong to the Lomé Convention entails a special responsibility on its part to provide increased assistance, and, equally important, to galvanise support from the wider international community. While it is true that the EEC countries have generally been positive in their support for IDA in its current problems, this support has not reached the extent justified by the Lomé connection and the responsibilities emanating from it. This is partly the fault of the ACP which have not sought to use the diplomatic potential of the Convention for assistance in wider North–South matters, even those in which ACP countries have a special interest. More directly, the current depressed economic conditions of most ACP countries mean that the Lomé III negotiators must press for greatly increased resource transfers. In current circumstances there is even a case for accelerating disbursements under Lomé II and to facilitate this by a supplementary provision. Increased provision of financial resources would necessitate a larger allocation under Stabex. A great advantage of Stabex is that, in the context of the whole aid programme under Lomé, it allows some adjustment of flows in relation to needs. It should be adapted, however, to meet more closely changes in needs arising from fluctuating export earnings. In this connection the discrimination against mineral exporters, which Sysmin is extremely inadequate to prevent, must be removed. It is not beyond the ingenuity of the Commission or the ACP to devise ways in which any support provided for minerals takes into account the involvement of transnational corporations in their production.

There is also a need to redirect EEC aid. Increasing the relevance of Lomé III to the development needs of the ACP would require much greater attention to food security and food production. In food aid the EEC has a ready means of assistance which does not impose a heavy burden, but it must ensure that distribution methods are used which avoid disincentive effects on local food production. More positively, food aid could be used directly to increase food production. There are indications that the EEC will be giving increased emphasis to small-scale projects in agriculture and small-scale farming. This emphasis is along the right lines, but it should not be carried too far since large-scale agricultural projects, e.g. river basin development, are not incompatible with the encouragement of small and medium sized farms. The large-scale river basin projects, although costly in capital, have the advantage of making large amounts of irrigated acreage available quickly, and for some African countries there is a premium on the availability of irrigated agricultural land.

Much greater attention should be given in Lomé III to encouraging commercial flows in the form of both loans and direct investment. ACP countries are now more amenable to accepting foreign direct investment and the avoidance in such investment of early painful reverse flows is very pertinent to development needs at this time. Serious consideration should be given to the need for a European investment guarantee arrangement and, in relation to both commercial lending and direct investment, the EIB should be given a substantial role. The rich mineral resources and potential of sub-Saharan Africa need to attract greater investment and this could be assisted by official involvement which would allow greater attention to the interests of recipient countries and which could be geared to assisting the establishment of joint ventures. It is unfortunate that at this time of great need, the resource endowment of ACP countries is not being used to attract financial flows. New mechanisms may be needed to enable long-term supply guarantees to be used as collateral for such investment.

The ACP must continue to pursue means of improving consultative procedures in relation to aid and of securing some participation in its administration. An area which offers scope for significant progress is a joint arrangement for the provision of technical assistance, in which ACP countries, by providing some financial contribution, would share in its management. This would facilitate greater use of technical assistance personnel from the ACP countries themselves.

In trade co-operation, the incorporation of safeguard provisions for use against ACP countries is an embarrassment to the Convention considering its trade and development objectives and the current minimal levels of import penetration from the ACP. The provisions offend the spirit of the Convention and should be removed. This could be facilitated by the adoption of positive adjustment assistance measures. There are indications that in order to avoid pressure from import penetration, EEC development policy is being orientated towards ldc industries which do not compete with EEC industries. Such an orientation would serve economic development badly and raise questions about the genuineness of the EEC's development intentions.

Conclusions

The institutional arrangements for a substantial and worthwhile economic co-operation arrangement between the EEC and ACP have been established but so far they have been supporting mechanisms which are severely limited in substantive terms. This does not do justice to the partnership concept of the Convention, its objectives, the claims made for it and its effectiveness in promoting the long-term interests of both the EEC and the ACP. The charge that the Convention is divisive will become increasingly significant unless more liberal arrangements are incorporated which do not stand in the way of wider co-operation between the EEC and the Third World. The ACP must adopt a strategy of exposing the Convention's defects in relation to its basic concept, objectives and the claims made for it by the EEC. The Convention offers scope for improvement in several areas. The amenability of the EEC to change and the prospect for world recovery at the time of the Lomé III negotiations indicate opportunities which must not be missed. The Convention could become a model for development co-operation between developed and developing countries. It is however a long way from realising this potential.

Avenues for Correcting the Imbalance

S. S. Saxena

The EEC's development policy has itself been developing over the past two decades, not according to some predetermined design but in response to changing circumstances and the collective empiricism of its population. It is now a complicated structure of many components. The Lomé Convention is only one of these, but it appears to have found a place much closer to the hearts of decision-makers than have the other components. This essay addresses itself to the implicit imbalance that has been produced by the halting evolution of the EEC's development policy.

Lomé versus NIEO

The obvious starting point for analysis leading to a prescription for the direction of EEC development policy after Lomé II is an understanding of the scenario leading to Lomé I itself. This Convention was eulogised[1] as 'a historical event', 'a gleam of commonsense in this world', 'a new model', and 'the beginning of new economic relations between industrial and non-industrial countries'. Even some critics have accepted that it goes a fair distance towards establishing a new international economic order (NIEO), since it addresses many of the complaints and contradictions in the old economic order. A salient feature of Lomé is its mobilisation of a panoply of instruments and their programmed application in the ACP countries according to the particular requirements and development priorities of those countries. Prominent among these instruments are the preferential arrangements for ACP access to the Community's market, the European Development Fund's budget for the life of the Conventions the scheme for the stabilisation of export earnings (Stabex) the loan capacity of the

European Investment Bank and industrial co-operation. In addition there are the provisions for food aid, emergency aid, and trade promotion applicable to both ACP and other developing countries.

Yet claims that Lomé is a genuine attempt to reduce the gap between North and South, weighted to the advantage of the weaker, do not cut much ice. If the principles expressed in the Declaration on the NIEO adopted by the UN General Assembly in 1974, are compared and contrasted with the professed and achieved objectives of the Lomé Convention, the picture that emerges is not very complimentary.[3] One assessment is that:

'It protects European markets and materials . . . for the minimal cost of Stabex and the European Development Fund. Its divisive impact retards progress towards Third World cohesion and self-reliance; it provides privileges for some, but not all . . . Lomé reinforces rather than transcends North–South divisions . . . Lomé and NIEO are not only incompatible but in opposition . . .'[4]

Beyond Lomé – avenues for action

It is undoubtedly true that a few innovative concepts and instrumentalities have been built into the Lomé Convention, but the latter ought not to be an end in itself and it is imperative that these concepts be extended to other regions too, especially the populous and most seriously affected (MSA) non-ACP countries. Although about half the number of Third World states are members of the Lomé Convention, it is much less significant in terms of population, covering only 15% of the people of the developing world, even excluding China. Quite clearly some EEC member states have a strong interest in developing closer economic relations with non-ACP countries. The European Community has unilaterally acknowledged its dependence on the developing countries for its economic advancement.[5] Deriving nearly 40% of its income from trade, the Community needs dependable sources of energy and raw materials, and also outlets for its manufactured products. Clearly therefore, it was self-interest rather than charity or *naïveté* which produced the innovative aspects of the Lomé Convention. One comment shortly after Lomé I was negotiated was: 'In short, it would appear that whatever one can say about the organisation, negotiating skills, persistence and compromise that allowed the Lomé Convention to be concluded, a much more fundamental matter underlay the proceedings – namely, the growing recognition that it pays to cultivate the attitude and institutions consistent with the growing reality of genuine economic interdependence on this globe.'

Several Third World countries, including the non-ACP states of South Asia (and especially India), welcomed the Lomé Convention on the grounds that it blazed a new trail in the evolving relationship between the developed and the developing world, and regarded it as a beginning of similar arrangements with other regions. It has been hoped that the trading advantages extended to ACP countries would be globalised to include other developing countries which also have a close relationship with EEC. While calling for the *globalisation* of the initiative, one does not necessarily visualise massive investment flows from the EEC to a non-ACP country such as India. Nor does one visualise massive technical assistance. These are specific to the context of the stage of development of the ACP countries. However, one does visualise the universalisation of the EEC's initiative in adopting a restrictionless trade regime. Indeed such globalisation will also protect non-ACP groups from the eventual discrimination that non-ACP exports to EEC will face from the competitive exports of ACP countries. In this connection, it can be recalled that the Commonwealth Heads of Governments' meeting at Kingston (29 April–6 May, 1975) while welcoming the Lomé Convention 'expressed the hope that the principles underlined in the Lomé Convention could usefully contribute to the further development of relations between the EEC and other industrialised countries, on the one hand, and developing countries including the Asian and other Commonwealth countries on the other'. It could be hoped that the coming year when the EEC will be preparing for Lomé III, will be most propitious for introducing this dimension to the Community's policy for giving easier access to imports from the developing countries.

There is yet another aspect of the Lomé Convention where the adoption of a more open approach would further strengthen international co-operation. The provisions of Lomé dealing with industrial, technical and financial co-operation constitute an important and forward looking feature. The major areas in which Lomé resources have been allocated in the ACP states are industrialisation and rural development, transport and communications, education, public health, housing and, finally, trade promotion activities. It is felt here that the experience which the non-ACP developing countries like India have gained in the development process would be relevant and could be made available for the benefit of other developing countries. For example, several Indian institutions and organisations have considerable experience and indeed have shared such experience with other developing countries through technical and economic co-operation. It could be hoped that in the preparations for renegotiations the Community institutions and the member states would take active account of this experience by making suitable provisions to make it possible for firms and organisations of other developing countries to participate in the various projects to be undertaken in the ACP. Such a move would not only give both ACP and non-ACP countries a more abiding interest in their respective relations with the EEC, but would also reinforce co-operation efforts within the developing world.

Prescriptions for a more global policy

In keeping with the empiricism and the evolved nature of the EEC's development policy, misgivings are bound to be aired about its somewhat *ad hoc* nature and lack of a global perspective.[7] In other words development policy cannot really be construed as fully developed as yet. The Community itself has decided that the principle on which its development policy is based should be 'to each according to his needs'.[8] Moreover it has prescribed four specific guidelines:[9]
(a) development co-operation should be taken into consideration in the common policies;
(b) national policies and action should be progressively co-ordinated;
(c) what the Community has already achieved in the sphere of development co-operation should be carried further;
(d) additional possibilities for financial and technical co-operation should be made available to the Community.

The acceptance in 1975 of Lomé I by all those Commonwealth countries eligible under Protocol 22 of the Treaty of Accession and its subsequent extension to other similar countries was a considerable achievement. But the Lomé pattern is not the only one for the Community and therefore innovations afresh would be quite in order. The programme for non-associates began in 1976 under stimulus from the European Parliament and the British Government, but is still very small. According to a report, the ACP countries received concessional aid worth £273.2 million in 1979; this contrasts with only £25 million disbursed to the non-associates in 1980, when just one of these non-associates, India, has twice the combined population of all ACP countries! The following suggestions, some of which have been supported by the UK House of Lords, would appear to merit attention:[10]
(a) The overall shape of the Community's aid programme should be substantially modified over time. Its selective nature, moulded by past historical circumstances, calls for conversion into a world-wide programme responding to the development needs of the Third World in the mid-1980s, matching the EEC's status in the world.
(b) European Development Fund aid to the ACP countries will remain unchanged until 1985. Any additional resources should not necessarily be used to increase the size of the EDF since this would imply pumping more aid to the relatively favoured group at the expense of EEC aid programmes in Asia and Latin America.
(c) Since the Mediterranean developing countries do not rank among the MSAs, the Maghreb and Mashreq need not be the beneficiaries of

any increase in Community aid. Instead more emphasis could be placed on loan finance, including EIB loans, for development in the Mediterranean region.

(d) The EEC's food aid programme is reported to be suffering from inefficiencies in planning, administration and delivery. However, the suitability for developing countries of some of the programmes (notably dairy foods) is questionable. There is a need for more streamlined planning and execution.

(e) Financial aid to non-associate developing countries in Asia and Latin America merits expansion. Savings on reduced dairy food aid could possibly be transferred to the non-associate programme.

(f) The EEC should consider increasing efforts within its existing aid programmes to work with OPEC countries to recycle surpluses to developing countries through co-financing and by attracting extra loan finance for developing countries.

(g) A system could be established to enable non-associate countries to use EEC aid to raise and service loans from other sources for development projects, thereby increasing the total amount of resources available to them.

It is interesting to read, in the 1981 Annual Report of the EEC the phrase 'To *balance* its relations with the ACP countries and the Mediterranean . . .' under the sub-heading 'Financial and technical co-operation with non-associated developing countries'.[11] The point, therefore, is to ask why progress towards this goal should proceed by such fits and starts, smacking of *adhocery*. The question is even more germane given the very apparent economic complementarity between the EEC and the Third World. Roy Jenkins remarked, during an address to the European Parliament (14 February 1978): 'We need a just international division of labour and resources because there is a close interdependence between the prosperity of the economies of the industrialised world and the rest. We need to ask ourselves how our economic relations should be adapted to growing industrial development in third countries at a time when the problems of inflation and unemployment in the industrialised nations hamper our ability to stimulate renewed growth. The impulse of the Third World has, in my view, a major part to play in improving the position.' In short, therefore, the time has come for the EEC to get cracking on carving out meticulously and substantially a kind of 'Doctrine' on development policy for the non-ACP Third World.

Sir Christopher Soames at Brussels once pointed out that while the EEC's members include former colonial powers, as a new collective entity it has no colonial past. One would wish to see this spirit implemented at least in the current decade to remove the negative features, that still remain to be remedied.[12] The suggestion here of spelling out a 'Doctrine' is a positive one, and not in the least in conflict or disharmony with any likely improvement in Lomé III. After all, both parties in the Lomé relationship tend to perceive it as a positive-sum game, normally conducted in a co-operative spirit, although conflict naturally occurs.[13]

In conclusion, one could do not better than repeat a recent remark of Sonny Ramphal:

'Lomé's strength was that it was not an act of charity; there was much in it for the EEC. Its weakness was that it was a bundle of promises; and not all have been fulfilled. But even while it disappointed in performance its potential lay revealed. The Convention has now provided 7 years of operational experience on which Europe and the ACP can build in terms of more effective co-operation under the Convention. Such improvement in itself would be a contribution to North–South Co-operation, a point that deserves attention as pre-paratory work starts on Lomé III.'[14]

Notes

1 Vide Hajo Hasenpflug, 'The Stabilisation of Export Earnings in the Lomé Convention: A Model Case?' in *The New International Economic Order* (eds) Karl P. Sauvant and Hajo Hasenpflug (Wilton House Publications, London) 1977, pp. 165–174.

2 Johan Galtung, 'The Lomé Convention and Neo-Capitalism', Paper No. 20, (1976) University of Oslo, pp. 1–16.

3 'The Lomé Convention: a Case Study' Paper 12 – *A third perspective Dominance and dependence,* The Open University, Milton Keynes (1981), pp. 4–42 esp. 39–40.

4 T. M. Shaw, 'EEC–ACP interactions and images as redefinitions of Eur Africa: exemplary, exclusive and/or exploitative?' *Journal of Common Market Studies,* Vol. XVIII, No. 2, (December 1979).

5 See e.g. 'The European Community' by Geoffrey Denton and Theo Peeters in *Economic Policies of Industrial States* (ed) Wilfried L. Kohl, (Lexington 1977), pp. 189–213 and Wolfgang Hager and Michael Noelke, *Community – Third World: The Challenge of Interdependence',* (documentation bulletin, Brussels, 1980), pp. 147–148.

6 Isebill Y. Gruhn, 'The Lomé Convention: inching towards interdependence', *International Organisation* 30 (no. 2), 1976, p. 259.

7 S. S. Saxena, 'The EEC, GSP, and the Third World' in K. B. Lall and H. S. Chopra (eds), *The EEC and the Third World,* Radiant, New Delhi, 1981, pp. 137–161.

8 Vide document 'Development Aid: Frescoe of Community Action Tomorrow' in *Bulletin of the European Communities,* Supplement 8/74 (Communication of the Commission transmitted to the Council on 5 November 1974), p. 4. The main guideline set therein reads: To each according to his needs, by bringing all our means to bear.

9 *Memorandum on a Community Policy on Development Co-operation: Synoptic and programme for initial actions* (Communications of the

Commission to the Council of 27 July 1971 and 2 February 1972), pp. 30–31.

10   Twenty-first Report from the House of Lords: Select Committee on the European Communities, Session 1980–81 Development Aid Policy Observations by the Government (Presented to Parliament by the Minister for Overseas Development, August 1981) Cmnd 8326; and also BIS B 309 (British High Commission in India, New Delhi) 'British White Paper on parliamentary report – Need for Global European Community Aid Policy by Robin Gordon Walker (7 August 1981).

11   Fifteenth General Report on the activities of the European Communities in 1981, Commission of the European Communities, Brussels-Luxembourg (1982), p. 243.

12   See S. S. Saxena, 'The EEC, GSP and the Third World' *ibid.* pp. 141–142, for further elaboration of these negative features.

13   John Ravenhill, 'Asymmetrical Interdependence: renegotiating the Lomé Convention', *International Journal,* Vol. XXV, No. 1, Winter 1979–80.

14   Commonwealth Secretary-General Shridath S. Ramphal opening Address at the Conference on 'Europe and the South in the 1980s: Prospects for Political Change' (Brighton, 16 June 1982) at the Institute for Development Studies, University of Sussex. Commonwealth Secretariat, London.

13

New Directions Under Commissioner Pisani

Christopher Stevens

During 1982 the style and direction of the EEC's new Commissioner for development, Edgard Pisani, became clear. He took office in Spring 1981 following the departure for the French foreign ministry of Claude Cheysson who was the principal architect of the Lomé Conventions, the main foundation for the EEC's claim that it is building a new relationship between North and South. The first indication of Pisani's approach to his new portfolio, and how it might differ from his predecessor, came within a few months of the changeover, when the Commission sent proposals to the Council of Ministers for a 'Plan of Action to Combat World Hunger'.[1] During 1982 the ideas outlined in this proposal were fleshed out as the Commission and a small group of ACP states discussed joint support for food sector strategies. By Spring 1982, the new Commissioner was ready to unveil a major restructuring of his department, the directorate-general for development (DG 8), which was put into effect in mid-September 1982. A few days later, on 29 September, the Commission adopted a major statement of development strategy which was presented to the European Parliament on the same day, and to Coreper on the following day; it was well-received by both bodies.

If 1982 has been the Year of Reflection which Pisani called for, 1983 will be the Year of Action as these new ideas are thrown into the renegotiation of the Lomé Convention. For Commissioner Pisani is not the president of an aid agency, still less a minister of development co-operation in a cabinet held together by party loyalty. As explained in *Survey 2* (Chapter 1) the Commissioner has a much broader mandate and can initiate proposals on a much wider front than can most ministers of development or aid agency chiefs.[2] But his power to implement these proposals is constrained by a system of checks and balances in which the checks predominate and are centred on the Council of Ministers. The proposals in the strategy paper of September

1982 must be transformed into a negotiating mandate for the successor to Lomé II by mid-1983 since negotiations between the EEC and ACP are scheduled to commence in September. When forming a mandate, the Commission proposes but the Council of Ministers disposes. Nonetheless, it is clearly vital to understand Commissioner Pisani's preferred strategy even if his ability to implement it will remain unclear until mid-1983 at the earliest. For this reason, excerpts from the strategy paper adopted in September 1982 are reproduced in the Documentary Appendix. The remainder of this chapter outlines the main ideas and the steps (in terms of policy and organisation) that have so far been taken to put them into effect.

Starting from first principles, the paper seeks to identify the distinctive elements in a Community-level development policy and in the process reveals attitudes that recur in relation to specific policies. The Community's Third World links, it asserts, are unlike either those of a multilateral agency or those of the member states. Unlike multilateral institutions, it is perfectly legitimate for the Community to pursue self-interested objectives, and to have geographical preferences. But its development co-operation is not an eleventh policy superimposed on the ten of the member states. 'It is the expression, not multilateral but collective, of a Community which has neither the attributes nor the ambitions of a state but which nevertheless has great capabilities'. It is therefore both an actor in its own right and 'a natural forum for concerting and coordinating' member state actions. This theme of harmonising the bilateral policies of the member states recurs throughout the paper, and clearly has some support outside as well as inside the Berlaymont. Stephane Hessel argues a similar viewpoint in the Forum (Chapter 12), although Michael Hofmann underlines the practical difficulties of harmonisation and Svendsen points to the wide differences between members in the priority accorded to the Community's development policy.

If the EEC's policies towards the Third World are to be made more consistent, in which direction should they point? The answer provided by the strategy paper is: to develop a set of concentric zones, with Africa at the centre, that tailor commercial and financial provisions to the needs of different Third World country groupings and the capabilities of the EEC; to find a golden mean in administering aid between the 'rigid conditionality imposed by financing bodies and the irresponsibility of non-conditionality'; and to emphasise predictability in trade relations on the grounds that this is more important 'than any limited progress which might be made towards liberalising trade'.

The focus on Africa clearly finds support in France and Germany, the two states that play the key role in determining Community development policy. It is significant that both Hessel and Hofmann emphasise this focus, because of 'solidarity and responsibility' for the former, and to compensate for Africa's inability to benefit from market forces, for the latter. Between them, these two essays sum up the consensus favouring Africa: some members (France, Belgium, Italy) have a clear political preference for Africa as Europe's sphere of involvement, while those with broader geographical horizons are either ineffectual (most notably the UK), or (as in the case of Germany) are happy to see the private sector in the role of flag bearer in other parts of the Third World. There is some evidence that during its passage through the Commission the strategy paper's emphasis on Africa was tempered somewhat, and broadened to the ACP. But it is also clear that there are no prospects for a significant broadening of the Community's development policy along the lines argued in the Forum by S. S. Saxena.

The ACP are to be at the centre of a set of concentric zones. Indeed, the possibility is raised of differentiation within the group 'if the ACP so wish'. The effect of this would be that the underlying principles, key features and institutional machinery of the relationship would be covered in an overall framework agreement of unlimited duration, which would be supplemented by more specific and limited sectoral and regional agreements tailored to the requirements of particular countries and problems. Beyond the ACP, the most favoured region would continue to be the Southern Mediterranean. The strategy paper identifies the region's main needs as continuing security of commercial relations in the face of EEC enlargement rather than financial assistance. Further out from the centre comes ASEAN, India and Latin America. These countries are offered the GSP for trade (see *Survey 2*, Chapter 5), 'greater enrichment of the contractual context' of their agreements with the EEC which, together with a proposed multiannual aid programme for non-associates, would provide them with greater predictability. The paper also calls for a wider interpretation of the statutes of the EIB which, at present, is limited in its activities to associated states (ACP, Maghreb, Mashreq) and, even then, by the willingness of its Board to lend outside the Community. The issue of graduation for the NICs is ignored despite early indications that the memorandum would put them in an additional category on the outer fringe.

In the zones of major concentration the proposed strategy emphasises action to promote 'self-reliant development' and 'genuine forms of international economic co-operation'. The first of these receives most attention in the strategy paper and is clearly closest to Commissioner Pisani's heart. As explained in *Survey 2* and elsewhere,[3] the Commissioner for Development Co-operation comes much closer to being a minister for North–South relations than do most of his counterparts in the Ten. Claude Cheysson played this role with skill and enthusiasm. The indications so far are that it has less appeal for Edgard Pisani, whose principal objective seems to be to transform his directorate-general into an effective aid agency with a focus on agricultural and rural development.

This orientation was first evident in the 1981 plan of action to combat world hunger. Subsequently, the Commissioner was closely involved in the formation of a plan to support food sector strategies in a select group of countries. At the time of going to press this plan still had not been fully worked out, but not only were its broad outlines clear but it also revealed the essence of Pisani's approach to aid for which he has coined the phrase 'conditionalité renversé'. The basic concept is that if ACP governments are prepared to formulate a convincing food sector strategy and implement those elements that fall within their domain (e.g. with respect to producer prices), the EEC will commit itself to supporting the strategy in two ways: by co-ordinating the activities of the Ten in their bilateral programmes, and by financing appropriate elements of the strategy from its own aid programme. There is a 'first batch' of three states – Kenya, Mali and Zambia – with whom Pisani has discussed the proposal and which have responded favourably and promised to draw up such strategies, although none had done so by early October 1982. Behind these there is a second group of 'possibles'. From the EEC side, the plan's success hinges on two points: whether the Commission can succeed in co-ordinating the Ten, and whether it can obtain additional finance for these strategies. The response of the Council has so far been positive, and the Commission is optimistic on co-ordination. The additional funds are more problematic. The Commission attempted twice in the first half of the year to have some Ecu 200mn transferred to the development budget from savings on agricultural support to finance not only the food strategies but also the Central American initiative (see Chapter 8), and other activities. Both attempts failed, but a third attempt using different tactics was scheduled for Autumn 1982.

The idea of co-ordinating aid and integrating it into the recipient's overall strategy is central to Pisani's thinking. The new organisation of his directorate-general reflects this (see Figure 13.1). The hope behind this re-organisation is twofold. First, overall responsibility for all EEC aid to a particular state is to be concentrated on the relevant country desk officer instead of, as in the past, being dispersed between geographical and functional specialists. Second, a new line has been created within the directorate-general to deal with development policy in particular sectors. Hence the agriculture, food and environment division, for example, should develop an institutional understanding of common rural problems and successful solutions, while the Sahelian Africa division should ensure that EEC aid to its region is appropriate to local conditions and internally consistent.

Will it all work? It is far too early to guess, but a judgment can be made of the new strategy's strengths and weaknesses. Edgard Pisani's aim is to put a cat among the pigeons: by throwing out broad and novel ideas he hopes to act as a spark that will ignite the latent interest (and interests) of all parties and enable the EEC to make a quantum leap in

Figure 13.1 *New structure of the directorate-general for development*

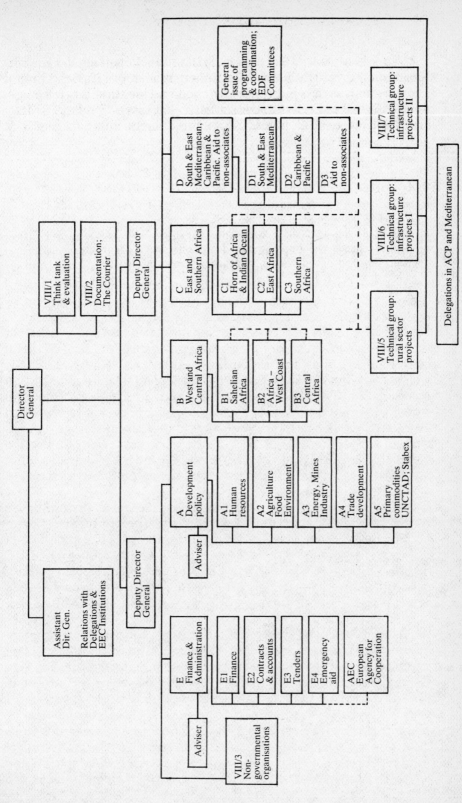

its Third World policy. It is a strategy akin to that guiding the Brandt Commission of which he was a member. A man of ideas and broad vision, he appears less interested in details and logistics. If his strategy succeeds it will radically transform EEC–Third World relations. If it fails, it will leave the Commission as a rather ineffectual aid agency.

Notes

1   COM (81) 560 final, 5 October 1981.
2   *Survey 2* Chapter 1, and Christopher Stevens, 'Policy-making on North–South issues – the importance of administrative organisation', *Millenium: Journal of International Studies* (London), vol. 11, no. 1, Spring 1982, pp. 14–26.
3   *Ibid.*

Statistical Appendix

A note on EEC units of account

The EEC has used a variety of units to express values. The most commonly used in the context of trade and aid flows are the European Currency Unit (Ecu), established in December 1978 for use in the European Monetary Co-operation Fund, and, until the end of 1980, the European Unit of Account (Eua), which expressed the aid provisions of the Lomé Convention. Both units were based on an identical basket of European currencies but, although the baskets were identical, the two units were not revalued at the same intervals and so at any one time they might have slightly different values in terms of other currencies. Since January 1981, all aid and trade values have been expressed in terms of Ecu alone. The contents of the Ecu basket are weighted according to the 1969–73 average of GNP and intra-Community trade of each member state, and in relation to the share of each country in the short-term monetary support between the EEC Central Banks. The Ecu is the sum of: German mark – 0.828; Pound sterling – 0.0885; French franc – 1.15; Italian lira – 109; Dutch guilder – 0.286; Belgian franc – 3.66; Luxembourg franc – 0.14; Danish krone – 0.217; Irish pound – 0.00759.

Table 1 *Source of EEC imports by value and by main trading bloc, 1975–81 (Ecu mn)*

Imports from:	1975[e]	1976[e]	1977[c]	1978[e]	1979[e]	1980[e]	1981[f]	1981 value as % of world total (excl. intra-EEC trade)
Class I[a]	60326	75818	82357	92750	111365	134114	138464	50
Class II[b]	54976	70021	75278	71192	88282	114562	118469	42
of which ACP[c]	8716	10480	12502	11892	14835	18924	15125	5
Class III[d]	9237	12362	13326	14008	17753	21943	22802	8
Miscellaneous	911	1388	782	436	721	947	453	—

[a] Western industrialised countries, excluding intra-EEC trade
[b] Developing countries, excluding Cuba 1976–1981
[c] 54 states, 1975–79, 59 states, 1980–81
[d] State trading countries – including Cuba 1976–81; excluding West German trade with East Germany
[e] 9 members
[f] 10 members

Source: Eurostat.

Table 2 *Direction of EEC (9 members) exports by value and by main trading bloc, 1975–80* (Ecu mn)

	1975	1976	1977	1978	1979	1980	1980 value as % of world total
Exports to:							
Class I[a]	62 505	74 131	85 643	89 983	104 904	118 978	53
Class II[b]	44 068	50 951	61 875	66 523	69 687	83 388	37
of which ACP[c]	8 124	9 888	12 519	12 723	11 816	15 684	7
Class III[d]	13 014	14 238	14 540	15 436	17 264	18 721	8
Miscellaneous	1 625	1 980	2 230	1 951	2 309	3 358	2

[a] Western industrialised countries, excluding intra-EEC trade.
[b] Developing countries, excluding Cuba 1976–80.
[c] 54 states, 1975–79, 59 states 1980.
[d] State trading countries – including Cuba 1976–80; excluding West German trade with East Germany.

Note: Because of the UK civil servants' strike of 1981 it is not yet possible to provide figures for 1981

Source: Eurostat

Table 3   *EEC trade with principal Third World trade partners 1980* (Ecu mn)[a]

Country	EEC Imports	EEC Exports	Balance[b]
Angola	214	320	+106
Algeria	4027	4710	+683
Argentina	1777	2221	+444
Brazil	4134	2535	−1599
Cameroon	712	743	+31
Chile	1316	596	−720
China	1889	1725	−164
Colombia	1060	561	−499
Congo	326	257	−69
Cuba	248	438	+190
Cyprus	265	522	+257
Ecuador	182	301	+119
Egypt	1746	3105	+1359
Gabon	776	394	−382
Ghana	391	315	−76
Hong Kong	3602	2133	−1469
India	1799	2298	+499
Indonesia	1192	1252	+60
Ivory Coast	1411	1165	−246
Kenya	456	750	+294
Liberia	464	334	−130
Libya	6373	4146	−2227
Malaysia	1788	1035	−753
Mexico	1063	2180	+1117
Morocco	1169	1479	+310
Netherlands Antilles	424	238	−186
Niger	329	215	−114
Nigeria	7872	6010	−1862
Pakistan	441	891	+450
Peru	527	417	−110
Philippines	820	591	−229
Senegal	192	445	+253
Singapore	1859	1713	−146
South Korea	1972	941	−1031
Sri Lanka	207	277	+70
Sudan	166	473	+307
Syria	930	1245	+315
Taiwan	2165	872	−1293
Tanzania	211	395	+184
Thailand	1237	726	−511
Trinidad	279	275	−4
Tunisia	1098	1541	+443
Uruguay	230	235	+5
Venezuela	1710	1551	−159
Yugoslavia	2057	4131	+2074
Zaire	1318	509	−809
Zambia	561	313	−248

[a] 9 member states
[b] Positive number means EEC has an export surplus.
See *Survey 2* for EEC trade balances with principal Third World partners, 1975–79.

Source: Eurostat

Table 4 *Commodity composition of EEC imports from Third World 1975–80[a] (Ecu mn)*

Commodity group:[b]	1975	1976	1977	1978	1979	1980	1980 value as % of total
0+1	7541	9805	13531	12574	13190	13284	12
2+4	5908	7304	7536	7118	8758	9330	8
3	33797	42104	41651	37677	48570	69233	60
5	490	566	663	605	821	1237	1
6+8	6202	8747	9959	10576	13448	16060	14
7	751	1064	1531	2022	2713	3423	3

[a] Nine EEC member states: Third World excludes Cuba 1976–80.
[b] Commodity groups: 0+1 – food, beverages and tobacco
2+4 – raw materials
3 – mineral fuels, lubricants and related materials
5 – chemicals and related products
6+8 – manufactured goods
7 – machinery and transport equipment

Source: Eurostat

Table 5 *EEC imports by member state and Third World region 1980–81 (Ecu mn)*

	EEC[a]	Germany	France	Italy	Netherlands	Belgium/ Lux.	UK	Ireland	Denmark	Greece
1980										
ACP[b]	19017	4369	4917	2255	3042	1680	2355	79	197	105
Mediterranean Basin	32220	9791	6557	8068	1840	1240	3417	102	244	1275
Latin America	13719	3866	2185	2764	1544	986	1741	41	356	189
ASEAN	6891	1998	1091	745	983	318	1568	30	125	31
1981										
ACP[b]	—	3307	4006	2284	2443	1651	—	57	224	221
Mediterranean Basin	—	11457	8759	9928	1987	1416	—	146	301	1121
Latin America	—	4146	3070	3801	1808	1196	—	56	366	114
ASEAN	—	1939	1044	711	1208	356	—	39	131	39

[a] 10 member states
[b] 59 countries

Source: Eurostat.

Table 6 *EEC exports by member state and Third World region 1980–81 (Ecu mn)*

	EEC[a]	Germany	France	Italy	Netherlands	Belgium/Lux.	UK	Ireland	Denmark	Greece
1980										
ACP[b]	15762	2576	4646	1385	1321	1000	4476	92	188	67
Mediterranean Basin	30373	10136	9629	7947	2167	2336	5248	317	399	
Latin America	11661	4356	2033	1977	665	613	1691	121	190	13
ASEAN	5323	1736	674	466	630	246	1417	28	120	5
1981										
ACP[b]	—	3366	5414	1674	1327	1049	—	120	323	93
Mediterranean Basin	—	14076	12490	12561	3263	2762	—	520	742	675
Latin America	—	5181	2691	2853	830	649	—	169	383	17
ASEAN	—	2514	1309	578	622	309	—	31	137	14

[a] 10 member states
[b] 59 countries

Source: Eurostat

Table 7 *Commitments of financial assistance under the First Lomé Convention up to end 1981 by method of financing and administering organisation* (Ecu mn)

| | Administered by | | | | | |
| | the Commission | | EIB | | Total | |
	Value	%	Value	%	Value	%
EDF IV Resources						
– Grants	1876.9	71	65.0	12	1941.9	61
of which:						
Micro-projects	18.2	1	—	—	18.2	—
Interest rate subsidies	—	—	65.0	12	65.0	2
Emergency aid	145.4	6	—	—	143.4	5
– Special loans	398.8	15	—	—	398.8	12
– Risk capital	—	—	98.4	18	98.4	3
– Stabex	377.5	14	—	—	377.5	12
EIB Resources						
– Loans	—	—	390.0	71	390.0	12
Total	2653.2	100	553.4	100	3206.6	100

Note: Columns may not add up due to rounding

Source: EEC Commission

Table 8 *Sectoral distribution of commitments from EDF IV (Lomé I) to ACP up to 31 December 1981*

Sector	Amount Ecu mn	%
Development of Production	1466.1	46
Industrial development	879.0	(27)
Tourism	16.7	(—)
Rural production	570.4	(18)
Transport and Telecommunications Infrastructure	634.1	20
Social Development	398.5	12
Trade Promotion	32.4	1
Emergency Aid	145.4	5
Stabex	377.5	12
Miscellaneous (including Delegations until 1 March 1980)	147.2	5

Note: Columns may not add up due to rounding

Source: EEC Commission

Table 9   *Commitments and disbursements from EDF IV (Lomé I) as at 31 December 1981 (Ecu mn)*

Recipient	Commitments	Disbursements	Disbursements as a % of Commitments
Bahamas	1.9	0.5	26.3
Barbados	4.2	2.9	69.0
Benin	55.6	43.6	78.4
Botswana	25.2	18.5	73.4
Burundi	56.6	37.1	65.5
Cameroon	80.1	47.8	68.2
Cape Verde	10.1	7.6	75.2
C.A.R.	47.6	32.6	68.5
Chad	67.3	43.1	64.0
Comoros	9.6	4.7	49.0
Congo	37.9	34.5	91.0
Djibouti	4.6	3.7	80.0
Dominica	4.6	4.4	95.6
Equatorial Guinea	7.1	2.0	28.2
Ethiopia	106.6	68.5	64.3
Fiji	20.4	15.8	77.4
Gabon	17.3	15.0	86.7
Gambia	22.7	15.3	67.4
Ghana	62.6	32.3	51.6
Grenada	2.6	1.6	61.5
Guinea	67.6	44.9	66.4
Guinea Bissau	31.4	26.3	83.8
Guyana	16.9	8.8	52.1
Ivory Coast	64.4	44.7	69.4
Jamaica	20.3	11.9	58.6
Kenya	85.9	61.6	71.7
Kiribati	0.5	0.1	0.2
Lesotho	20.7	13.0	62.8
Liberia	34.1	20.7	60.7
Madagascar	81.4	43.0	52.8
Malawi	75.0	48.8	65.1
Mali	89.1	77.6	87.1
Mauritius	20.6	9.4	45.6
Mauritania	76.6	66.6	86.9
Niger	101.9	82.2	80.7
Nigeria	19.0	12.9	67.9
Papua New Guinea	9.1	4.6	47.2
Rwanda	70.0	52.5	75.0
St. Lucia	2.3	1.9	82.6
St. Vincent	0.5	0.5	100.0
Sao Tomé & Principe	2.2	1.3	59.1
Senegal	138.1	113.2	82.0
Seychelles	2.9	1.7	58.6
Sierra Leone	31.6	19.8	62.7
Solomon Islands	6.7	0.9	13.4
Somalia	73.5	48.0	65.3
Sudan	146.5	88.9	60.7
Suriname	8.7	4.4	50.6

Table 9 *– contd*

Recipient	Commitments	Disbursements	Disbursements as a % of Commitments
Swaziland	28.5	23.5	82.5
Tanzania	133.9	78.6	58.7
Togo	48.7	35.2	72.3
Tonga	4.3	3.9	90.7
Trinidad & Tobago	8.2	4.0	48.8
Tuvalu	0.6	0.3	50.0
Uganda	87.2	43.7	50.1
Upper Volta	82.3	54.0	65.6
Western Samoa	7.5	6.3	84.0
Zaire	123.0	58.1	47.2
Zambia	67.8	51.1	75.4
Regional Projects	255.6	137.3	53.7
Unspecified	33.8	21.8	64.5
Total	2 813.5	1 859.5	66.1

Source: EEC Commission

Table 10 *Breakdown of EDF IV funded contracts according to nationality of suppliers, up to 31 December 1981*

Country of firm	Works contracts	Supply contracts	% share of Technical Co-operation contracts	All contracts
Belgium	6.6	4.4	8.3	6.5
Denmark	0.3	0.6	2.0.	0.7
France	23.4	22.8	20.0	22.6
Germany	7.6	20.1	20.8	12.8
Ireland	0	0	1.7	0.3
Italy	11.2	14.8	11.4	12.0
Luxembourg	0	0	1.5	0.3
Netherlands	3.4	4.3	7.3	4.3
United Kingdom	3.4	18.5	14.2	8.7
Total EEC	56.0	85.5	87.2	68.3
ACP and TOM	42.9	8.5	12.3	29.7
Third countries	1.1	6.0	0.5	2.0
Total in Ecu '000	928 076	334 404	299 384	1 561 855

Note: Columns may not add up due to rounding

Source: EEC Commission

Table 11 *Commitments of financial assistance under the Second Lomé Convention up to end 1981 by method of financing and administering organisation* (in Ecu mn)

| | Administered by | | | |
| | the Commission | | EIB | |
	Value	%	Value	%
EDF IV Resources				
– Grants	277.9	61	0	—
of which:				
Interest rate subsidies	—	—	36.3	15
Emergency aid	24.4	5	—	—
– Special loans	13.5	3	—	—
– Risk capital	—	—	48.5	20
– Stabex	138.0	30	—	—
EIB Resources				
– Loans	—	—	158.4	65
Total	453.8	100	243.2	100

Source: EEC Commission

Table 12 *Sectoral distribution of commitments from EDF V (Lomé II) to ACP up to 31 December 1981*

Sector	Amount Ecu mn	%
Development of Production	311.0	45
Industrial development	236.2	(34)
Tourism	0.2	(—)
Rural production	74.6	(11)
Transport and Telecommunications Infrastructure	85.0	12
Social Development	117.6	17
Education and training	22.2	(3)
Health	7.6	(1)
Water engineering, housing and urban administration	87.8	(13)
Trade Promotion	12.8	2
Emergency Aid	24.4	4
Stabex	138.0	20
Miscellaneous	8.1	1

Note: Columns may not add up due to rounding

Source: EEC Commission

Table 13   *Stabex transfers 1975–81 by country*

Recipient	1981 Ecus mn	1975–1981 Ecus mn	%
Belize		0.3	—
Benin		20.4	3
Burundi	11.0	23.5	4
Cameroon		4.1	1
Cape Verde	0.2	1.6	—
C.A.R.	1.0	9.8	2
Chad	2.6	12.5	2
Comoros	1.1	4.5	1
Congo		7.4	1
Djibouti		0.7	—
Dominica	2.5	7.9	1
Ethiopia		14.4	2
Fiji	0.8	3.8	1
Gabon		6.7	1
Gambia	8.1	23.7	4
Ghana		5.2	1
Guinea Bissau	1.5	14.3	2
Ivory Coast	19.2	53.4	8
Jamaica	3.3	5.5	1
Kenya	10.0	20.0	3
Kiribati	0.5	3.3	1
Lesotho	0.2	0.4	—
Liberia		7.6	1
Madagascar	1.2	8.2	1
Malawi	1.3	2.6	—
Mali	2.6	14.9	2
Mauritania		37.0	6
New Hebrides		1.4	—
Niger		22.7	3
Rwanda	6.6	13.8	2
St. Lucia	1.3	2.7	—
St. Vincent	0.9	1.8	—
Senegal	38.6	142.3	21
Sierra Leone	1.0	5.9	1
Solomon Islands		2.2	—
Somalia	1.9	5.7	1
Sudan	13.4	66.0	10
Swaziland		13.2	2
Tanzania	6.3	33.3	5
Togo		3.6	1
Tonga	0.6	2.4	—
Tuvalu	0.01	0.2	—
Uganda		20.6	3
Upper Volta		7.3	1
Vanuatu	4.2	8.4	1
Western Samoa	1.2	5.3	1
Total	143.1	673.4	

Note: Columns may not add up due to rounding

Source: EEC Commission

Table 14 *Commitments and disbursements from EDF V (Lomé II) as at 31 December 1981 (Ecu mn)*

Recipient	Commitments						Disbursements
	Grants & Special Loans	Stabex	Emergency Aid	EIB Interest Subsidy	EIB Risk Capital	Total	Total
Bahamas	0.1	0	0	0	0	0.1	—
Barbados	1.6	0	0	0	0	1.6	0.9
Benin	0.6	0	0	0	0	0.6	0
Botswana	2.0	0	0	0	0	2.0	0
Burundi	0.5	11.0	0	0	4.0	15.5	11.0
Cameroon	0.7	0	0	3.8	0	4.5	3.9
Cape Verde	0.2	0.2	0.5	0	0	0.9	0.2
C.A.R.	0.2	1.0	0.5	0	0	1.7	1.5
Chad	0.5	2.6	1.5	0	0	4.6	3.0
Comoros	0.4	1.1	0.2	0	0.2	1.9	1.1
Congo	3.2	0	0	0	0	3.2	0.2
Djibouti	0.1	0	0.1	0	1.8	2.0	0.3
Dominica	0.2	2.5	0.5	0	0	3.2	2.9
Equatorial Guinea	0.05	0	0.2	0	0	0.05	0
Ethiopia	53.6	0	0.2	0	0	53.8	0.2
Fiji	0.4	0.8	0.3	4.0	0	5.5	4.8
Gabon	0.1	0	0	7.2	0	7.3	7.2
Gambia	3.6	0	0.06	0	0	11.8	8.2
Ghana	8.1	0	0.1	0	0	8.2	0.03
Grenada	0.2	0	0	0	0	0.2	0.08
Guinea	0.9	0	0.5	0	0	1.4	0.2
Guinea Bissau	0.8	1.5	0	0	0	2.3	1.5
Guyana	0.6	0	0	0	0	0.6	0.04
Ivory Coast	14.3	19.2	0	0	0	33.5	19.2
Jamaica	0.3	3.3	0	0	0	3.6	3.2
Kenya	16.2	10.0	0.3	1.6	1.5	29.6	12.3
Kiribati	0.1	0.5	0	0	0	0.6	0.5
Lesotho	0.7	0.2	0	0	3.0	3.9	0.2

Madagascar	8.2	1.2	0.2	0	2.2	11.8	3.0
Malawi	4.0	1.3	0.1	0	0	5.4	1.3
Mali	17.5	2.6	0.6	0	0	20.7	3.1
Mauritius	1.7	0	0	0	0	1.7	0
Mauritania	1.3	0	0	0	0	1.3	0
Niger	20.4	0	0.8	3.6	0	24.8	3.6
Nigeria	0.4	0	0.3	0	0	0.7	0.3
Papua New Guinea	0.2	0	0	0	12.0	12.2	0.01
Rwanda	17.6	6.6	0	0	0	24.2	6.6
St. Lucia	1.2	1.3	0	0	0	2.5	1.4
St. Vincent	2.3	0	0.2	0	0	2.5	0
Sao Tomé & Principe	0.1	0	0	0	0	0.1	0.02
Senegal	3.5	38.6	0.2	2.9	2.3	47.5	41.8
Seychelles	0	0	0.04	0	0	0.04	0
Sierra Leone	1.7	1.0	0	0	0	2.7	1.0
Solomon Islands	0	0	0	0	0	0	0
Somalia	11.6	1.9	10.5	0	0	24.0	9.1
Sudan	1.5	13.4	0.5	0	0	15.4	14.3
Suriname	1.0	0	0	0	0	1.0	0
Swaziland	0.4	0	0	1.9	0	2.3	1.9
Tanzania	5.1	6.3	0.1	0	7.5	19.0	6.3
Togo	4.0	0	0	1.5	0	5.5	1.6
Tonga	0	0.6	0.2	0	1.0	1.6	0.6
Trinidad & Tobago	1.2	0.01	0	0	0	1.2	0
Tuvalu	0.1	0	0	0	0	0.1	0.01
Uganda	5.1	0	3.3	0	0	8.4	0.3
Upper Volta	29.3	0	0.02	0	0	29.5	1.0
Vanuatu	0	0	0	0	0	0	0
Western Samoa	5.1	1.2	0	0	3.0	9.3	1.2
Zaire	1.2	0	2.0	0	6.0	9.2	1.5
Zambia	6.9	0	0.8	8.5	1.5	17.7	2.5
Zimbabwe	0	0	0	0	0	0	0
Regional projects	28.4	0	0	1.3	1.8	31.5	5.6
Total	291.4	138.0	24.4	36.3	48.5	538.6	190.7

Total disbursements = 35.4% of total commitments   *Source:* EEC Commission

Table 15 *Stabex transfers to ACP and OCT, 1975–81, by commodity*

Commodity	1981 Ecus mn	1975–1981 Ecus mn	%
Groundnut products	63.9	284.8	42
Coffee	54.1	122.6	18
Iron ore		61.8	9
Cotton	2.6	48.5	7
Rough timber		39.0	6
Bananas	9.7	25.2	4
Sisal		20.6	3
Copra and copra products	1.31	11.1	2
Palm nuts and palm oil	1.3	10.3	2
Raw hides, skins & leather	0.4	9.9	2
Tea	1.3	9.7	1
Vanilla	1.2	5.3	1
Cocoa	1.6	4.3	1
Cloves		2.3	—
Essential oils	0.9	1.8	—
Coconut oil	0.8	1.6	—
Gum arabic		0.69	—
Pyrethrum		0.6	—
Cocoa paste		0.5	—
Mohair	0.2	0.4	—
Ylang-ylang		0.2	—

Note: Excludes Ecu 7.6mn to Vanuatu for copra and coconut oil, for which no breakdown between two products is available.

Source: EEC Commission

Table 16 *EIB lending to the Third World 1981 (Ecu mn)*

Recipient	From EIB own resources	Special section operations
Maghreb	52.0	0
Morocco	30.0	0
Tunisia	12.0	0
Algeria	10.0	0
Mashreq	15.0	0
Jordan	3.0	0
Lebanon	12.0	0
Africa	106.4	34.0
Burundi	0	4.0
Cameroon	10.0	0
Comoros	0	0.2
Djibouti	0	1.8

Table 16 – *contd*

Recipient	From EIB own resources	Special section operations
Gabon	22.0	0
Lesotho	0	3.1
Liberia	0	0.7
Madagascar	0	2.2
Malawi	0	0.4
Mali	0	0.2
Mauritius	7.5	0.04
Niger	10.0	0
Senegal	10.0	2.7
Swaziland	7.0	0
Tanzania	0	7.5
Togo	4.4	0
Zambia	31.5	1.5
Caribbean	0	0.2
St. Lucia	0	0.2
Pacific	52.0	16.2
Fiji	12.0	0.2
Papua New Guinea	40.0	12.0
Tonga	0	1.0
Western Samoa	0	3.0
OCT (New Caledonia)	0	1.0

Source: EIB Annual Report 1981 (Luxembourg)

Table 17 *Allocations to the non-associate aid programme*

	Eua mn
1976	20
1977	45
1978	70
1979	110
1980	138.5
1981	150
1982	185[a]

[a] in Ecu million

Source: EEC Commission

Table 18 *Exchange rates: member states of the EEC and the United States*[a]

Period	Germany	France	Italy	Netherlands	Belgium/ Luxembourg	United Kingdom	Ireland	Denmark	Greece	United States
	1000 DM = ...Ecu	1000 FF = ...Ecu	1000 L = ...Ecu	1000 Fl = ...Ecu	1000FB/Flux = ...Ecu	1000 £ = ...Ecu	1000 £ = ...Ecu	1000 DKr = ...Ecu	1000 Dr = ...Ecu	1000 $ = ...Ecu
1975	327.934	187.997	1.235	318.989	21.945	1785.631		140.397	25.004	805.951
1976	355.183	187.096	1.075	338.392	23.167	1608.809		147.890	24.459	894.414
1977	377.599	178.378	0.993	357.130	24.460	1529.751		145.865	23.790	876.332
1978	391.252	174.217	0.925	363.112	24.963	1506.142		142.462	21.375	784.720
1979	398.268	171.543	0.878	363.816	24.897	1547.051	1493.694	138.714	19.695	729.581
1980	396.164	170.388	0.841	362.283	24.632	1670.880	1479.297	127.757	16.857	718.221
1981	397.788	165.565	0.792	360.347	24.216	1807.959	1447.134	126.222	16.228	895.696

[a] The Ecu is a 'basket' unit, based on a certain quantity of each Community currency, weighted on the basis of the 5 years (1969–1973) average of the gross national product (GNP) and of the intra-Community trade of each member state. This weighting also takes account, for each currency, of the share of the country concerned in the short-term monetary support between the central banks of the Community.

Source: Eurostat

Documentary Appendix

Extracts from 'Memorandum on the Community's Development Policy' – COM (82) 640 Final

Summary

Objectives

1.1 The following objectives must be pursued if the developing countries, and in particular the poorest among them, are to achieve lasting, autonomous development:
- help countries to apply development policies based on self-reliance;
- help people attain food self-sufficiency by providing support for active rural development policies and for the framing of economic policies which promote food production;
- help to develop human resources and foster awareness of the cultural aspects of development;
- develop independent capacity for scientific research and technical applications and the use of the whole range of science and technology in the service of development;
- systematically exploit all natural resource potential;
- restore and preserve the ecological balances and control the growth of urbanisation.

1.2 The Community will continue to promote international economic co-operation, bilateral and multilateral, by:
- establishing and consolidating between Europe and its partners durable contractual relations based on solidarity and mutual interest;
- introducing via the North–South Dialogue 'a new system of international economic relations based on the principles of equality and mutual benefit as also to promote the common interest of all countries';[1]
- contributing towards the strengthening of economic relations between developing countries ('South–South co-operation').

[1] UN General Assembly Resolution 34–138

2 Methods

2.1 In its development activities, the Community will seek ways to take political dialogue beyond mere negotiations on projects to be financed. The Community respects the sovereign right of beneficiary countries over the use of the resources it puts at their disposal; it also considers it has a right and a duty to engage in a dialogue with the governments of those countries concerning the effectiveness of the policies it is supporting. Such a dialogue is being tried out for the first time with regard to food strategies.

The Community also believes it should look again with the ACP States at ways to help them improve their capacity to administer aid better.

2.2 In support of consistent food strategies, the Community will, among other things, deploy food aid which, emergencies apart, should be integrated into its development activity instead of existing as an end in itself.

2.3 The Community will supplement food aid with funds allocated according to the same criteria in all cases where other types of action and the supply of agricultural inputs would be more suitable (e.g. in the form of agricultural inputs or support for structural measures).

2.4 As regards co-operation in fields of mutual interest (mineral resources, energy, industry, fisheries, etc.), the Community will seek ways of ensuring more consistent use of existing instruments, or of reforming them, in line with strategies worked out jointly with its partners. The Commission will in due course be presenting communications on these various questions.

2.5 The Community and the Member States will maintain a continuous process of co-ordination and harmonisation to improve the coherence and efficiency of their assistance to developing countries and the consistency of their internal and external policies with their development and co-operation policy.

3 The institutional framework

3.1 The Community confirms the special importance it attaches to the co-operation links set up with the ACP countries under the Lomé Conventions and will expand the joint development work undertaken within that framework.

The Community is willing to organise its relations with the ACP countries under a framework Convention of unlimited duration. It will take as its basis the institutional system already established with them in order to help them reverse the trend towards ever greater dependence on food imports and ever greater poverty and to contribute to their development.

3.2 Recognising that the stability and prosperity of the Mediterranean developing countries are linked to their own political and economic interests, the Community and its Member States will contribute to their development by every means available and undertake to honour the commitments undertaken in the co-operation agreements. Further, the Community is willing to organise its relations with the southern Mediterranean countries, in due course, within the framework of a comprehensive region-to-region convention.

3.3 The Community is willing to improve the content of the co-operation agreements with developing countries in Asia and Latin America, in particular by making available under these agreements certain funds to help carry out specific operations of mutual interest.

The Community will continue its development activities outside the framework of the agreements, concentrating its efforts in places where it can help fight poverty and hunger by means of financial assistance for rural development in the poorest countries and the poorest communities within them. In order to make such aid more effective the Community will endeavour to programme operations on a multi-annual basis.

3.4 Often, development operations cannot be fully effective unless they are undertaken over several countries concurrently, in the areas of trade relations and industrial co-operation.

In its co-operation ties with the various groups of developing countries, the Community will continue to press for the necessary regional aspect of development work to be taken into account; it will adjust its co-operation instruments to give greater weight than in the past to this important factor, with the aim of building up complementarity and contributing to the economic balance of regional groupings.

3.5 On the multilateral front the Community and the Member States will improve the effectiveness of their work within the multilateral development financing bodies by jointly defining and implementing a European position in those institutions. In this connection the idea of financial participation in certain multilateral institutions by the Community as such should be examined.

In the North–South context, with particular reference to the global negotiations, the Community will endeavour to promote achievement of the objectives adopted by The European Council in June 1981 and subsequently broadened.

4 Means

4.1 The Community will set itself a development aid target level of 1% of Community GNP and will try to achieve it by stages over the next ten years, in order to affirm the continuity of its operations and make them more predictable.

4.2 Money allocated by the Community to development aid will henceforth be brought together in a single budget framework, to reflect the uniformity and consistency and improve the flexibility of Community development policy in both its forms:
(i) contractual (Lomé Convention and Mediterranean agreements, instruments incorporated in co-operation agreements with other developing countries);
(ii) autonomous (financing operations by NGOs, aid to NADCs, emergency aid in line with the Commission's proposals, food aid and support for food strategies, support for scientific research of benefit to developing countries, operations under co-operation agreements where not financed on a contractual basis).
4.3 The Community will seek every possible means of increasing the flow of non-budget money to the developing countries by mobilising money on the capital markets and encouraging private investment. It will examine the possibility of putting its own borrowing capacity directly at the service of developing countries.

In the shorter term, a more liberal interpretation of Article 18 of the EIB's Statute could enable the Bank to undertake operations in developing countries linked to the Community by co-operation agreements to finance operations of mutual interest.
4.4 The establishment of the EMS and the extension of its currency unit, the ECU, could be used as a stabilising factor for developing countries or groups of countries willing to take it as a reference.
4.5 The Community's first priority in the trade field is to keep access as open and predictable as possible, especially where the arrangements are based on a contract negotiated with its partners.
4.6 As regards commodities, the Community will continue, as in the past, to work at the international level for the stabilisation of commodity markets.

When the Lomé Convention comes up for renewal, the Community is willing to review with the ACP countries the Stabex and Sysmin systems and the sugar, bananas and rum protocols, in the light of experience, in order to improve their effectiveness.

IV. Action for development: methods and areas of application

4.3 Areas of application

The pursuit of the basic objectives proposed by the Commission runs up against geographical constraints, as the Community cannot claim to cover every corner of the globe where development action is desirable. The fact that funds (even if they are increased) are limited dictates that

Community action be concentrated where its effectiveness is most assured, i.e. in areas where the strength of the European presence, the experience acquired and the responsibilities assumed in the past have given rise to a special obligation.

Africa is the first area for Community development action, particularly the poorest African countries, whose economic record and growth prospects stand in stark contrast with results achieved elsewhere in Africa and the Third World.

These poor countries account for 54% of the population of sub-Saharan Africa. Their total population will rise from 190 million in 1980 to over 330 million by the end of the century. Just in the last ten years, their food production per head of population has fallen by around 10%.

Imports of cereals have increased accordingly and over 20% of those imports are now financed by food aid. These keep the towns – whose population is doubling every ten to twelve years (and already accounts for 20% of the total population) – supplied with food which the rural sector is no longer able to provide. Such imports are responsible for introducing largely artificial patterns of consumption and economic practices into a process of urbanisation which is becoming potentially explosive and uncontrollable.

The Caribbean and Pacific countries, though characterised by less acute poverty and a generally more favourable development of their economies, are nonetheless experiencing the same deterioration in their food balances. In addition, their whole development effort is conditioned by their insularity and, for many of them, by the small area of their territory – in some cases spread over extensive archipelagos.

Faced with these problems, the Community, which has forged with the African, Caribbean and Pacific States a unique model of co-operation, must assume the responsibilities that flow therefrom. With the ACP countries it must use the institutional system of Lomé in order to reverse the trend towards greater food dependence and impoverishment. It is necessary to create the conditions for lasting development taking account of the interdependence between development, the environment, population and resources. The same effort must be made to exploit the ACP States' mineral and energy resources in the service of their development and to encourage on a regional basis forms of industrialisation which are both internationally competitive and geared to meeting domestic requirements.

Without in any way usurping the decision-making powers of individual states, the Community must, through its analyses of the situation and the resources it intends to deploy, convince Africa that its future depends primarily on the mobilisation and nurturing of peasant labour, development of the huge land resources available and protection of the currently endangered vegetation. It is not sufficient for

Europe merely to spend money on Africa; it must ensure that the policies applied enable a possible future to take shape.

Another important area for development action is the Mediterranean, which is linked to the Community by the co-operation or association agreements but first and foremost by virtue of geography and historical ties. The Community, in the implementation of the overall approach established in 1972, and in the application of the association agreements, has demonstrated its willingness to participate in the development of its Mediterranean partners, while respecting their individual political philosophies.

The sociological, ecological and economic context is not the same as in the case of Black Africa, but the development problems, particularly in respect of agriculture, are considerable and are increasing as the population expands. If those problems are to be solved a new impetus must be given to financial co-operation which, while under no circumstances being able to replace the trade commitments entered into by the Community in the context of the agreements, remains a basic pillar of the Community's role in the Mediterranean.

In the case of other developing countries of Asia and Latin America, the very scale of their financing requirements means that the Community must concentrate on those countries and sectors to which a constant flow of official development assistance remains essential; a Community presence is imperative in those countries where its aid, along with that of other donors, can help to combat poverty and hunger. The Commission therefore recommends that the Community extend its aid programmes directed towards the poorest countries of Asia and Latin America, programmes mainly designed to promote rural development, to help the neediest sections of the population. To make this type of action more effective, the Commission considers it would be desirable to embark upon multiannual programming of the aid provided, independently of the funds intended to help implement the co-operation agreements, which are the expression of the traditional links which the Community maintains with the countries of Latin America and Asia (see section 5.3 below).

In addition to these direct contributions there are those which the Community and the Member States make to multilateral development financing institutions (World Bank, IDA, regional banks) which devote a substantial share of their resources to development in Asian and Latin American countries. In view of the danger of curtailment of the scope of these institutions' activities, the Community and the Member States should act jointly to increase their resources and influence their methods of action.

V. The system of co-operation

Although world interdependence has grown steadily over the last twenty years, collective capacity to overcome insecurity – which should go hand-in-hand with such interdependence – has instead become weaker.

As the most deeply involved of all the major industrial powers in the workings of world economic interdependence, the Community shares with the developing countries a fundamental interest in the construction of a system of international economic co-operation that offers the participating countries a minimum standard of security and predictability. The policies pursued to that end, on a basis of mutual interest, are complementary to action for development, the results of which are constantly in danger of being undermined by world economic instability.

Despite its unfinished state, the Community constitutes by its very existence a call for the reorganisation of international economic relations and a challenge to move away from the traditional framework of relations between nation states and gradually replace it with a system of relations between regional groups or major continental units basing their relations on the predictability and security of a contract negotiated between equals and administered jointly in their mutual interest.

The Community is neither a nation nor a state, but it is an actor on the world stage and cannot remain passive before the current trend of international relations. It supports the development of the North–South Dialogue as a means of achieving greater justice and regrets the resurgence of East–West confrontation as the sole mode of classifying and organising the powers. Though a fully committed member of the West, whose values it shaped and defends, the Community cannot bring itself to look on the world in black-and-white terms. In defending the values of liberty and in following its natural inclination towards the workings of the market and enterprise, it also intends to preserve its own vision of the world. Such is its constant endeavour.

Internally, this is the very essence of the Community, founded upon the Treaties. That is the thrust of the plan to make the EMS a factor for stability in the international monetary system. It is also the principle underlying the Community system of co-operation, most fully articulated to date in the Lomé Convention.

5.1 The Lomé policy

At the appropriate time the Commission will present proposals to the Council with a view to the adoption of directives for the negotiations due to open on 1 September 1983 between the Community and the

ACP countries. The proposals will fall within the framework of the guidelines laid down by this memorandum.

But even at this stage the Commission proposes that the Council confirm the importance it attaches to the co-operation links forged with the ACP countries, and also its readiness to continue and expand the joint action for development begun in this framework.

The Lomé co-operation framework serves the interest of the ACP: they demonstrated this by deciding, in the light of experience of the first Convention, to renew the contract while making a number of improvements. In an uncertain world, the security of access to the Community market and the predictability of financial assistance under the Lomé Convention help them to plan ahead. The Convention can and must be improved not only as a factor making for security but also as an instrument of development.

It is a framework that can also serve the basic interests of the Community inasmuch as the Community's own economic aims can be dovetailed with its partners' development objectives, particularly in the industrial, energy and mining fields.

But the action provided for in the Convention can only be developed over time. The Commission has therefore been looking at ways of bestowing greater continuity on a co-operation system which has the manifest support of the Community and the ACP but is thrown into the melting pot at each renegotiation.

The implementing arrangements and the financial provisions of the Convention will have to continue to be reviewed at intervals. But to call the whole system into question every five years[1] is to inject uncertainty into the objectives, the permanence of the guarantee machinery[2] and the security of conditions of access to the Community market, all to no purpose. Unnecessary confrontations are caused, when everyone knows from the outset that the Convention will be renewed in one form or another.

The Commission therefore proposes that the Community declare its readiness – if the ACP so wish – to negotiate with the ACP a framework convention for an unlimited period establishing the principles, objectives, key features and institutional machinery of their co-operation; this would not preclude protocols on sectoral or regional implementation, the duration of which would have to be tailored to their specific object. This would ensure a proper balance between continuity of a Convention which remains a fundamental political instrument and the adaptability of its machinery in line with circumstances and differences in the situation of the ACP countries or in the way in which they evolve.

Such continuity would make it possible to undertake certain activi-

---

[1] Every three years, in fact, given the length of the negotiations.
[2] E.g. Stabex, Sysmin and emergency aid.

ties which are indispensable for development but for which lead times are long; the fight against desertification, the preservation of tropical forests, soil management and the management of natural and energy resources, the development of indigenous scientific and technical research capacity, the fight against the major endemic diseases – these are not tasks on which the Community and the ACP can embark without allowing themselves a more ample time scale than that of the five-year conventions and without giving themselves scope for action beyond the limits of national frontiers or even regional boundaries.

Are these long-term operations not precisely those that governments, at grips with immediate needs, sometimes tend to neglect? If EEC–ACP co-operation did not help to meet the cost and if resources for such major undertakings were not guaranteed as a matter of principle, development operations would soon become futile since the natural environment itself would already be destroyed.

With regard, finally, to extending the geographical scope of the future Convention, the Commission hopes that ways will be found of enabling Angola, Mozambique and an independent Namibia to participate.

Then the group of ACP countries would bring together – with the exception of one country – all of sub-Saharan Africa, in addition to all those Caribbean and Pacific countries which have their own vision of the Convention to which they attach unquestionable value. But the diversity of the countries covered by the Convention constitutes a *de facto* argument in favour of a regionalised approach under the Convention. Without involving any departure from the framework convention suggested, the existence of forms of regional co-operation geared to practicalities can offer substantial advantages. There will be no question of regions being devised either by Europe or the Convention. But the European Community, drawing on its rich experience, may be able to establish the conditions for fruitful forms of regional co-operation, though only time will tell whether they can or should be institutionalised or take on a political form.

In any case the Commission will propose in due course that the measures for encouraging regional co-operation, whether between ACP countries or between the ACP and neighbouring developing countries, should be further strengthened. In addition to the case of southern Africa, this will embrace European aid for development in the countries of Central America and the Caribbean, some of which belong to the ACP group, and the strengthening of co-operation with the Mediterranean countries.

Select Bibliography of Recent Publications on EEC–Third World Relations

Belgium

EEC publications

The Courier, periodical, published bi-monthly on EEC–ACP relations.
European Information: 51/81, 'ASEAN and the European Community', July 1981, 11pp. 50/81, 'The European Community and India', June 1981, 14pp.
Commission of the European Communities, *Commission Report to the ACP–EEC Council of Ministers on the administration of financial and technical co-operation in 1980, under the Lomé Convention,* (COM (81) 686 final), 1981.
– *How to Participate in Contracts financed by the EDF,* Dossiers Development Series 3, 1981, 42pp.
– *European Development Fund Procedures,* Dossiers Development Series 4, 1981, 34pp.
– *Annual Report of the ACP–EEC Council of Ministers, 1 March 1980–28 February 1981,* 1981, 129pp.
– *Practical Guide to the use of the EEC's Scheme of Generalised Tariff Preferences,* 1 May 1981, 354pp.
ACP–EEC Council of Ministers, *The Second ACP–EEC Convention, signed at Lomé on 31 October 1979 and related documents* (L 2985) 1981 edition, 549pp.
EC Statistics Office, *EC–China: a statistical analysis of foreign trade, 1970–79,* 1981, 98pp.
– *ACP Basic Statistics,* 1981, 137pp.
Court of Auditors, *Special Report on European Community Food Aid* (mimeo).
European Investment Bank, *Statute and other provisions* (text updated to 31/12/81), EIB, 34pp.

Other

Friedrich Ebert Stiftung
Outlook for EEC Policy of Co-operation with Developing Countries; conclusions of a conference held by the German Friedrich Ebert Foundation with the Socialist Group of the European Parliament (English, French, German).

Hage, R. W., Taylor, R. and Noelke, M.
EEC Protectionism: Present Practice and Future Trends, vol. 2, Brussels, European Research Associates, 1981.
Jamar, Joseph (ed)
Intégrations régionales entre pays en voie développement, Bruges, Tempelhof, 1982, 274pp.
La Communauté européenne et l'Amerique Latine
Editions d l'Univ. de Bruxelles, 1981, 234pp.
Leroy, Olivier
Nord-Sud, le dossier des produits de base, Brussels, La Lettre Européenne, 2 vols., 1981, 500pp.
Pitrone, Antonio
The EEC GSP in the 80s, Brussels, Agence Européenne d'Informations, 1981, 307pp. (Contains all regulations in force).

Denmark

Harboe, J. and Wangel, A.
Fælleskab eller mods ætning. EF og den 3 verden, Copenhagen, FN-forbundet, 1982, pp. 120. (FN, Orientering, Sænummer/April 1982).
Hoffmeyer, B.
EEC's Common Agricultural Policy and the ACP States, Copenhagen, Centre for Development Research, 1982 (forthcoming).
Neersø, P.
'EF, Danmark og u-landene', *Tidens Stemme,* vol. 36, 5, 1981, pp. 38–40.
Torm, U.
'EF's nye Lome-konvention og u-landenes krav om an ny økonomisk verdensorden', *Kontakt,* no. 5, 1980/81, p. t.1–8.

France

Association Française pour l'Étude du Tiers-Monde
Colloque, 1977: 'Le Tiers Monde et le CEE', Paris, Berger-Levrault, 1978, 258 pp.
Balleux, Aymeric
'La Communauté Economique Européene et les pays en voie de développement', *Révue Juridique et Politique,* vol. 35, no. 4, October–December 1981.
Barthalay, Bernard
'L'Europe dans la problematique Nord-Sud', *Europe en formation,* no. 242, March–April, 1981, pp. 45–55.
Catalans, Yves
'Aide internationale: credits amputés d'un tiers', *Actuel Développement,* no. 47, March–April, 1982, pp. 13–16.
Durant, Remy
'Le Dialogue Nord-Sud', *Défense Nationale,* no. 37, August–September, 1981, pp. 7–20.

Fontaine, Andre
'Du conflit Est–Ouest au dialogue Nord–Sud: la voie à suivre; interview recueillie par Patrick Wajsman', *Politique Internationale,* no. 15, Spring 1982, pp. 9–18.

Institut Français des Relations Internationales
Les pays les plus pauvres: quelle cooperation pour quel développement? Paris, Dunod, 1981, 291 pp.

Ikonicoff, Moises
'Le système économique mondial: désordre ou rationalité?', *Revue Tiers Monde,* no. 81, January, 1981.

Lietaer, B., *Le Grand Jeu Europe–Amerique Latine,* Press Universitaires Françaises, 1981, 400 pp.

Nouaille-Degorge, Brigitte
'Bilan politique de la cooperation', *Projet,* no. 165, May 1982, pp. 547–558.

Paoloni, Marc
'L'Europe dans le dialogue Nord–Sud', *Problèmes économiques,* no. 1756, 13 Janvier 1982, pp. 26–32.

Saint Geourgs, Jean
L'Imperatif de cooperation Nord–Sud: la synergie des mondes, Paris, Dunod, 1981, 291 pp.

Touscoz, Jean
'Le Parti Socialiste Francais et le cooperation avec le Tiers Monde', *Politique Etrangere,* vol. 46, no. 4, December 1981, pp. 875–889.

Uri, Pierre and Fabre, Renaud
Aider le Tiers Monde a se nourrir lui-même, Economica, 1981, 192 pp.

Germany

Becker, J.
Die Partnerschaft von Lome – Eine neue zwischenstaatliche Kooperationsform des Entwicklungsvölkerrechts, Baden-Baden, Nomos-Verlag, 1979.

Bergmann, C. and Grundmann, H. E.
Interdependenz zwischen Industrie- und Entwicklungsländern, Baden-Baden, Nomos-Verlag, 1980.

Bley, H. and Tetzlaff, R. (eds)
Afrika und Bonn. Versäumnisse und Zwänge deutscher Afrika-Politik, Reinbeck, Rowolt, 1978.

Dauderstädt, M. *et al*
EG-Politik der Zusammenarbeit mit Entwicklungsländern – Perspektiven im Lichte des Wandels der Nord–Süd Beziehungen und der EG-Fortentwicklung, Köln, Weltforum-Verlag, 1982.

'Neue Perspektiven fur das Verhaltnis des Europäischen Gemeinschaft zu Latinamerika?', *DIW Wochenbericht,* 13–14/82, 186–90.

Pfaller, A.
Industrieexporte aus Entwicklungsländern in weltwirtschaftlichen Interessenkonflikt, Opladen, Westdeutscher Verlag, 1981.

Schmuck, Otto
'Das europäische Parlament vor den Herausforderungen der Dritten Welt' (the European Parliament and the demands of the Third World – English summary), *Vierteljahresberichte,* June 1981, 133–146.

Schultz, S., Schumacher, D. and Wilkens, H.
Wirtschaftliche Verflechtung der Bundesrepublik Deutschland mit den Entwicklungsländern, Baden-Baden, Nomos-Verlag, 1980.
Schumacher, D. and Hollmann, K.
'Handel mit Entwicklungsländern und Beschäftigung in der Europeäischen Gemeinschaft', *Schriftenreihe des Deutschen Institut für Wirtschaftsforschung*, no. 66, Berlin, 1981.
Senghaas, D.
Von Europa lernen. Entwicklungsgeschlichtliche, Frankfurt, Suhrkamp-Verlag, 1982.
Steinweg, R. (ed)
Hilfe+Handel = Frieden? – Die Bundesrepublik in der Dritten Welt, Frankfurt, Suhrkamp-Verlag, 1982.
Wilson, Rodney
'The Middle East and the EEC: an analysis of trade flows', *Inter Eeconomics*, May/June 1982, 118–124.

Greece

Ioakimidis, P. C.
External Economic Relations and European Community Policy, Athens, Papazisis, 1982, 245pp. (in Greek).

Ireland

Fitzpatrick, J.
Industrialisation, Trade and Ireland's Development Cooperation Policy, Dublin, Advisory Council on Development Cooperation, 1982.
Fitzpatrick, J. (ed)
Ireland, *The Common Agricultural Policy and Developing Countries*, Seminar Proceedings, Dublin, Comhlamh/Gorta, 1982.
Matthews, A. and Fitzpatrick, J.
'The European Community's food aid policy: a role for Ireland', *Administration*, vol. 28, no. 3, 1981.
O'Neill, H.
'Irish aid: performance and policies', in O. Stokke (ed), *European Aid: Performance and Policies*, Oslo, Norwegian Institute for International Affairs, 1982.

Italy

Lala, Riccardo
Les Procedures de la coopération financière et techniques dans le cadre de la

Deuxième Convention de Lomé, Torino, G. Giapplchelli Editore, 1981, 248pp. (author is an official at the Court of Justice).
Rivista di Diritto Europeo, July–September XX1–3, Rome, includes article on Lomé II.
'Studi e ricerche: la convenzione di Lome' *Politica Internazionale,* 5, 1982, 95–114. (Several articles).

The Netherlands

Centre for Development Studies, University of Antwerp
'Europe and the South Asian countries' problems of trade policy', symposium 11 December 1979, pub. 1980.
Cochius, M. I.
'De EG-voedselhulp: van overschottenpolitiek naar een waar ontwikkelings-beleid', *Nieuw Europa* 7 (1981) 3, pp. 88–96.
Dijck, P. v. & Verbruggen, H.
'Het multivezelakkoord, de EG en de werkgelegenheid in ontwikkelingslan-den', *Economische Statistische Berichten,* 3353, pp. 472–476.
Faber, Gerit
The European Community and Development Cooperation, Assen, Van Gor-cum, 1982, 260 pp.
Groot, G. de
'Het multivezelakkoord', *Economische Statistische Berichten* 66 (1982) 3335, pp. 1240–1244.
Maandschrift Economie vol. 46 (1982) 4: 'Nieuw Protectionisme':
  (a) Jepma, C. J., 'De veranderingen in de internationale arbeidsverdeling; een tweede industriële revolutie?'.
  (b) Groot, G. de, 'Nieuw protectionisme in Nederland'.
  (c) Tharakan, P. K. M., 'Nieuw protectionisme in België'.
Mierlo, T. J. M. v.,
'Ein nieuw perspectief voor de bestrijding van technische handelsbelemmer-ingen', *Nieuw Europa,* 7 (1981), 3, pp. 112–123.

Norway

Hermansen, Olav
'U-landene, Lome-konvensjonene og industrisamarbeidet – forhapninger og realiteter', *Internasjonal Politikk,* 1982, no. 1, pp. 95–115.
Isachsen, A. J.
Økonomiske betraktninger omkring den nye økonomiske verdensordning', *Statsøkonomisk Tidsskrift,* vol. 94 (1980) no. 2, pp. 119–140.
Isaksen, Jan
'NIEO-positions and economic interest. West European reaction on four specific issues.' Paper prepared for the TFID Workshop, Ottawa, May 14–15, 1980. (DERAP Working Paper A176.) Also published in *Development and Peace,* Budapest, vol. 1 (1980) no. 2, pp. 42–54.

Norbye, Ole David Koht
'The international restructuring process; EEC, the European periphery and the other developing countries', Bergen, Chr. Michelsen Institute, 1981, (DERAP Working Paper A236).
Sengupta, Arjun
'The leverages of the South in the North–South relations: non-alignment as a source of power.' Bergen, Chr. Michelsen Institute, 1981, pp. 62. (DERAP Working Paper A 217.)
Vargas, Ines and Felipa Aguero
The impact of the evolving and new international economic order on the situation of the workers. Project Report. Oslo, Institute of Peace Research, 1981, pp. 42. (PRIO publication S-23/81.)

United Kingdom

Asante, S. K. B.
'The Lome convention: towards perpetuation of dependence or promotion of interdependence', *Third World Quarterly,* October 1981, 658–672.
Curzon, G. *et al*
MFA for ever? Future of the Arrangement for Trade in Textiles, Trade Policy Research Centre, 1981, 47 pp.
Frank, Isaiah
Trade Policies of Interest to the Third World, Trade Policy Research Centre, 1981, 68 pp.
Gaines, D. B., Sawyer, W. C. and Sprinkle, R.
'EEC Mediterranean policy and US trade in citrus', *J. World Trade Law,* September/October 1981, 431–439.
House of Commons Select Committee on the European Communities
Development Aid Policy: Session 1980/81, presented to Parliament by the Minister of Overseas Development, HMSO, July 1981.
Jepma, C.
'An application of the constant market shares technique on trade between the associated African and Malagasy states and the European Community (1958–1978)', *J. Common Market Studies.* December 1981, 175–192.
Josling, T. E., Langworthy, M. and Pearson, S.
Options for Farm Policy in the European Community, Trade Policy Research Centre, 1981, 84 pp.
Latin America Bureau
The European Challenge: Europe's New Role in Latin America, LAB, 1982.
McQueen, Matthew
'Lome and the protective effects of rules of origin', *J. World Law,* March/April, 1982, 119–132.
Marsh, J. S. and Mahe, L. P.
The CAP in the 1980s: Two Views on Revision, Ashford, Wye College, Centre for European Agricultural Studies, 1981, 66 pp.
Musto, Stefan
'The Canary Islands and the EC – options for integration', *J. Common Market Studies,* December 1981, 115–137.

Pearce, Joan
'The CAP: a guide to the Commission's new proposals', *The World Today*, September 1981, 339–347.
Rodbielski, G.
'The Common Agricultural Policy and the Mezzagiorno', *J. Common Market Studies*, June 1981, 331–350.
Serre, Françoise de la
'The Community's Mediterranean policy after the second enlargement', *J. Common Market Studies*, June 1981, 377–388.
Smith, Ian
'GATT:EEC sugar export refunds dispute', *J. World Trade Law,* November/December 1981, 534–543.
Von Braun, J. and De Haen, H.
'Egypt and the enlargement of the EEC: impact on the agricultural sector', *Food Policy*, February 1982, 46–56.

Other

Sharma, Yojana
'The EEC's inconsistent development policy', Geneva, *IFDA Dossier,* May/June 1982, 80–82.
Amin, Samir
'Strategies alternatives de développement de la region mediterranéenne – relations entre les strategies nationales, regionales et mondiales', Geneva, *IFDA Dossier,* March/April 1982, 74–80.
Forster, Jacques
'L'aide publique au développement de six petits pays européens: Autrriche, Danemark, Finlande, Norvege, Suede, Suisse', Berne, *E & D, Entwicklung Developpement* no. 8, 1981, 2–14.
Just, Wolf-Dieter
'The world as a trading place – on cultural presuppositions and effects of the Lome Convention', IFDA Dossier (Geneva) March/April 1982, 33–44.
Rajana, Cecil
'The Lome Convention: an evaluation of EEC economic assistance to the ACP states', *Canadian J. of Development Studies,* 1981, 2:2, 301–340.
Chopra, H. S. and Mitra, S. K.
'India–EEC relations', *Indian & Foreign Review,* New Delhi, 19:13, 15 April 1982, 12–14.
Rajana, Cecil
'Europe undermined: the Lome response: an evaluation of the EEC–ACP non fuel minerals arrangement', *African Development,* Dakar, April–June 1981, VI 2, 5–42.

Annex (to Chapter 10)

ACP sub-groupings

1 Yaoundé ACP: Benin, Burundi, Cameroon, Central African Republic, Chad, Congo, Gabon, Ivory Coast, Madagascar, Mali, Mauritania, Niger, Rwanda, Senegal, Somalia, Togo, Upper Volta, Zaire.

2 Commonwealth ACP: Bahamas, Barbados, Botswana, Dominica, Fiji, Gambia, Ghana, Grenada, Guyana, Jamaica, Kenya, Kiribati, Lesotho, Malawi, Mauritius, Nigeria, Papua New Guinea, St Lucia, St Vincent and the Grenadines, Seychelles, Sierra Leone, Solomon Islands, Swaziland, Tanzania, Tonga, Trinidad and Tobago, Tuvalu, Uganda, Western Samoa, Zambia.

3 Previously non-associated ACP: Cape Verde, Ethiopia, Equatorial Guinea, Guinea, Guinea Bissau, Liberia, Sudan.

4 Non-oil ACP: ACP group excluding Nigeria, Trinidad and Tobago, Gabon, Bahamas, Congo.

5 Non-oil Commonwealth ACP: Commonwealth ACP group excluding Nigeria, Trinidad and Tobago, Bahamas.

6 Non-oil Yaoundé ACP: Yaoundé ACP group excluding Gabon, Congo.

Major oil-exporting developing countries

Iraq, Iran, Libya, Nigeria, Saudi Arabia, Kuwait.

Other developing countries

World excluding industrialised countries, South Africa, European developing countries, major oil-exporting developing countries, ACP.

Index